Literary Criticism Series

— 8 —

Cover photo by Branko Gorjup

Northrop Frye

Mythologizing Canada
Essays on the Canadian Literary Imagination

Edited by

Branko Gorjup

LEGAS

New York Ottawa Toronto

Canadian Cataloguing in Publication Data

Frye Northrop, 1912-1991
Mythologizing Canada. Essays on the Canadian Literary Imagination

(Literary criticism series ; 8)
ISBN 0-921252-57-9

1. Canadian literature (English) — History and criticism. I. Gorjup, Branko II. Title II. Series: Literary criticism series (Legas); 8.

PS8077.F79 1996 C810.9 C96-900725-6
PR9184.6.F79 1996

For further information and for orders:

LEGAS

P. O. Box 040328
Brooklyn, New York
11204

68 Kamloops Ave.
Ottawa, Ontario
K1N 8T9

2908 Dufferin St.
Toronto, Ontario
M6B 3S8

Printed and bound in Canada

For Francesca
and Francesco

Acknowledgments

In the fall of 1990 I had the honour of accompanying Professor Northrop Frye to Europe: to the University of Zagreb to receive an honorary doctorate; and to Sicily, where he was to be awarded the Mondello Prize. There we joined Agostino Lombardo, Professor of English at the University of Rome "La Sapienza". It was during discussions among the three of us that the idea of this book was born. I am deeply grateful to Professor Lombardo for raising the concept, and for his many years, before and since, of guidance and encouragement.

I would like to acknowledge the Estate of Dr. H. Northrop Frye for its support of this project; particularly, Mrs. Jane Widdicombe, for the direction she gave me in my research.

Many very special thanks to Maude McCarty, who, as my friend and editor, has seen this project through to its publication, and who has given me over the years an accurate voice.

I am indebted to Laura Pietropaolo for her invaluable commentary on the introduction to this collection. My thanks go also to Margaret Atwood, Rosemary Sullivan, Barry Callaghan, Rosamaria Plevano, and Jane Varnus for their interest and support.

I shall be forever grateful to Francesca Valente, who first introduced me to Northrop Frye and to the wonders of the Canadian imagination, and whose dedication and critical acumen were indispensable to the realization of this project.

Finally, I would like to thank Professor Leonard G. Sbrocchi, my publisher, for his astute counsel and commitment to this book.

Contents

Introduction

The selection of the essays in this book is a direct response to Northrop Frye's interdisciplinary body of writing produced over a period of almost five decades. My intent is twofold: first, to assemble the essays specifically concerned with the Canadian literary imagination — some of them published in *The Bush Garden* and *Divisions on a Ground* but dispersed among the essays on culture and education — and second, to illustrate Frye's initial insights into Canadian writing and to trace their subsequent changes.

Arranged in chronological order, these essays document Frye's expanding and changing critical consciousness about Canada. They reveal his remarkable insights into cultural differences between Canada's past and its present, and particularly between Canada and the United States. In the earlier essays, Frye examined and assessed the achievement of Canadian writing, and set out to develop his primary conceptual and organizational categories for its criticism. In the later essays, however, in spite of frequent 'disruptions,' he constructed a cogent theoretical frame of reference within which Canadian literature can be read in terms of a distinctive Canadian imagination. These essays also disclose Frye's notion of the Canadian context as an unfinished literary construct, one that is bound to be superseded by new ideals and conventions, and absorbed at times by the Canadian imagination to serve as a cohesive force for different models of national unity and identity. And finally, these essays demonstrate Frye's significance within an already-existing Canadian literary tradition, revealing both the affinities and the differences between his discourse and traditional patterns of thinking.

The subject of Canadian literature and culture in Frye's work constitutes a smaller but highly significant segment of critical writing. Commonly described as 'occasional,' it stands somewhat apart from his *summa,* not only thematically but also theoretically. The discrepancy between Frye's 'international' criticism, with its predilection for abstraction, systematization and universalization — best represented by his *Anatomy of Criticism, The Great Code: The Bible and Literature* and *Words with Power* — and his 'domestic' criticism, espousing literature's mimetic and non-autonomous status — as collected in *The Bush*

Garden, Divisions on a Ground and the present volume — has been the subject of extensive debate and controversy in Canada in recent years.

Eli Mandel was one of several critics who identified this discrepancy, apparent as early as Frye's first influential essay on the Canadian literary imagination, "Canada and Its Poetry," published in 1943. This essay, argued Mandel, reveals Frye to be "oddly" preoccupied with the "geographical" or "political" rather than with the "literary" context of Canadian writing (Mandel, 289). Mandel's observation echoes those made by others, including Frank Davey in "Surviving the Paraphrase," Russell Brown in "Critic, Culture, Text: Beyond Thematics" and Dermot McCarthy in "Early Canadian Literary Histories and the Function of a Canon." They all called into question the validity of Frye's reading of Canadian literature in terms of environmental determinism, to which he had theoretically committed himself as early as 1965 in his Conclusion to the first edition of *Literary History of Canada.*

In this influential essay Frye recommended that Canadian writing be studied "as part of Canadian life" rather than "as part of an autonomous world of literature." To some critics, this sounded not only inconsistent with Frye's theoretical stance regarding non-Canadian literary texts but also protectionist, designed to exempt Canadian writing from the rigorous and universally sanctioned critical standards that are applied to the world's great classics. While Frye's detractors quickly accused him of being patronizing towards Canada's literary achievement, his followers saw him as an important ally in their quest for a national literature. For the latter group, Frye's Canadian criticism represented a powerful endorsement of their belief that literature's distinctive character is realizable only in relation to its context, to its geography and its history.

Among the critics just mentioned, McCarthy has located Frye in a Canadian critical tradition dating to the middle of the nineteenth century (MacCarthy, 32), according to which imaginative writing is perceived in primarily utilitarian terms. Literature's autonomous status is dismissed, while its production — and its formation into a literary canon — is subordinated to a larger and more important task — that of nation-building. This view of literature reached its climax in the post-Confederation period in the works of such promoters of Canadian writing as William Kirby, Charles G. D. Roberts, Isabella Valancy Crawford, Edward Hartley Dewart and Graeme Mercer Adam. The more recent upsurge of cultural nationalism — particularly buoyant between 1967, the year of Expo, and the 1989 Free Trade debate — is closely related to this particular ideological stance.

Frye's two 'contradictory' readings of literature — the 'literary,' founded on "humanist/universalist" or "modernist/internationalist" principles, and the 'extra-literary,' based on "the Canadian contextual specifics" — can be approached, however, as Linda Hutcheon has proposed, in terms of a typically postmodern tension. What, she asks, if we choose "to examine Frye's position from a postmodern perspective ...?" What if we assess Canadian writing without applying 'universal' standards and ideals? Then, she answers, we might negotiate a radically different perception of Canada which, "instead of sounding like a failed nation with a deficient or at least immature culture (according to the model of modernity), might start to sound postmodernly open and provisional." From a postmodern position, the contradictions that have irritated some of Frye's critics, particularly those who have argued from within the modernist frame of reference, are overcome — the modern binary either/or worldview is displaced by one in which the postmodern both/and thinking prevails.

Hutcheon acknowledges that there is, however, little doubt of Frye's belief in the autonomous status of literature. But, she reminds us that he also engaged in practical criticism: for Frye, the study of society was a natural extension of the study of literature. This position is most evident in his essays on the Canadian literary imagination and culture, and critics "who have not looked at these writings," warns Hutcheon, "miss this important tension in his thought" (Hutcheon, 110-113).

Undoubtedly, Frye's writing has profoundly influenced both the Canadian imagination and Canadian literary scholarship. The list of his supporters and detractors is impressively long and still growing, strong evidence of his continuing relevance. Such prominent writers and critics as Margaret Atwood, George Bowering, James Reaney, Robert Kroetsch, David Staines, Brown Russell, Sandra Djwa and Rosemary Sullivan are only a few of those who have felt compelled to address Frye's engaging perception of the Canadian literary representation. Their work reflects an eloquent and, at times, a passionate "dialogue" with Frye, as well as amongst themselves. While it embodies, on the one hand, the contesting views of individual critics and schools, influenced as they are by diverse theoretical and ideological conventions, on the other, it documents an important period in the development of Canadian criticism.

Some of Frye's supporters, like Margaret Atwood, D. G. Jones, John Moss, Margot Northey, Tom Marshall and Warren Tallman, skilfully absorbed Frye's key concepts — 'environmental determinism' and 'garrison culture,' for example — into their own critical discourse. They created a theoretical framework that subsequent critics have designated as the basis of the so-called 'school' of thematic criticism. They were quick to sense in Frye's work the establishment of "the nationalist and literary contexts within which it would be possible to speak of a Canadian literary tradition" (Mandel, 288). Interestingly, recent post-colonial criticism has re-stated the validity of such an approach, pointing out its dependence on the conception of national literary uniqueness, which is essential for the establishment of difference within English writing.

According to post-colonial critics, the development of a national literature begins with the individual's desire for self-recognition within a post-colonial context, which, in turn, sets in motion the process for group identification. Members of such a group can then begin challenging forms of cultural imperialism still submerged in their society. Without "such development at the national level..., no discourse of the post-colonial could have emerged" (Ashcroft, 17). In reference to Frye's brand of nationalism, however, the real threat to Canada's continuing existence as a nation no longer came from the British imperial connection — though frequently Frye would point out its frostbiting effect on the Canadian imagination — but rather from the 'new,' more aggressive type of American imperialism. As most of the essays in this collection attest, Frye devoted much of his energy to the construction of a distinctive model for Canadian literary and cultural traditions — and he did so largely in contrast to American ones — in order to break the inevitable pattern of reference to the United States as a standard.

Other critics — detractors, such as Frank Davey, Barry Cameron, George Bowering and David Jackel — challenged Frye's thinking by criticizing those who fell under his influence and who propagated a narrow and exclusionary approach to Canadian writing. These critics feared that the conception of a national literature could not support the necessary checks to prevent the rise to the level of myth of half-truths or stereotypes. In a somewhat similar but more politically focused manner, post-colonial critics have been voicing their concern with extreme forms of nationalism, particularly in its "essentialist formulation," which would inevitably lead to "nationalist and racist orthodoxies" (Ashcroft, 17). But Frye had already expressed this wariness of nationalism's potentially dangerous side. Yet, he was convinced, as he stated in 1976 in his Conclusion to the second edition of *Literary History of Canada*, that the Canadian brand of nationalism was "on the whole a positive development, in which self-awareness ha[d] been far more important than aggressiveness."

The commotion that Frye's Canadian criticism caused within literary and academic establishments during the 1960s and 1970s paralleled the dramatic social change that was rapidly redefining Canada's cultural map. When Frye, as a young reviewer for *The Canadian Forum* and *The University of Toronto Quarterly* in the late 1930s and early 1940s, was starting to explore the meaning and definition of the Canadian imagination, the representation of the immigrant experience in literature and in art was still exclusively European and White. It proposed a vision of Canada as a homogenized nation fulfilling its destiny as a Western political and cultural construct.

As the Canadians of this period — the 1960s and the 1970s — intensified their quest for a distinctive national identity and its representation in literature, they almost simultaneously began to question the meaning, and indeed the very appropriateness, of such a quest. Most of all, they questioned its relevance to a society that had already, by and large, begun to embrace and officially endorse the ideals of multiculturalism and multiracialism. Thus, the dual response to Frye's Canadian critical thought — one that saw his work as a useful paradigm for the construction of a unified vision of Canada, and the other that could no longer validate such a model in a context of an increasing number of non-European immigrants — becomes synonymous, especially in more recent critical discourse, with the country's transition from colonial to post-national status.

By the mid 1970s, notwithstanding opposition from numerous detractors, Frye's Canadian critical thought — derived, as I shall later discuss in more detail, from the notion that the imagination is essentially vegetable in character, thriving best in a specific environment — had moved to the very centre of a burgeoning Canadian literary criticism. For Sandra Djwa, for example, Frye's work has provided a "critical framework for much of the present writing and study of Canadian poetry" (Djwa, 24). David Staines, concurring with Djwa's assessment, tells Frye's detractors to stop finding "fault with his theories" and start realizing how "much of their writing uses Frye's enunciated myths as a point of departure" (Staines, 162). In a more recent post-colonial study of the Canadian literary sensibility, Arnold Harrichand Itwaru has observed that Frye's search for an ideal or "intangible" Canada, situated in the place where Canada physically is, ends in failure: instead of finding a social ideal in Canada's pastoral myths, Frye finds territorial insularity and regionalism. Itwaru ultimately commends Frye's "inconclusive" search, which he sees as an acknowledgment that the "Canada which is located in the landscape of the mind ... must be constantly sought" (Itwaru, 20). This observation echoes Hutcheon's description of "Frye's Canada" as a cultural construct that "might start to sound postmodernly open and provisional" (Hutcheon, 111), or as a conception that is re-constituted by each succeeding generation of newcomers.

* * *

When in 1864 Edward Hartley Dewart edited the first major anthology of Canadian poetry, *Selections from Canadian Poets,* he reflected in his introduction on the nationally held belief in literature's utilitarian role. Literature's function, he maintained, was to be "an essential element in the formation of national character." Literature could achieve this, he continued, by becoming the porte-parole of national "intellectual life, the bond of national unity, and the guide of national energy" (Dewart, 50). Dewart, however, did not substantiate this abstract set of guidelines, leaving unanswered the question of what, in fact, might constitute Canada's national character.

A quarter of a century later, another major anthology of Canadian poetry, *Songs of the Great Dominion,* was published. Its editor, William Douw Lighthall, optimistically reiterated the inseparability of literature from its national context. What was new and distinctive about Lighthall's analysis was his conviction that the poets he anthologized consciously reflected Canada's environment and its peoples' perception of their place within it. He suggested that his reader might "catch" in the poems, as he did himself, a glimpse of Canada as it had been transformed from a state of wilderness into a state of civilization.

However emphatic his insistence on Canada's "young might, public wealth, and heroism" (Lighthall, 128), imbued with the Imperialist spirit of Victorian positivism and idealism, Lighthall's vision of Canada betrayed something of which he and his contemporaries were unaware: that Canada's future would lie in subduing and controlling its environment, which in practical terms meant exploitation and destruction of nature and native cultures. It was Frye who articulated half a century later this unvoiced belief. Nevertheless, Lighthall did inadvertently suggest that in the "cheerful" voices of his anthology a darker and more negative tone could be found. That tone alluded to the "death-song" of "vanishing races" as they disappeared, along with the Canadian wilderness, into "Arcadias," or into what Frye would later call the 'garrisons' of European civilization.

Despite this dark undercurrent, what prevailed throughout the latter part of the nineteenth century was a perception marked by an abstract rhetoric, celebrating Western man's courage, dedication, ingenuity and nobility. In fact, most of the cultural critics or commentators of that period, such as Goldwin Smith, Graeme Mercer Adam, William Kirby, J. G. Bourinot and J. D. Logan, subordinated literature to political ends. By popularizing its utilitarian function and by ascribing to it a belief in civilization's superiority over nature, they constructed a pattern of thinking that reflected the Canadian version of a social utopia: a late-Victorian concept of rational man endowed with a vision in which human surpasses nature.

With the advent of Realism in the 1920s, and of Modernism in the 1930s, Romantic/Victorian thinking began to be challenged. The critical debunking of the paradisiacal vision of the Canadian West, rooted in the Cartesian celebration of reason, was best manifested in what is now termed Prairie Realism. Similarly in poetry, Modernism rejected the romantic, simplified version of the man-nature relationship and replaced it with one characterized by ironic tension and ambiguity. Nature was perceived, in the words of critic A. J. M. Smith, as "harsh and lovely," and humans, despite their vitality, intelligence and will to power, as insecure and self-destructive. This change in literary and cultural conventions seems to have influenced significantly Frye's perception of the cultural context, from which his Canadian literary criticism was just beginning to emerge.

In fact, it was while reviewing Smith's *Book of Canadian Poetry* in 1943 that Frye, as he would later acknowledge in his "Preface" to *The Bush Garden,* discovered that his thinking on the subject of Canadian poetry had come into focus and received a sense of direction. In "Canada and Its Poetry," as the review was called, Frye began by commenting that Smith's anthology possessed "unity of tone" which, rather than being imposed by the author on the collection of texts, arose from the "material itself." And it was this unified tone that for the first time unconsciously proved "the existence of a definable Canadian genius," described by Frye as "neither British nor American but, for all its echoes and imitations and second-hand ideas, peculiarly our own." What, in fact, made it peculiarly our own was a distinctly Canadian "attitude of mind" and a "recognizable Canadian accent," both relating to and emanating from a specific environment or context.

At this phase of Frye's thinking, that specific environment implied the concept of nation. A Canadian poet who consciously tried to "avoid being Canadian" would have sounded "like nothing on earth" because "poetry is not a citizen of the world: it is conditioned by language, and flourishes best within a national unit." Because of Canada's specific historical, political and cultural development, a Canadian poet had to choose his creative locus from among three possible environments — the imperial, the national and the provincial. The imperial, because of its abstract nature, and the provincial, because of its narrowness and inwardness, were both, according to Frye, "inherently anti-poetic environments," and the poetry they inspired was conditioned by "the colonial in Canadian life."

However, Frye would soon abandon this tripartite concept of the Canadian context and replace it with a binary one — the regional versus the national, whereby the regional was regarded as the real source of the poet's imagination. While the imperial and the provincial were altogether dismissed, the national fell into the category of opposition to the regional.

Having alerted the reader to certain problematic aspects of the Canadian context in relation to literary representation, Frye then turned his attention to the issue of "unity of tone" in Canadian poetry, of which Smith's anthology had so powerfully made him aware. Frye understood "unity of tone" as captured by Smith's poets to imply a preponderance of sombre tones, united in the evocation of a sense of "stark terror." This terror was the poet's response to the "frightening loneliness of a huge and thinly settled country." The perception of nature as easily dominated and exploited, readily yielding abundance, gave way to the image of an incomprehensible and sinister monster that mocked man's "thrifty little heaps of civilized values." Frye saw this re-defined and acutely focused representation of the phenomenal world in three ways: first, as a powerful and expanding metaphor in which nature is identified initially as unconsciousness; second, as "a kind of existence which is cruel and meaningless;" and third, as the "source of cruelty and subconscious stampeding within the human mind."

However, this perception, Frye argued, is also a predominant and specifically Canadian response to the relationship between the civilized human and an alien world of wilderness; predominant because Frye acknowledged in Smith's anthology the presence, albeit sporadic, of a "vision beyond nature," in which the individual refuses to be "bullied by space and time" and attempts to affirm "the supremacy of intelligence and humanity over stupid power." It is this unconvincing representation of the relationship between humans and nature that was embodied in Lighthall's "cheerful" voices. Frye identified this attitude to nature as being typically a product of the American imagination.

In the essay "The Narrative Tradition in English-Canadian Poetry," Frye made a direct connection between the environment Canada was perceived to be and Canada as represented in literature over the previous hundred and fifty years. He observed that most of the best poems of Canada's best poets were lyrical. However, the narrative poem occurred with surprising frequency and with "uneven but frequently remarkable success." What facilitated the evolution of the narrative tradition in Canada was, in Frye's view, the peculiar relationship between the poet and the language. The language, inherited and old, "with a thousand years of disciplined utterance behind it," was now interacting with a new landscape, with a "young" country. The country, of course, was not chronologically young, but appeared to be so to "the imaginative eye" of the artist which saw everywhere a crude, unfinished face, as yet untempered by European civilization.

However, Frye also recognized the existence of a parallel context. Canada was not only "a thinly settled country under a bleak northern sky" but also a "highly sophisticated civilization." The understanding of the Canadian environment as a paradox allowed Frye to acknowledge the Canadian poet's complex nature, manifested in the long narratives — from Oliver Goldsmith's *Rising Village,* Charles Heavysege's *Jephthah's Daughter,* Charles Mair's *Tecumseh,* Archibald Lampman's "At the Long Sault," to E. J. Pratt's *Brébeuf and His Brethren.* In such poems Frye found a similar contrast of "human and civilized values with nature's disregard of them" and a tendency for "God to disappear behind the mask of nature," a nature perceived as mindlessly destroying "the higher forms of life." The tension between the primitive and the civilized, Frye concluded, remained one of the central characteristics of the Canadian imagination.

In 1954, by the time he published his essay significantly entitled "Preface to an Uncollected Anthology," Frye believed that the only imaginative space for the poet was not the nation but the poetic "environment." This change of view had to do with another idea Frye was beginning to develop, which would take into account the cultural and political differences between Canada and the United States. Unlike the States, Canada had grown, Frye argued, in "one dimension": it was a nation founded on "the stops on two of the world's longest railway lines." Each stop represented a small community separated from the next by space, such that the nation's frontier consisted of a series of circumferences rather than a single boundary line. Its unity was, therefore, purely conceptual and maintained only by political will. Eventually Frye came to believe that it was not "a nation but an environment" that influenced poets, and that poetry could "deal only with the imaginative aspects of that environment." If a cultural development were to follow a political one — which, Frye observed, had already occurred by the time he wrote this article — the result would be an "anonymous international art."

In the Conclusion to *Literary History of Canada,* published in 1965, Frye reiterated his observation on the link between the Canadian context and the Canadian imagination's response to it. Canadian literature, which in *Literary History of Canada* meant Canadian writing whatever "its inherent merits," was seen by Frye as being "an indispensable aid to the knowledge of Canada." It was not surprising, then, that he began his synthesis by returning to a discussion of the Canadian context. Once again, he contrasted perceptions of Canada and the United States — of each country's transformation from an untamed to a conquered wilderness to a nation — in order to conceptually differentiate them. Canada, Frye maintained, immediately "swallowed the European newcomer on his continuous and longitudinal penetration of the continent which, as he had described earlier, rendered the "frontier into a circumference rather than a boundary." The American experience was different. For the Europeans entering the land that would become the United States, emigration was a "matter of crossing the ocean" and arriving at the Atlantic seaboard "with a western frontier that moved irregularly but steadily back until it reached the other coast.

The east-west movement not only made the "growth of Canada geographically credible" but also "attracted to itself" almost everything that had been "heroic and romantic in the Canadian tradition." However, in counterpoint, Frye acknowledged as part of the Canadian imagination another movement: the southward pull, which is more "critical and analytical, more inclined to see Canada as an unnatural and politically quixotic aggregate of disparate northern extensions of American culture." These two movements — one preoccupied with a social covenant based on the continuity of tradition, linking Canada to Britain, the other celebrating the energy of the individual, a product of the American Revolution — Frye identified as the alternating currents in the Canadian mind.

Another enduring observation Frye made in the Conclusion concerning the relationship between context and imagination entered the Canadian vocabulary as the term "garrison mentality," which denotes two of Frye's previously stated and related ideas: the imagination's horror-stricken response to nature and the frontier's circumferential character. Each small community along the long line from east to west represented, Frye argued, a small garrison, enclosed by the European immigrant's fear of the vastness of nature and of the indigenous population.

With the publication of a second edition of *Literary History of Canada,* Frye enlarged the scope of his central argument. Reviewing Canada's literary production of the past decade, he favorably assessed the development of Canadian nationalism. He referred to the book's "creative vitality," which he identified as "an emerging form of Canadian self-definition." This self-definition, however, presupposed the recognition of "the American parallel development" which, as Frye explained, had been fostered by an historical distinction between the two countries. The imaginative foundation of the United States was rooted in the revolutionary eighteenth-century sensibility, in "the age of rationalism and enlightenment." Believing in "the rational continuity of life," the Americans saw their context as expandable, as being in a perpetual state of technological transformation. In contrast, Frye argued, Canada had had no similar "enlightenment;" it had gone "directly from the Baroque expansion of the seventeenth century to the Romantic expansion of the nineteenth." Consequently, the Canadian counterpart of American positivism was predominantly a tragic vision of life manifested by a deep sense of discontinuity, by a "feeling for sudden descent or catastrophe." Such an imaginative response to the Canadian context, Frye believed, rendered the Canadian sensibility much more introspective and undogmatic.

In "Haunted by Lack of Ghosts," Frye continued to contrast the American and Canadian contexts by means of the Cartesian notion of environment as object. Such an environment, Frye explained, is governed by an "egocentric consciousness" that sees nature as something external, as an extension of the individual's power to reason. Although in Canada such consciousness never developed, attempts were made during the nineteenth century to impress it onto the Canadian imagination. The result, Frye said, was a poetry that found expression through "prefabricated rhetoric about the challenge of a new land and the energetic optimism demanded to meet it." But the more genuine response to the new land had been the one of "solitude and loneliness, of hostility or indifference of nature." According to Frye, this response formed a poetic consciousness that arose from the experience from within the leviathan of Canadian nature.

* * *

Frye's Canadian criticism encompasses disparate elements of a vast and loosely defined country and assembles them into an illuminating pattern of perception. As shown in the following essays, Frye's means to acquiring his perception was through a close interrogation of existing traditions and of a changing context; it was a perception, though, that saw the imagination as a transformative and re-creative force. Unlike Lighthall in the previous century, Frye did not have to strain his ear to "catch" something distinctively Canadian in Canadian writing. He heard clearly, right past the white noise of "prefabricated rhetoric," what he believed were writers' genuine responses to forces larger than themselves.

It was this "curious schizophrenia" in Canadian writing that Frye manipulated and examined on numerous occasions. Each transformation added to both the scope of his argument and its cogency. It was an argument that envisaged the uniqueness of the Canadian imagination in terms of its "alternate current." And, of course, this "alternate current" could not be diminished by Canada's regional character. The region, as Frye frequently repeated in these essays, was the only true home for the imagination, although many writers from various parts of Canada would produce a body of literature that would be felt by both Canadian and non-Canadian readers as "distinctive of the country." At the heart of this distinctiveness was the link between context and text or, as Frye called it, an "imaginative continuum" that would keep both defining and redefining the representation of the writer's experience of Canada as a physical and cultural environment.

It would be difficult for a student of Canadian literature to grasp fully the complexity of contemporary Canadian writing without exposure to Frye's illuminating inquiry into its earlier stages of development, when the writer's key preoccupation was still with the conception of feeling genuinely at home in a new country. And to feel genuinely at home, Frye observed, the writer had to humanize or — mythologize — the environment; he had to transform it imaginatively through cultural representation. And writing was the most compelling way to do so. The interfacing of context and text, as Frye saw it in Canadian writing, generated a distinctive literary production, which facilitated the first major step toward a national literature and, eventually, toward the liberating realization that literary standards can only be made, not met.

Branko Gorjup
York University

WORK CITED

Mandel, Eli. "Northrop Frye and the Canadian Literary Tradition." In *Centre and Labyrinth: Essays in Honour of Northrop Frye,* edited by Eleonor Cook, Chaviva Hosek, Jay Macpherson, Patricia Parker and Julian Patrick. Toronto: University of Toronto Press, 1983.

McCarthy, Dermot. "Early Canadian Literary Histories and the Function of a Canon." In *Canadian Canons: Essays in Literary Value.* edited by Robert Lecker. Toronto: University of Toronto Press, 1991.

Ashcroft, Bill, Griffiths, Gareth, and Tiffin, Ellen. *The Empire Writes Back.* London and New York: Routledge, 1989.

Hutcheon, Linda. "Frye Recoded: Postmodernity and Conclusions." In *The Legacy of Northrop Frye,* edited by Alvin A. Lee and Robert Denham. Toronto: University of Toronto Press, 1994.

Djwa, Sandra. "*The Canadian Forum:* Literary Catalyst." *Studies in Canadian Literature* 1 (Winter 1976).

Staines, David. "Frye: Canadian Critic/Writer." In *The Northrop Frye Legacy,* edited by Alvin A. Lee and Robert Denham. Toronto: University of Toronto Press, 1994.

Itwaru, Harrichand Arnold. *The Invention of Canada.* Toronto: Tsar, 1990.

Dewart, Edward Hartley. Introduction to *Selection from Canadian Poets.* In *Towards a Canadian Literature,* Vol. 1, edited by Douglas M. Daymond and Leslie G. Monkman. Ottawa: The Tecumseh Press, 1984.

Lighthall, William Douw. Introduction to *Songs of the Great Dominion.* In *Towards a Canadian Literature,* Vol. 1, edited by Douglas M. Daymond and Leslie G. Monkman. Ottawa: The Tecumseh Press, 1984.

Canada and Its Poetry

The appearance of Mr. A.J.M. Smith's new anthology[1] is an important event in Canadian literature. For instead of confining his reading to previous compilations, as most anthologists do, he has made a first-hand study of the whole English field with unflagging industry and unfaltering taste. A straightforward research job is simple enough to do if one has the time: but Mr. Smith has done something far more difficult than research. He had to read through an enormous mass of poetry ranging from the lousy to the exquisite, the great bulk of which was that kind of placid mediocrity which is always good verse and just near enough to good poetry to need an expert to detect its flat ring. He had to pronounce on all this not only with a consistent judgment but also with historical sense. He had to remember that a modern poet may hold deeply and sincerely to the more enlightened political views and become so gnarled and cryptic an intellectual that he cannot even understand himself, and still be just as conventional a minor poet as the most twittering Victorian songbird. In dealing with many of the older writers, Campbell[2] for instance, or Carman,[3] he had to trace the thin gold vein of real imagination through a rocky mass of what can only be called a gift of metrical gab. He had to remember that occasionally a bad poem is of all the greater cultural significance for being bad, and therefore should go in. In judging his younger contemporaries he had to remember both that a flawed talent is better than a flawless lack of it

[1]A.J.M. Smith, ed., *Book of Canadian Poetry* (Chicago: W. Gage & Co., University of Chicago Press, 1943) p.452.

[2]William Wilfred Campbell (1858-1918). A popular literary figure in Canada around the turn of the nineteenth century. His fiction, poetic drama and poetry embodied aesthetic and political values against which the succeeding generation of Modernist poets, including A. J. M. Smith, defined itself.

[3]Bliss Carman (1861-1929) was one of the leading representatives of the group called the 'Confederation Poets' -- a term that has been in use since the publication of Malcolm Ross's anthology, *Poets of the Confederation,* in 1960. Other poets associated with the group include Charles G. D. Roberts, Archibald Lampman and Duncan Campbell Scott. In his own time Carman was an influential literary figure, one of the first Canadian poets to transform the external landscape into an aesthetic symbol.

and that still it is performance and not "promise" that makes the poet, of whatever age.

It is no easy job; but Mr. Smith has, on the whole, done it. Of course there are omissions, of which he is probably more acutely aware than his readers. In any case anthologies ought to have blank pages at the end on which the reader may copy his own neglected favorites. In my judgment, a few people are in who might well have been out, and a few out who might well have been in: some dull poems are included and many good ones are not; and one or two poets have been rather unfairly treated — including, I should say, one A. J. M. Smith. But no kind of book is easier to attack than an anthology; and in any case the importance of this one is not so much in the numbers or merits of the poems included as in the critical revaluations it makes.

Mr. Smith's study of the pre-Confederation poets is the only one that has been made from anything like the modern point of view. In Charles Heavysege he has unearthed — the word will not be too strong for most of his readers — a genuine Canadian Beddoes, a poet of impressive power and originality[4]: and he has given Isabella Crawford[5] enough space to show that she is one of the subtlest poets that Canada has produced. The more famous writers of the so-called Maple Leaf school come down to a slightly more modest estimate, and, though Mr. Smith is scrupulously fair to them, he cannot and does not avoid saying that they talked too much and sang too little, or sang too much and thought too little. In any case the supremacy of Lampman[6] over the whole group comes out very clearly. In the next period Pratt[7] gets his deserved prominence, and the younger poets are generously represented. Here is, in short, what Canada can do: the reader who does not like this book simply does not like Canadian poetry, and will not be well advised to read further. Of course, as Mr. Smith says in his Preface, French-Canadian poetry is a separate job — still to be done, I should

---

[4]Charles Heavysege (1816-76) wrote predominantly long, dark, verse epics based on Biblical themes. His two most celebrated works are *Saul: A Drama in Three Parts*, 1857, and *Jephthah's Daughter*, 1865.

[5]Isabella Valancy Crawford (1850-87) is best known today for her long narrative poems, including *Malcolm's Katie*, published in 1884. Virtually unknown in her own time, she died young and impoverished.

[6]Archibald Lampman (1861-99), probably the best known and the most respected of the Confederation Group of poets, wrote mostly lyrical nature poems.

[7]E. J. Pratt (1882-1964) is considered one of Canada's major twentieth-century poets. His long, epic narratives, in which the Canadian landscape and experience are mythologized, are seen as the link between tradition and innovation.

think, for Fournier's[8] *Anthologie des Poètes Canadiens* is, as its editor Asselin[9] frankly admits, more a collection of poets than of poems. But we cannot leave the French out of our poetry more than we can leave Morrice[10] or Gagnon[11] out of our painting, and one can only hope for some French-speaking philanthropist to produce a companion volume.

The thing that impresses me is the unity of tone which the book has, and to which nearly all the poets in various ways contribute. Of course any anthologist can produce a false illusion of unity by simply being a critic of limited sympathies, responding only to certain kinds of technique or subject-matter. But Mr. Smith is obviously not that: his notes and introduction show a wide tolerance, and his selections, though bold and independent, are certainly not precious. No: the unity of tone must come from the material itself, and the anthology thus unconsciously proves the existence of a definable Canadian genius (I use this word in a general sense) which is neither British nor American but, for all its echoes and imitations and second-hand ideas, peculiarly our own.

Now admittedly a great deal of useless yammering has been concerned with the "truly Canadian" qualities of our literature, and one's first instinct is to avoid the whole question. Of course what is "peculiarly our own" is not what is accidentally our own, and the poet may talk forever about forests and prairies and snow and the Land of the North and not be any more Canadian than he will be Australian if he writes a sonnet on a kangaroo. One of F. R. Scott's poems included by Mr. Smith notes a tendency on the part of minor poets to "paint the native maple." This is like saying that because the quintuplets are Canadian, producing children in litters is a Canadian characteristic. Nevertheless, no one who knows the country will deny that there is something, say an attitude of mind, distinctively Canadian, and while Canadian

---

[8]Jules Fournier (1884-1918), was a prominent journalist with *La Press* and editor of several books, including *Anthologie des Poètes Canadiens*, published posthumously, in 1920.

[9]Olivar Asselin (1874-1937), another well-known journalist and co-founder of *Le Nationaliste* and *Le Devoir*. Asselin's books include *A Quebec View of Nationalism*, 1909. He wrote the preface for Fournier's *Anthologie des Poètes Canadiens*.

[10]James Wilson Morrice (1865-1924), painter of international reputation and one of the earliest Canadian modernists. He spent his adult life in France. His fame in Canada was almost entirely posthumous.

[11]Clarence Gagnon (1881-1924), etcher and painter, best known for his scenes of rural Quebec and for his numerous book illustrations.

speech is American, there is a recognizable Canadian accent in the more highly organized speech of its poetry.

Certainly if a Canadian poet consciously tries to avoid being Canadian, he will sound like nothing on earth. For whatever may be true of painting or music, poetry is not a citizen of the world: it is conditioned by language, and flourishes best within a national unit. "Humanity" is an abstract idea, not a poetic image. But whether Canada is really a national unit in any sense that has a meaning for culture I could not decide myself until I saw Mr. Smith's book; and even then one has misgivings. The patriotic avarice that claims every European as "Canadian" who stopped off at a Canadian station for a ham sandwich on his way to the States is, no doubt, ridiculous; but apart from that, does not any talk about Canadian poetry lead to some loss of perspective, some heavy spotlighting of rather pallid faces? Every Canadian has some feeling of sparseness when he compares, for example, Canada's fifth largest city, which I believe is Hamilton, with the fifth largest across the line, which I believe is Los Angeles. And the same is true of poetry. Every issue of the *New Yorker* or *New Republic*, to say nothing of the magazines which really go in for poetry, contains at least one poem which is technically on a level with five-sixths of Mr. Smith's book. With so luxuriant a greenhouse next door, why bother to climb mountains to look for the odd bit of edelweiss? The only answer is, I suppose, that in what Canadian poems have tried to do there is an interest for Canadian readers much deeper than what the achievement in itself justifies.

The qualities of our poetry that appear from this book to be distinctively Canadian are not those that one readily thinks of: a fact which was an additional obstacle in Mr. Smith's path. For Canada is more than most countries a milieu in which certain preconceived literary stereotypes are likely to interpose between the imagination and the expression it achieves. What a poet's imagination actually can produce and what the poet thinks it ought to produce are often very different things. They never should be, but they sometimes are; and it is hard to judge accurately the work of a man who is a genuine poet but whose poetry only glints here and there out of a mass of verse on conventional themes he has persuaded himself he should be celebrating. If a poet is a patriot, for instance, there may be two natures within him, one scribbling ready-made patriotic doggerel and the other trying to communicate the real feelings his country inspires him with. If he is religious, the poet in him may reach God in very subtle ways; but the man in him who is not a poet may be a more commonplace person, shocked by his own poetic boldness. If he is revolutionary, the poet in him may have to argue with a Philistine materialist also in him who does not really see the point of poetry at all. This is at least one reason why so much patriotic, religious and revolutionary verse is bad.

Now this creative schizophrenia is, we have said, common in Canada, and the most obvious reason for it is the fact that Canada is not only a nation but a colony in an empire. I have said that culture seems to flourish best in national units, which implies that the empire is too big and the province too small for major literature. I know of no poet, with a very dubious exception of Virgil, who has made great poetry out of what Shakespeare calls "the imperial theme": in Kipling, for instance, this theme is largely a praise of machinery, and of the Robot tendencies within the human mind. The province or region, on the other hand, is usually a vestigial curiosity to be written up by some nostalgic tourist. The imperial and the regional are both inherently antipoetic environments, yet they go hand in hand; and together they make up what I call the colonial in Canadian life.

This colonial tendency has been sharpened by the French-English split, the English having tended to specialize in the imperial and the French in the regional aspects of it. The French are on the whole the worse off by this arrangement, which has made Quebec into a cute tourist resort full of ye quainte junke made by real peasants, all of whom go to church and say their prayers like the children they are, and love their land and tell folk tales and sing ballads just as the fashionable novelists in the cities say they do. True, I have never met a French-Canadian who liked to be thought of as an animated antique, nor do I expect to: yet the sentimental haze in which the European author of *Maria Chapdelaine*[12] saw the country is still quite seriously accepted by Canadians, English and French alike, as authentic. A corresponding imperial preoccupation in English poets leads to much clearing of forests and planting of crops and tapping vast natural resources: a grim earnestness of expansion which seems almost more German than British. The more naive expressions of this do not get into Mr. Smith's book. Instead, he sets Isabella Crawford's song, "Bite Deep and Wide, O Axe, the Tree," in its proper context, a viciously ironic one; and Anne

---

[12]Louis Hémon (1880-1913) wrote *Maria Chapdelaine* during his brief sojourn in Canada in 1911, first in Quebec City and later in the Lac Saint-Jean area, where the novel is set. Hémon died tragically the same year in Ontario. Since its posthumous publication in Canada in 1916, the novel has had immense appeal, particularly in Quebec, where it has been received as a sympathetic and unpatronizing treatment of Quebecois society.

Marriott's "The Wind Our Enemy" and Birney's[13] "Anglo-Saxon Street" are also there to indicate that if we sow the wind of empire with too little forethought we shall reap a dusty whirlwind of arid squalor.

The colonial position of Canada is therefore a frostbite at the roots of the Canadian imagination, and it produces a disease for which I think the best name is prudery. By this I do not mean reticence in sexual matters: I mean the instinct to seek a conventional or commonplace expression of an idea. Prudery that keeps the orthodox poet from making a personal recreation of his orthodoxy: prudery that prevents the heretic from forming an articulate heresy that will shock: prudery that makes a radical stutter and gargle over all realities that are not physical: prudery that chokes off social criticism for fear some other group of Canadians will take advantage of it. One sees this perhaps most clearly in religion, because of the fact that the division of language and race is approximately one of religion also. Mr. Smith has included a religious poem called "Littlewit and Loftus,"[14] which, though in some respects a bad poem, is at any rate not a prudish one in the above sense: it ends with the authentic scream of the disembodied evangelical banshee who has cut herself loose from this world and who has the sense of release that goes with that, even if she is not wholly sure what world she is now in. It is a prickly cactus in a desert of bumbling platitudes and the pouring of unctuous oil on untroubled waters; or else, as in Bliss Carman, prayers of a stentorian vagueness addressed to some kind of scholar-gypsy God.

I wish I could say that the tighter grip of religion on the French has improved matters there; but it has done nothing of the kind. In French poetry too one feels that the Church is often most vividly conceived not as catholic but as a local palladium to be defended for political reasons: as a part of the parochial intrigue which is given the title of "nationalism." The type of prudery appropriate to this is a facile and mawkish piety. In short, the imperial tendency may call itself "Protestant" and the regional one "Catholic"; but as long as both are colonial, both will be essentially sectarian. Similarly, the imperial tendency may call itself British and the regional one French; but as long

---

[13]Earle Birney (1904-94), was an innovative and versatile poet, best known for his long narrative poem, *David*, 1942. In his poetry, Birney captured the disillusionment inherent in twentieth-century industrialized civilization.

[14]"Littlewit and Lotfus," a poem, written by Marjorie Pickthall (1883-1922), best remembered for her two collections of poetry, *The Drift of Pinions*, 1913, and *The Lamp of Poor Souls*, 1916. *The Selected Poems of Marjorie Pickthall*, edited by Lorne Pierce, appeared in 1957.

as both are colonial, these words will have only a sectional meaning. It is an obvious paradox in Canadian life that the more colonial the English or French speaking Canadian is, and the more he distrusts the other half of his country, the more artificial his relation to the real Britain or France becomes. The French-Canadian who translates "British Columbia" as "Colombie canadienne" and flies the tricolor of the French Revolution on holidays, and the English-Canadian who holds that anything short of instant acquiescence in every decision of the British Foreign Office is treason, are the furthest of all Canadians from the culture of what they allege to be their mother countries.

But even when the Canadian poet has got rid of colonial cant, there are two North American dragons to slay. One is the parroted *cliché* that this is a "new country" and that we must spend centuries cutting forests and building roads before we can enjoy the by-products of settled leisure. But Canada is not "new" or "young": it is exactly the same age as any other country under a system of industrial capitalism; and even if it were, a reluctance to write poetry is not a sign of youth but of decadence. Savages have poetry: the Pilgrim Fathers, who really were pioneers, started writing almost as soon as they landed. It is only from the exhausted loins of the half-dead masses of people in modern cities that such weary ideas are born.

The other fallacy concerns the imaginative process itself, and may be called the Ferdinand the Bull theory of poetry. This theory talks about a first-hand contact with life as opposed to a second-hand contact with it through books, and assumes that the true poet will go into the fields and smell the flowers and not spoil the freshness of his vision by ruining his eyesight on books. However, practically all important poetry has been the fruit of endless study and reading, for poets as a class are and must be, as an Elizabethan critic said, "curious universal scholars." There are exceptions to this rule, but they prove it; and it is silly to insist on them.

In looking over Mr. Smith's book one is struck immediately by the predominance of university and professional people; and it is in the classical scholarship of Lampman, the encyclopedic erudition of Crémazie[15] which is said to have included Sanskrit, and the patient research and documentation of Pratt's *Brébeuf*[16] and sea narratives,

---

[15]Octave Crémaize (1827-79) was an active member of the Institut Canadien de Quebec, founded in 1847 to promote French culture and language. His lyrics, some of which were set to music, celebrate the courage and nobility of the ordinary Quebecois through reflections on his land, his language and his traditions.

[16]The full title of this long poem, portraying the clash between Native Canadian and European civilizations, is *Brébeuf and His Brethren*, 1940.

that Canadian poetry has become most articulate. There is nothing especially Canadian about this, but one point may be noted. To an English poet, the tradition of his own country and language proceeds in a direct chronological line down to himself, and that in its turn is part of a gigantic funnel of tradition extending back to Homer and the Old Testament. But to a Canadian, broken off from this linear sequence and having none of his own, the tradition of Europe appears as a kaleidoscopic whirl with no definite shape or meaning, but with a profound irony lurking in its varied and conflicting patterns. The clearest statement of this is in that superb fantasy the *Witches' Brew*, Pratt's first major effort, a poem of which apparently I have a higher opinion than Mr. Smith. It is also to be found, I think, in the elaborate Rabbinical apparatus of Klein.[17]

American even more than Canadian poetry has been deeply affected by the clash between two irreconcilable views of literature: the view that poets should be original and the view that they should be aboriginal. Originality is largely a matter of returning to origins, of studying and imitating the great poets of the past. But many fine American poets have been damaged and in some cases spoiled by a fetish of novelty: they have sought for the primitive and direct and have tried to avoid the consciously literary and speak the language of the common man. As the language of the common man is chiefly commonplace, the result has been for the most part disastrous. And here is one case where failing to achieve a virtue has really warded off a vice. There has on the whole been little Tarzanism in Canadian poetry. One is surprised to find how few really good Canadian poets have thought that getting out of cities into God's great outdoors really brings one closer to the sources of inspiration. One reason for this is that there has been no revolution in Canada, and less sense of building up a new land into what the American Constitution calls a more perfect state. A certain abdication of political responsibility is sharply reflected in our poetry, and is by no means always harmful to it. We can see this clearly if we compare Bliss Carman with his American friend Hovey,[18] who sang not only of

---

[17]Abraham Moses Klein (1909-72) was a member of the McGill Fortnightly Review group, which included Leon Edel, Leo Kennedy, F. R. Scott and A. J. M. Smith. Like them, Klein practiced and promoted Modernist tendencies in poetry. He was the first Canadian poet to fully assimilate in his writing a rich Hebrew culture.

[18]Richard Hovey (1864-1900), American poet, playwright and a personal friend of Bliss Carman with whom he collaborated on three collections of poetry: *Songs from Vagabondia;* 1894, *More Songs from Vagabondia;* 1896 and *Last Songs from Vagabondia,* 1901.

freedom and the open road but also of America's duty to occupy the Philippines and open up the Pacific. The Canadian likes to be objective about Americans, and likes to feel that he can see a bit of Sam Slick[19] in every Yankee: as a North American, therefore, he has a good seat on the revolutionary sidelines, and his poetic tendencies, reflective, observant, humorous, critical and quite frankly traditional, show it.

The closest analogy to Canadian poetry in American literature is, as one would expect, in the pre-1776 period: in Anne Bradstreet and Philip Freneau and the Hartford Wits.[20] We have many excellent counterparts to these, and to the tradition that runs through Emerson, but few if any good counterparts to Whitman, Sandburg, Lindsay, Jeffers or MacLeish. Early American poetry is traditional, but its tradition is a great one: and when the Americans gained maturity in government they lost some in poetry; for there is an assurance and subtlety in Bradstreet and Freneau that Longfellow and Whittier and many of those mentioned above do not possess. This is not to say that the best American poetry appeared before 1776, but as we seem to be stuck with at least some colonial characteristics, we may as well appreciate what virtues they have.

Nature in Canadian poetry, then, has little of the vagueness of great open spaces in it: that is very seldom material that the imagination can use. One finds rather an intent and closely focused vision, often on something in itself quite unimportant: in Birney's slug, Finch's[21] station platform, the clairvoyance of hatred in MacKay's[22]

---

[19]Sam Slick is the main character in T. C. Haliburton's *The Clockmaker; or, the Sayings and Doings of Samuel Slick, of Slickville.* As an energetic and aggressive Yankee peddler, Sam Slick is the embodiment of American entrepreneurship; the character's main function was to satirize Nova Scotian colonial apathy.

[20]Hartford Wits, a group of Connecticut professional men and literary aspirants who met in Hartford to discuss literary issues in post-revolutionary America. Members of the group included Richard Aslop, Theodore Dwight and David Humphreys. Their writing was known for its biting political satire.

[21]Robert Finch (1900-95), a distinguished professor of French at the University of Toronto, whose poetry was first published in the anthology, *New Provinces,* 1936, which also includes the work of other Modernists such as F. R. Scott, A. J. M. Smith and E. J. Pratt.

[22]L.A. MacKay published his first collection of poems, *Viper's Bugloss,* 1938, under a pseudonym "John Smalacombe." His second collection, *The Ill-Tempered Lover and Other Poems,* 1948, appeared under his own name.

"I Wish My Tongue Were a Quiver," Hambleton's[23] sharply etched picture of salmon fishing. The first poet Mr. Smith includes, the Canadian Oliver Goldsmith, makes an accurate inventory of a country store, and he sets a tone which the rest of the book bears out. The vocabulary and diction correspond: the snap and crackle of frosty words, some stiff with learning and others bright with concreteness, is heard wherever there is the mental excitement of real creation, though of course most obviously where the subject suggests it: in, for instance, Charles Bruce's "Immediates":

> An ageless land and sea conspire
> To smooth the imperfect mould of birth;
> While freezing spray and drying fire
> Translate the inexplicit earth.

or in P.K. Page's "Stenographers":

> In the felt of the morning, the calico minded,
> sufficiently starched, insert papers, hit keys,
> efficient and sure as their adding machines.

But, according to Mr. Smith's book, the outstanding achievement of Canadian poetry is in the evocation of stark terror. Not a coward's terror, of course; but a controlled vision of the causes of cowardice. The immediate source of this is obviously the frightening loneliness of a huge and thinly settled country. When all the intelligence, morality, reverence and simian cunning of man confronts a sphinx-like riddle of the indefinite like the Canadian winter, the man seems as helpless as a trapped mink and as lonely as a loon. His thrifty little heaps of civilized values look pitiful beside nature's apparently meaningless power to waste and destroy on a superhuman scale, and such a nature suggests an equally ruthless and subconscious God, or else no God. In Wilfred Campbell, for instance, the Canadian winter expands into a kind of frozen hell of utter moral nihilism.

> Lands that loom like spectres, white regions of winter,
>   Wastes of desolate woods, deserts of water and shore;
> A world of winter and death, within these regions who enter,
>   Lost to summer and life, go to return no more.

---

[23]Ronald Humbleton (1917-) edited in 1944 an important anthology of a younger generation of Modernists, *Unit of Five*, which included P. K. Page, Louis Dudek and others. His only volume of poetry, *Object and Event*, was published in 1953.

And the winter is only one symbol, though a very obvious one, of the central theme of Canadian poetry: the riddle of what a character in Mair's[24] *Tecumseh* calls "inexplicable life." It is really a riddle of inexplicable death: the fact that life struggles and suffers in a nature which is blankly indifferent to it. Human beings set a high value on their own lives which is obviously not accepted in the world beyond their palisades. They may become hurt and whimper that nature is cruel to them; but the honest poet does not see cruelty: he sees only a stolid unconsciousness. The human demands that Patrick Anderson's Joe hurls at nature are answered by "a feast of no;" a negation with neither sympathy nor malice in it. In Birney's *David* a terrible tragedy of wasted life and blasted youth is enacted on a glacier, but there is no "pathetic fallacy" about the cruelty of the glacier or of whatever gods may be in charge of it. It is just a glacier. D. C. Scott's "Piper of Arll" is located in an elusive fairyland, but the riddle of inexplicable death is still at the heart of the poem. The same theme is of course clearer still in Pratt's sea narratives, especially *The Titanic.*

Sometimes this theme modulates into a wry and sardonic humour. In the laughter of that rare spirit Standish O'Grady, who in his picture of freezing Canadians huddling around "their simpering stove" has struck out one of the wittiest phrases in the book, something rather sharper sounds across the laughter:

> Here the rough Bear subsists his winter year,
> And licks his paw and finds no better fare.

In Drummond's[25] finest poem, "The Wreck of the Julie Plante," the grim humour of the ballad expresses the same tragedy of life destroyed by unconsciousness that we find in Pratt and Birney:

> For de win' she blow lak hurricane,
> Bimeby she blow some more.

---

[24]Charles Mair (1838-1927), as a member of the Canada First movement, passionately promoted Canadian cultural nationalism. He urged writers and poets to follow his example of using Canada's heroic past as subject matter. His best-known work is a verse play, *Tecumseh: A Drama,* 1886, dealing with one of Canada's most important historical events, the War of 1812.

[25]William Henry Drummond (1854-1907) achieved great popularity at the turn of the nineteenth century with his lyrics on Quebec *habitant* life, written in what some critics have described as an 'invented' local idiom.

Tom MacInnes has the same kind of humour, though the context is often fantastic, and his "Zalinka" is a parody of Poe which somehow manages to convey the same kind of disturbing eeriness. But whether humorous or not, even in our most decorous poets there are likely to be the most startling flashes of menace and fear. A placid poem of Charles G. D. Roberts about mowing is suddenly punctured by the line "The crying knives glide on; the green swath lies." Archdeacon Scott writes a little poem on Easter Island statues which ends in a way that will lift your back hair.

But the poetic imagination cannot remain for long content with this faceless mask of unconsciousness. Nature is not all glacier and iceberg and hurricane; and while there is no conscious cruelty in it, there is certainly a suffering that we can interpret as cruelty. Hence the poet begins to animate nature with an evil or at least sinister power: night in Heavysege becomes a cacodemon, and spring in Dorothy Livesay a crouching monster. Mr. Smith's book is full of ghosts and unseen watchers and spiritual winds: a certain amount of this is faking, but not all: Lampman's "In November," with its ghastly dead mullens and the wonderful *danse macabre* in which it closes, is no fake. The "crying in the dark" in Lampman's "Midnight," the dead hunter in Eustace Ross's "The Death," the dead "lovely thing" in Neil Tracey's poem, the married corpses in Leo Kennedy's "Epithalamium": all these are visions, not only of a riddle of inexplicable death, but of a riddle of inexplicable evil. Sometimes, of course, this evil takes an easily recognized form: the Indians in Joseph Howe's spirited narrative and the drought wind in Anne Marriott have no spectral overtones. But it is obvious that man must be included in this aspect of the riddle, as it is merely fanciful to separate conscious malice from the human mind. Whatever sinister lurks in nature lurks also in us; and Tom MacInnes's "tiger of desire" and the praying mantis of a remarkable poem by Anne Dalton have been transformed into mental demons.

The unconscious horror of nature and the subconscious horrors of the mind thus coincide: this amalgamation is the basis of symbolism on which nearly all Pratt's poetry is founded. The fumbling and clumsy monsters of his "Pliocene Armageddon," who are simply incarnate wills to mutual destruction, are the same monsters that beget Nazism and inspire *The Fable of the Goats*;[26] and in the fine "Silences," which Smith includes, civilized life is seen geologically as merely one clock-tick in eons of ferocity. The waste of life in the death of the Cachalot and the waste of courage and sanctity in the killing of the Jesuit missionaries are tragedies of a unique kind in modern poetry: like the tragedy of Job,

---

[26]*The Fable of the Goats*, E.J. Pratt, 1937.

they seem to move upward to a vision of a monstrous Leviathan, a power of chaotic nihilism which is "king over all the children of pride." I admit that "Tom the Cat from Zanzibar" in *The Witches' Brew* is good fun, but when Mr. Smith suggests that he is nothing more, I disagree.

In the creepy ambiguity of the first line of Malzah's song in Heavysege, "There was a devil and his name was I," the same association of ideas recurs, and it recurs again in what is perhaps the most completely articulate poem in the book, Lampman's "The City of the End of Things"; which, though of course it has no room for the slow accumulation of despair that *The City of Dreadful Night*[27] piles up, is an equally terrifying vision of humanity's Iron Age. In the younger writers the satire on war and exploitation is more conventional and anonymous, but as soon as they begin to speak with more authority they will undoubtedly take their places in the same tradition — Patrick Anderson especially.

To sum up. Canadian poetry is at its best a poetry of incubus and *cauchemar*, the source of which is the unusually exposed contact of the poet with nature which Canada provides. Nature is seen by the poet, first as unconsciousness, then as a kind of existence which is cruel and meaningless, then as the source of the cruelty and subconscious stampedings within the human mind. As compared with American poets, there has been comparatively little, outside Carman, of the cult of the rugged outdoor life which idealizes nature and tries to accept it. Nature is consistently sinister and menacing in Canadian poetry. And here and there we find glints of a vision beyond nature, a refusal to be bullied by space and time, an affirmation of the supremacy of intelligence and humanity over stupid power. One finds this in Kenneth Leslie:

> Rather than moulds invisible in the air
> into which petals pour selective milk
> I seem to sense a partnered agony
> of creature and creator in the rose.

One finds it in Dorothy Livesay's apostrophe to the martyred Lorca:

> You dance. Explode
> Unchallenged through the door

---

[27] *The City of Dreadful Night*, 1880, was written by a British author, James Thomson (1834-82), best known by his signature 'B.V.' His poetry is somber in tone and evokes a feeling of loneliness and futility of human existence.

As bullets burst
Long deaths ago, your breast.

One finds in Margaret Avison's very lovely "Maria Minor" and her struggle to divine "the meaning of the smashed moth" in a poem which makes an excellent finale to the book. And one begins thereby to understand the real meaning of the martyrdom of Brébeuf, the theme of what with all its faults is the greatest single Canadian poem. Superficially, the man with the vision beyond nature is tied to the stake and destroyed by savages who are in the state of nature, and who represent its mindless barbarity. But there is a far profounder irony to that scene: the black-coated figure at the stake is also a terrifying devil to the savages, *Echon*, the evil one. However frantically they may try to beat him off, their way of savagery is doomed; it is doomed in their Nazi descendants; it is doomed even if it lasts to the end of time.

This is not, I hope, a pattern of thought I have arbitrarily forced upon Canadian poetry: judging from Mr. Smith's book and what other reading I have done this seems to be its underlying meaning, and the better the poem the more clearly it expresses it. Mr. Smith has brought out this inner unity quite unconsciously because it is really there: just as in his "Ode on Yeats" he has, again quite unconsciously, evoked a perfect image of the nature of poetic feeling in his own country:

An old thorn tree in a stony place
Where the mountain stream has run dry,
Torn in the black wind under the race
Of the icicle-sharp kaleidoscopic white sky,
  Bursts into sudden flower.

"Canada and Its Poetry." First published in *Canadian Forum,* December 1943.

The Narrative Tradition in English-Canadian Poetry

The Canadian poet cannot write in a distinctively Canadian language; he is compelled to take the language he was brought up to speak, whether French, English, or Icelandic, and attempt to adjust that language to an environment which is foreign to it, if not foreign to himself. Once he accepts a language, however, he joins the line of poets in the tradition of that language, at the point nearest to his immediate predecessors. A nineteenth-century Canadian poet writing in English will be emulating Keats and Tennyson; writing in French, he will be emulating Victor Hugo or Baudelaire. It may be thought that it would be a pure advantage to the Canadian poet to put an old tongue into a new face; that the mere fact of his being a Canadian would give him something distinctive to say, and enable him to be original without effort. But it is not as simple as that. His poetry cannot be "young," for it is written in a European language with a thousand years of disciplined utterance behind it, and any attempt to ignore that tradition can only lead to disaster. Nor is Canada a "young" country in the sense that its industrial conditions, its political issues, or the general level of its civilization, are significantly different from contemporary Europe. Nevertheless, to the imaginative eye of the creative artist, whether painter or poet, certain aspects of Canada must, for a long time yet, make it appear young. Its landscape does not have, as that of Europe has, that indefinable quality which shows that it has been lived in by civilized human beings for millennia. Its villages do not "nestle;" they sprawl awkwardly into rectangular lines along roads or railways. Its buildings do not melt into their backgrounds; they stand out with a garish and tasteless defiance. It is full of human and natural ruins, of abandoned buildings and despoiled countryside, such as are found only with the vigorous wastefulness of young countries. And, above all, it is a country in which nature makes a direct impression on the artist's mind, an impression of its primeval lawlessness and moral nihilism, its indifference to the supreme value placed on life within human society, its faceless, mindless unconsciousness, which fosters life without benevolence and destroys it without malice. There is, of course, much more to be said about nature than this, even by the Canadian artist, but this is an aspect of nature which the sensitive Canadian finds it impossible to avoid. It is all very well for a European poet to see nature in terms of a settled order which the mind can interpret, like Wordsworth, or even in terms of oracular hints and suggestions, like Baudelaire in *Correspondances;* but the Canadian poet receives all his initial impressions in the environment of Rimbaud's *Bateau Ivre.*

What the poet sees in Canada, therefore, is very different from what the politician or businessman sees, and different again from what his European contemporaries see. He may be a younger man than Yeats or Eliot, but he has to deal with a poetic and imaginative environment for which, to find any parallel in England, we should have to go back to a period earlier than Chaucer. In certain Old English poems, notably "The Wanderer" and "The Seafarer," there is a feeling which seems to a modern reader more Canadian than English: a feeling of the melancholy of a thinly-settled country under a bleak northern sky, of the terrible isolation of the creative mind in such a country, of resigning oneself to hardship and loneliness as the only means of attaining, if not serenity, at least a kind of rigid calm. It is a feeling which in later centuries becomes very rare, though there is something of it in some romantic poems, such as Keats's "La Belle Dame Sans Merci."

Now of course modern Canadian life is far less simple and homogeneous than Old English life. The Canadian poet, though he must try to express something of what the Old English poet felt, cannot afford to forget either that a highly sophisticated civilization is as much a part of Canadian life as deep snow and barren spaces. If we can imagine a contemporary of the *Beowulf* poet, with equal genius and an equally strong urge to write an archaic epic of the defeat of a monster of darkness by a hero of immense strength and endurance — a theme which should appeal powerfully to a Canadian — yet writing for the same public as Ovid and Catullus, and forced to adapt their sophisticated witticisms and emotional refinements to his own work, we shall begin to get some idea of what the Canadian poet is up against.

This if why nearly all good Canadian poets have much less simple poetic natures than they appear to have at first glance. The "framework" of Lampman, for instance, is that of a placid romantic nature poet beating the track of Wordsworth and Keats. But there are also in Lampman many very different characteristics. He has, for instance, a spiritual loneliness, a repugnance to organized social life, which goes far beyond mere discontent with his provincial environment. This is a quality in Lampman which links him to the great Canadian explorers, the solitary adventurers among solitudes, and the explorer-painters like Thomson[1] and Emily Carr who followed them, with their eyes continually straining into the depths of nature. And in the terrible clairvoyance of "The City of the End of Things," a vision of the Machine Age slowly freezing into idiocy and despair, something lives again of the spirit of the Old English Wanderer, who, trudging from castle to castle in the hope of finding food and shelter in exchange for his songs, turned to the great Roman ruins, the "eald enta geweorc" (the ancient work of giants), to brood over a greater oppression of man by nature than his own.

Similarly, the "framework" of Isabella Crawford is that of an intelligent and industrious female songbird of the kind who filled so many anthologies in the last century. Yet the "South Wind" passage from *Malcolm's Katie* is only the most famous example of the most remarkable mythopeic imagination in Canadian poetry. She puts her myth in an Indian form, which reminds us of the resemblance between white and Indian legendary heroes in the New World, between Paul Bunyan and Davy Crockett on the one hand and Glooscap[2] on the other. The white myths are not necessarily imitated from the Indian ones, but they may have sprung from an unconscious feeling that the primitive myth expressed the imaginative impact of the country as more artificial literature could never do.

Some of the same affinities appear in those aspects of our literature that a poet would naturally be most interested in, though very few of them have received adequate poetic treatment. The martyrdom of the Jesuit missionaries, the holding of the Long Sault against the Iroquois, the victories over incredible odds in the War of 1812, the desperate courage of the Indians who died with Tecumseh and Riel, the 1837 outbreak, the fight without gasmasks against gas at St. Julien, the spearheading of the plunge into Amiens, the forlorn hope at Dieppe — there is a certain family resemblance among all these events which makes each one somehow typical of Canadian history. Is there not something in the character of such themes that recalls the earliest poetry of our mother countries, of the lost battle of Maldon where courage grew greater as the strength ebbed away, or of the reckless heroism at Roncesvalles which laid the cornerstone of French literature? It is perhaps not an accident that the best known of all Canadian poems, "In

---

[1]Tom Thomson (1877-1917) was one of Canada's leading painters before his tragic early death by drowning. Thomson, who broke from the mannerism of the previous generation of painters, is considered a precursor of the Group of Seven.

[2]Glooscap is a central figure in Micmac legends. Of unknown origin, he was endowed with magical powers which he used for the good of his people.

Flanders' Fields," should express, in a tight, compressed, grim little rondeau, the same spirit of an inexorable ferocity which even death cannot relax, like the old Norse warrior whose head continued to gnash and bite the dust long after it had been severed from his body.

Hence it is at least possible that some of the poetic forms employed in the earlier centuries of English literature would have been more appropriate for the expression of Canadian themes and moods than the nineteenth-century romantic lyric or its twentieth-century metaphysical successor. It is inevitable that the Canadian poetry should have been cast in the conventional forms of our own day; but though the bulk of it is lyrical in form, a great deal of it is not lyrical in spirit, and when a Canadian poem has failed to achieve adequate expression, this may often be the reason. It has been remarked, for instance, that sexual passion is a theme that our poets have not treated very convincingly. This emotion is also lacking in Old English poetry, and perhaps for some of the same reasons. But sexual passion is one of the essential themes of the lyric: Canadian poetry is lyrical in form and Old English poetry is not, hence the failure to deal with sexual passion is felt as a lack in Canadian poetry but is not missed in Old English. On the other hand, it occasionally happens that a successful Canadian poem has owed its success to its coincidence, deliberate or otherwise, with one of the forms of pre-Chaucerian literature. Thus Drummond's best poem, "The Wreck of the Julie Plante," is not merely a modern imitation of the ballad; it has the tough humour and syncopated narrative of the authentic ballad at its best. Consider too the subject of many of D. C. Scott's finest poems, the lovers destroyed in a long jam, the lonely Indian murdered in the forest for his furs, the squaw who baits a fish hook with her own flesh to feed her children. These are ballad themes; and his longest poem "Dominique de Gourges," a narrative filled with the sombre exultation of revenge, is curiously archaic in spirit for the author of a poem on Debussy. Something medieval has also crept in to the religious emotions of A. J. M. Smith and to Leo Kennedy's exercises in the *macabre*.

All this may help to explain a phenomenon of our poetry which must have puzzled many of its students. In looking over the best poems of our best poets, while of course the great majority are lyrical, we are surprised to find how often the narrative poem has been attempted, and attempted with uneven but frequently remarkable success. I say surprised, because good narratives are exceedingly rare in English poetry — except in the period that ended with the death of Chaucer. And this unusual prominence of the narrative is one of the things that makes Canadian poetry so hard to criticize with the right combination of sympathy and judgment. We tend to form our canons of criticism on carefully polished poetry, but such standards do not always apply to the narrative, for the test of the great narrative is its ability to give the flat prose statement a poetic value. And as there has been no connected tradition of narrative in English literature since 1400, the Canadian poet who attempts the form has to depend largely on his own originality, and no one except Pratt has worked hard enough and long enough at the form to discover its inherent genius. Hence among Canadian narratives there are many failures and many errors of taste and stretches of bad writing, but to anyone who cares about poetry there may be something more interesting in the failure than in a less ambitious success.

At the outset of Canadian literature we find many long poems, Goldsmith's[3] *Rising Village,* O'Grady's[4] brilliant but unfinished *Emigrant,* Howe's[5] *Acadia,* also unfinished, and two dramatic poems by Duvar[6], *The Enamorado* and *De Roberval,* the last of which illustrate the fact that the Canadian narrative is frequently cast in the form of dialogue or literary drama. All of these follow well established European conventions, and so do the first two productions of the clumsy but powerfully built genius of Heavysege. *Saul* belongs to the tradition of the Victorian leviathan, the discursive poem combining a Biblical subject with middle class morality, represented by the better known Bailey's[7] *Festus. Count Filippo,* too, is in the manner of nineteenth-century reactions to Jacobean drama and the Italian Renaissance, and might almost have served as the model for Max Beerbohm's *Savanarola Brown*. But *Jephthah's Daughter,* his third effort, strikes its roots

---

[3]Oliver Goldsmith (1794-1861) was the first Canadian-born poet to publish a book of verse. He is best known for his long narrative poem, *The Rising Village,* 1825, reprinted in David Sinclair's *Nineteenth-Century Narrative Poems,* 1972.

[4]Standish O'Grady (1793-1841). *The Emigrant: A Poem in Four Cantos,* self-published, was the poet's only printed work.

[5]Joseph Howe (1804-73) was a renowned politician of nineteenth-century Nova Scotia, a publisher of *Novascotian,* the leading journal in the Colony, a journalist and a poet. His poetry, including his long narrative poem, "Acadia," came out in local newspapers and was posthumously published as *Poems and Essays,* 1874. "Acadia" is also reprinted in Sinclair's *Nineteenth-Century Narrative Poetry.*

[6]John Hunter-Duvar (1830-99) wrote verse dramas of which *The Enamorado,* 1879, and *De Roberval,* 1888, are the best known — and lyrical poetry, including "The Emigration of the Fairies," considered by some critics to be his most technically accomplished work.

[7]Jacob Bailey (1731-1808) published in 1853 his moving and well-documented account of a Loyalist before his flight to Nova Scotia in *The Frontier Missionary: A Memoir of the Life of the Rev. Jacob Bailey.*

deeply into Canada, and is the real commencement of a distinctively Canadian form of the narrative poem.

Heavysege begins by saying that the story of Jephthah's daughter is very similar to the story of Iphigenia, and that he has chosen the Hebrew legend because there is a spiritual loneliness about it which attracts him more profoundly. Iphigenia was sacrificed in the midst of great bustle and excitement, and was, as Samuel Johnson said of the victim at a public hanging, sustained by her audience: Jephthah's daughter is destroyed by the mute anguish of uncomprehending superstition. To Heavysege, a man who, like Jephthah, worships a God who demands fulfillment of a rash vow of sacrifice even if it involves his own daughter, is really a man in the state of nature: he has identified his God, if not with nature, at any rate with a mindless force of inscrutable mystery like nature, and all Jephthah's questionings and searchings of spirit are the looks of intelligence directed at blankness, the attempts of a religious pioneer to find a spiritual portage through the heart of darkness. The passage in which Heavysege described this most clearly cannot be beaten in James Thomson[8] for the sheer starkness of its mood, a grimness that is far deeper than any ghost-haunted horrors. Jephthah prays to be delivered from the blood of his daughter, and asks for a sign of divine mercy. There is a slight pause, then Jephthah hears:

> The hill-wolf howling on the neighbouring height,
> And bittern booming in the pool below.

That is all the answer he gets.

In this poem Heavysege has put together certain essential ideas: the contrast of human and civilized values with nature's disregard of them in a primitive country, the tendency in the religion of such a country for God to disappear behind the mask of nature, and the symbolic significance, when that happens, of human sacrifice and the mutilation of the body (a theme already elaborated by Heavysege in the episode in *Saul* about the hewing of Agag in pieces). Once one has carefully read this narrative, the essential meaning of many fine Canadian poems leaps out of its derivative and conventional context. Thus in Isabella Crawford's *Malcolm's Katie* there is a superbly ironic scene in which the hero sings of the irresistible advance of capitalist civilization and its conquest of nature, symbolized by the axe, and links his exu-

---

[8]James Maurice Thompson (1844-1901) was one of many turn-of-the-century writers who produced popular historical romances, usually set in remote and exotic places. He is the author of *Alice of Old Vincennes*, 1901.

berant belief in the enduring power of the nation he is building with his belief in the enduring power of his love for the heroine. He is answered by the villain, in a passage of far greater eloquence, who points out the cyclic progress of all empires from rise to decline and the instability of woman's love. As the hero turns indignantly to refute his slanders, the tree which he has not quite chopped down falls on him and crushes him. True, he recovers and marries the heroine and forgives the villain and lives happily ever after and love conquers all and nature is grand, but somehow the poem reaches an imaginative concentration in that scene which it never afterwards recaptures. In the same poem the heroine is caught in a log jam, and, though of course she is rescued, the sudden glimpse of the trap of nature, the endless resources it has for suddenly and unconsciously destroying a fragile and beautiful human life, is far more effective without the rescue, and is so developed in D. C. Scott's "At the Cedars."

Mair's *Tecumseh* and Lampman's "At the Long Sault" apply the same pattern to Canadian history. The former has been charged with lack of unity, but the theme of the drama is the sacrifice of Tecumseh, to which everything else leads up, the various conflicts between his own fierce loyalties and vacillations of his friends and enemies being merely the struggles of a doomed victim who now arouses and now disappoints our hopes for his escape. Lampman, too, seems most deeply impressed, not only by the sacrificial nature of what the Long Sault heroes did, which is obvious enough, but by its symbolic connection with, again, a state of nature in which the higher forms of life are so often destroyed by the lower. That is why he introduces the beautiful picture of the moose pulled down by wolves, the symbol of the exceptional and unblemished hero who falls a victim to the agents of a careless fate.

Pratt has studied the technique and resources of the narrative form more carefully that his predecessors, and so it is not surprising to find the themes we have been tracing much more explicitly set forth in his work. He delights in describing big and even monstrous things, and whenever he can he shows them exulting in their strength. In the antics of Tom the Cat from Zanzibar in *The Witches' Brew*, in the almost equally feline sense of relaxed power in "The 6000," in the ferocious but somehow exuberant massacres in *The Great Feud*, there is more enthusiasm than in his other works, for naturally he greatly prefers the Othellos of this world to the Iagos, and hates to see the latter victorious. But the Canadian narrative demands a tragic resolution. *The Cachalot* is not perhaps a tragic poem, but is there really so much moral difference between the whale caught by men and the moose in Lampman pulled down by wolves? In *The Titanic* the mindlessness of the agent of destruction is the imaginative centre of the poem: the tragic theme of hubris, the punishment of man by fate for his presumption in defying it, is, though a very obvious and in fact ready-made aspect of the theme, deliberately played down. If *Dunkirk* seems less wholly convincing than some of his other narratives, it may well be because the absence of the theme of wasted life gives it a resolutely optimistic quality which seems rather forced, more the glossed and edited reporter's story than the poet's complete and tragic vision.

Brébeuf is not only the greatest but the most complete Canadian narrative, and brings together into a single pattern all the themes we have been tracing. Here the mutilation and destruction of the gigantic Brébeuf and the other missionaries is a sacrificial rite in which the Indians represent humanity in the state of nature and are agents of its unconscious barbarity. It is curious that, just as the poet minimizes the theme of hubris in *The Titanic*, so in *Brébeuf* he minimizes the awareness of the Indians, their feeling that they are disposing of a real enemy, a black-coated emissary of an unknown God and an unknown race that may soon wipe them out. In any case, Indians, even Iroquois, are not merely wolves; and while the conflict of mental and physical values is certainly present, there is a greater range of suggestiveness. In the first place, the scene is related to its universal archetype: Brébeuf is given the courage to endure the breaking of his body because the body of God was in a very similar way broken for him. Thus the essential tragedy of Jephthah's daughter, as a pointless and useless waste of life, ceases to exist. In the second place, the Indians represent the fact that the unconscious cruelty of nature is recreated by the partly conscious cruelties of ignorant and frightened men. This point is already implicit in *Jephthah's Daughter;* we have seen that Jephthah is really sacrificing his daughter to nature. But it is clearer here, and it is clear too that the monsters of *The Great Feud*, who are animated only by an impulse to mutual destruction, prefigure the stampeding and maniacal fury of Nazism as much as their descendants in *The Fable of the Goats* do.

In *Brébeuf* the poet makes a comment which may well be prophetic for the future of Canadian poetry:

> The wheel had come full circle with the visions
> In France of Brébeuf poured through the mould of St. Ignace.

For a wheel does come full circle here: a narrative tradition begotten in the nineteenth century, and heir to all the philosophical pessimism and moral nihilism of that century, reaches its culmination in *Brébeuf* and is hardly capable of much future development. True, Birney's *David* is a fine example of the same sort of tragedy that is in "At the Cedars" or even *The Titanic,* and in the phrase "the last of my youth" with which the poem ends there is even a faint suggestion of a sacrificial symbolism. And in Anne Marriott's "The Wind Our Enemy," it is significant that the enemy is still the wind rather than the forces of economic breakdown that helped to create the wind. But neither of these poets seems likely to go on with this theme, and in such poems as "The Truant," where man confronts the order of nature undismayed, it is evident that Pratt is abandoning it too. The poet's vision of Canada as a pioneer country in which man stands face to face with nature is bound to be superseded by a vision of Canada as a settled and civilized country, part of an international order, in which men confront the social and spiritual problems of men. That this development is now taking place and will greatly increase in future needs no detailed proof: but it is to be hoped that the poets who do deal with it will maintain an interest in the traditional narrative form. For the lyric, if cultivated too exclusively, tends to become too entangled with the printed page: in an age when new contacts between a poet and his public are opening up through radio, the narrative, as a form peculiarly well adapted for public reading, may play an important role in reawakening a public respect for and response to poetry. There are values in both tradition and experiment, and in both the narrative has important claims as Canadian poetry hesitates on the threshold of a new era.

"La tradition narrative dans la poésie canadienne-anglaise." First published in *Gants du Ciel,* No. 11 (1946), (French translation by Guy Sylvestre.) English text published as "The Narrative Tradition in English-Canadian Poetry" in *The Bush Garden,* 1971.

Preface to an Uncollected Anthology

The author imagines he has collected his ideal anthology of English Canadian poetry, with no difficulties about permission, publishers, or expense, and is writing his preface.

Certain critical principles are essential for dealing with Canadian poetry which in the study of English literature as such are seldom raised. Unless the critic is aware of the importance of these principles, he may, in turning to Canadian poets, find himself unexpectedly incompetent, like a giraffe trying to eat off the ground. The first of these principles is the fact that the cultivated Canadian has the same kind of interest in Canadian poetry that he has in Canadian history or politics. Whatever its merits, it is the poetry of his own country, and it gives him an understanding of that country which nothing else can give him. The critic of Canadian literature has to settle uneasily somewhere between the Canadian historian or social scientist, who has no comparative value-judgment to worry about, and the ordinary literary critic, who has nothing else. The qualities in Canadian poetry which help to make Canada more imaginatively articulate for the Canadian reader are genuine literary values, whether they coincide with other literary values or not. And while the reason for collecting an anthology can only be the merit of the individual poems, still, having made such a collection, one may legitimately look at the proportioning of interests, at the pattern of the themes that seem to make Canadian poets eloquent.

It is not a nation but an environment that makes an impact on poets, and poetry can deal only with the imaginative aspect of that environment. A country with almost no Atlantic seaboard, which for most of its history has existed in practically one dimension; a country divided by two languages and great stretches of wilderness, so that its frontier is a circumference rather than a boundary; a country with huge rivers and islands that most of its natives have never seen; a country that has made a nation out of the stops on two of the world's longest railway lines: this is the environment that Canadian poets have to grapple with, and many of the imaginative problems it presents have no counterpart in the United States, or anywhere else.

In older countries the works of man and of nature, the city and the garden of civilization, have usually reached some kind of imaginative harmony. But the land of the Rockies and the Precambrian Shield impresses painter and poet alike by its raw colours and angular rhythms, its profoundly unhumanized isolation. It is still "The Lonely Land" to A. J. M. Smith, still "A Country without a Mythology" to Douglas LePan. The works of man are even more imaginatively undigested. A Canadian village, unlike an English one, does not "nestle": it sprawls awkwardly along a highway or railway line, less an inhabited centre than an episode of communication. Its buildings express an arrogant defiance of the landscape; its roads and telephone wires and machinery twist and strangle and loop. Irving Layton says, looking at an abstract picture,

> When I got the hang of it
> I saw a continent of railway tracks
> coiling about the sad Modigliani necks
> like disused tickertape, the streets
> exploding in the air
> with disaffected subway cars.

The Wordsworth who saw nature as exquisitely fitted to the human mind would be lost in Canada, where what the poets see is a violent collision of two forces, both monstrous. Earle Birney describes the bull-dozers of a logging camp as "iron brontosaurs;" Klein compares grain elevators to leviathans.

Poets are a fastidious race, and in Canadian poetry we have to give some place, at least at the beginning, to the anti-Canadian, the poet who has taken one horrified look at the country and fled. Thus Standish O'Grady, writing of *The Emigrant:*

> Here forests crowd, unprofitable lumber,
> O'er fruitless lands indefinite as number;
> Where birds scarce light, and with the north winds veer
> On wings of wind, and quickly disappear,
> Here the rough Bear subsists his winter year,
> And licks his paw and finds no better fare...
> The lank Canadian eager trims his fire.
> And all around their simpering stoves retire;
> With fur clad friends their progenies abound,
> And thus regale their buffaloes around;

Unlettered race, how few the number tells,
Their only pride a cariole and bells...
Perchance they revel; still around they creep,
And talk, and smoke, and spit, and drink, and sleep!

There is a great deal of polished wit in these couplets of the modern ambiguous kind: the word "lumber," for example, has both its Canadian meaning of wood and its English meaning of junk. We notice that "Canadian" in this poem means French Canadian *habitant:* O'Grady no more thinks of himself as Canadian than an Anglo-Indian colonel would think of himself as Hindu. Here is an American opinion, the close of a folk song about a construction gang that spent a winter in Three Rivers:

And now the winter's over, it's homeward we are bound,
And in this cursed country we'll never more be found.
Go back to your wives and sweethearts, tell others not to go
To that God-forsaken country called Canaday-I-O.

Thanks to the efforts of those who remained, this particular theme is now obsolete, although Norman Levine in 1950 spoke of leaving the land of "parchment summers and merchant eyes" for "the loveliest of fogs," meaning England. Still, it will serve as an introduction to two central themes in Canadian poetry: one a primarily comic theme of satire and exuberance, the other a primarily tragic theme of loneliness and terror.

It is often said that a pioneering country is interested in material rather than spiritual or cultural values. This is a *cliché,* and it has become a *cliché* because it is not really true, as seventeenth-century Massachusetts indicates. What is true is that the imaginative energy of an expanding economy is likely to be mainly technological. As a rule it is the oppressed or beleaguered peoples, like the Celts and the Hebrews, whose culture makes the greatest imaginative efforts: successful nations usually express a restraint or a matter-of-fact realism in their culture and keep their exuberance for their engineering. If we are looking for imaginative exuberance in American life, we shall find it not in its fiction but in its advertising; not in Broadway drama but in Broadway skyscrapers; not in the good movies but in the vista-visioned and technicoloured silly ones. The extension of this life into Canada is described by Frank Scott in "Saturday Sundae," by James Reaney in "Klaxon," a fantasy of automobiles wandering over highways without drivers, "Limousines covered with pink slime / Of children's blood," and by many other poets.

The poet dealing with the strident shallowness of much Canadian life is naturally aware that there is no imaginative change when we cross the American border in either direction. Yet there is, I think, a more distinctive attitude in Canadian poetry than in Canadian life, a more withdrawn and detached view of life which may go back to the central fact of Canadian history: the rejection of the American Revolution. What won the American Revolution was the spirit of entrepreneur capitalism, an enthusiastic plundering of the natural resources of a continent and an unrestricted energy of manufacturing and exchanging them. In *A Search for America,* which is quite a profound book if we take the precaution of reading it as a work of fiction, Grove[1] speaks of there being two Americas, an ideal one that has something to do with the philosophy of Thoreau and the personality of Lincoln, and an actual one that made the narrator a parasitic salesman of superfluous goods and finally a hobo. At the end of the book he remarks in a footnote that his ideal America has been preserved better in Canada than in the United States. The truth of this statement is not my concern, but some features of my anthology seem to reflect similar attitudes.

In the United States, with its more intensively indoctrinated educational system, there has been much rugged prophecy in praise of the common man, a tradition that runs from Whitman through Sandburg and peters out in the lugubrious inspirationalism of the Norman Corwin school. Its chief characteristics are the praise of the uncritical life and a manly contempt of prosody. One might call it the Whitmanic-depressive tradition, in view of the fact that it contains Robinson Jeffers. It seems to me significant that this tradition has had so little influence in Canada. I find in my anthology a much higher proportion of humour than I expected when I began: a humour of a quiet, reflective, observant type, usually in fairly strict metre, and clearly coming from a country with a ringside seat on the revolutionary sidelines.

A song from a poem by Alexander McLachlan called, like O'Grady's, "The Emigrant," will illustrate what I mean:

> I love my own country and race,
>   Nor lightly I fled from them both,
> Yet who would remain in a place
>   Where there's too many spoons for the broth.

---

[1]Frederick Philip Grove (1879-1948), born Felix Paul Greve in Prussia, spent most of his adult life in Canada where he is regarded as one its foremost writers of realistic fiction.

The squire's preserving his game.
    He says that God gave it to him,
And he'll banish the poor without shame,
    For touching a feather or limb....

The Bishop he preaches and prays,
    And talks of a heavenly birth,
But somehow, for all that he says,
    He grabs a good share of the earth.

In this poem there is nothing of the typically American identification of freedom with national independence: the poet is still preoccupied with the old land and thinks of himself as still within its tradition. There is even less of the American sense of economic competition as the antidote to social inequality. The spirit in McLachlan's poem is that of a tough British radicalism, the radicalism of the Glasgow dock worker or the Lancashire coal miner, the background of the Tom Paine who has never quite fitted the American way of life.

We may find something similar in a totally different context: an episode in the *Malcolm's Katie* of that very shrewd woman Isabella Crawford. The hero is engaged in cutting down a tree and singing the praises of the axe as the agent of progress. He is interrupted by the villain, who is something of a Spenglerian and who speaks of the eventual downfall of all cycles of civilization. The hero turns indignantly to refute this unhealthy pessimism, whereupon the tree, which he has forgotten about, falls over and flattens him. The irony of the scene is all the more striking for being somewhat out of key with the general romantic tone, as of course the hero gets up again, and his simple-minded view of life eventually baffles the villain and annexes the heroine. If we are to read Canadian poetry sympathetically we must often keep an eye out for such disturbers of poetic convention.

It is not surprising to find a good deal of satiric light verse in this imaginative resistance to industrial expansion and the gum-chewing way of life. Frank Scott we have mentioned: his "Canadian Social Register" is a ferocious paraphrase of an advertising prospectus, and his "Social Notes" are also something un-American, social poems with an unmistakably socialist moral. The observations of Toronto by Raymond Souster and of Montreal by Louis Dudek, Miriam Waddington, and Irving Layton have much to the same effect: of golfers Layton remarks "that no theory of pessimism is complete / Which altogether ignores them." But of course it is easy for the same satiric tone to turn bitter and nightmarish. Lampman's terrible poem, "The City of the End of Things," is not only social but psychological, and warns of the dangers not simply of exploiting labour but of washing our own brains. There are other sinister visions in A. J. M. Smith's "The Bridegroom," in Dudek's "East of the City," in Dorothy Livesay's "Day and Night," in P. K. Page's "The Stenographers," and elsewhere. Canadian poems of depression and drought, like Dorothy Livesay's "Outrider" or Anne Marriott's "The Wind Our Enemy," often have in them the protest of a food-producing community cheated out of its labour not simply by hail and grasshoppers but by some mysterious financial finagling at the other end of the country, reminding us of the man in Balzac's parable who could make his fortune by killing somebody in China. The same feeling comes out in a poignant folk song that could have come from only one part of the world, southeastern Newfoundland:

> Oh, mother dear, I wants a sack
> With beads and buttons down the back...
> Me boot is broke, me frock is tore, But
> Georgie Snooks I do adore...
> Oh, fish is low and flour is high,
> So Georgie Snooks he can't have I.

There are of course more positive aspects of industrial expansion. In Canada the enormous difficulties and the central importance of communication and transport, the tremendous energy that developed the fur trade routes, the empire of the St. Lawrence, the transcontinental railways, and the northwest police patrols have given it the dominating role in the Canadian imagination. E. J. Pratt is the poet who has best grasped this fact, and his *Towards the Last Spike* expresses the central comic theme of Canadian life, using the term "comic" in its literary sense as concerned with the successful accomplishment of a human act.

The imagery of technology and primary communication is usually either avoided by poets or employed out of a sense of duty: its easy and unforced appearance in Pratt is part of the reason why Pratt is one of the few good popular poets of our time. Technology appears all through his work, not only in the poems whose subjects demand it, but in other and more unexpected contexts. Thus in "Come Away, Death":

> We heard the tick-tock on the shelf,
> And the leak of valves in our hearts.

In "The Prize Cat," where a cat pounces on a bird and reminds the poet of the deliberately summoned-up brutality of the Fascist conquest of Ethiopia, the two themes are brought together by the inspired flash of a technical word:

Behind the leap so furtive-wild
Was such ignition in the gleam
I thought an Abyssinian child
Had cried out in the whitethroat's scream.

As a student of psychology, before he wrote poetry at all, he was preoccupied with the problems of sensory response to signals, and the interest still lingers in the wireless messages of The Titanic, the radar and asdic of "Behind the Log", and the amiable joggle of "No. 6000," one of the loveliest of all railway poems:

A lantern flashed out a command,
A bell was ringing as a hand
Clutched at a throttle, and the bull,
At once obedient to the pull,
Began with bellowing throat to lead
By slow accelerating speed
Six thousand tons of caravan
Out to the spaces — there to toss
The blizzard from his path across
The prairies of Saskatchewan.

In *Behind the Log*, Canadians undertake a mission of war in much the spirit of an exploration: there is a long journey full of perils, many members of the expedition drop off, and those that reach the goal feel nothing but a numb relief. Nothing could be less like the charge of the Light Brigade. Yet perhaps in this poem we may find a clue to the fact that Canada, a country that has never found much virtue in war and has certainly never started one, has in its military history a long list of ferocious conflicts against desperate odds. The Canadian poem best known outside Canada, MacCrae's[2] "In Flanders Fields," breathes the spirit like that of a Viking warrior whose head continued to gnaw the dust after it had been cut from his body; and it comes from the country of the Long Sault, Chrysler's Farm, St. Julien and Dieppe. Douglas LePan's "The Net and the Sword," the title poem of a book dealing with the Italian campaign of the Second World War, mentions something similar:

---

[2]John MacCrae (1872-1918) had a prominent medical career, which led him in 1914 to join the Canadian Forces in Europe as a medical officer. His most famous poem, "In Flanders' Fields," was written during the battle of Ypres and was subsequently included in a volume of twenty-nine of his war poems, edited by Sir Andrew MacPhail in 1919.

In this sandy arena, littered
And looped with telephone wires, tank-traps, mine-fields,
Twined about the embittered
Debris of history, the people whom he shields
Would quail before a stranger if they could see
His smooth as silk ferocity.

LePan finds the source of the ferocity in the simplicity of the Canadian soldier's vision: "Skating at Scarborough, summers at the Island," but perhaps it is also a by-product of engineering exuberance. We notice that the looped litter of telephone wires and the like belongs here to Europe, not to Canada, and the same kind of energy is employed to deal with it.

The tragic themes of Canadian poetry have much the same origin as the comic ones. The cold winter may suggest tragedy, but it may equally well suggest other moods, and does so in Lampman's sonnet "Winter Evening," in Patrick Anderson's "Song of Intense Cold," in Roberts' "The Brook in February," in Klein's "Winter Night: Mount Royal," and elsewhere. Other seasons too have their sinister aspects: none of Lampman's landscape poems is finer than his wonderful Hallowe'en vision of "In November," where a harmless pasture full of dead mullein stalks rises and seizes the poet with the spirit of an eerie witches' sabbath:

And I, too, standing idly there
With muffled hands in the chill air
Felt the warm glow about my feet,
And shuddering betwixt cold and heat,
Drew my thoughts closer, like a cloak,
While something in my blood awoke,
A nameless and unnatural cheer,
A pleasure secret and austere.

Still, the winter, with its long shadows and its abstract black and white pattern, does reinforce themes of desolation and loneliness, and more particularly, of the indifference of nature to human values, which I should say was the central Canadian tragic theme. The first poet who really came to grips with this theme was, as we should expect, Charles Heavysege. Heavysege's first two long poems, *Saul* and *Count Filippo,* are Victorian dinosaurs in the usual idiom: *Count Filippo* in particular, like the Albert Memorial, achieves a curious perverted beauty by the integrity of its ugliness. His third poem, *Jephthah's Daughter,* seems to me to reflect more directly the influence of his Canadian environment.

He tells us in the introduction that he decided on Jephthah's daughter rather than Iphigenia because Iphigenia was, as Samuel Johnson said of the victim of a public hanging, sustained by her audience; the Biblical theme had a solitary bleakness about it that was nearer to what he wanted. During the action Jephthah goes out in the darkness to pray for release from his vow, asking for some sign of that release. He listens a moment and then hears:

> The hill wolf howling on the neighbouring height,
> And bittern booming in the pool below.

He gets of course no other answer, and it is clear that what Jephthah is really sacrificing his daughter to is nature, nature as a mystery of mindless power, with endless resources for killing man but with nothing to respond to his moral or intellectual feelings. The evolutionary pessimism of the nineteenth century awoke an unusual number of echoes in Canada, many of them of course incidental. In a well-known passage from Charles Mair's *Tecumseh,* Lefroy is describing the West to Brock, and Brock comments: "What charming solitudes! And life was there!" and Lefroy answers: "Yes, life was there! inexplicable life, / Still wasted by inexorable death;" and the sombre Tennysonian vision of nature red in tooth and claw blots out the sentimental Rousseauist fantasy of the charming solitudes.

In the next generation the tragic theme has all the more eloquence for being somewhat unwanted, interfering with the resolutely cheerful praise of the newborn giant of the north. Roberts, Wilfred Campbell, Wilson Macdonald,[3] and Bliss Carman are all romantics whose ordinary tone is nostalgic, but who seem most deeply convincing when they are darkest in tone, most preoccupied with pain, loss, loneliness, or waste. We notice this in the poem which would go immediately into anyone's anthology, such as Campbell's "The Winter Lakes," Wilson Macdonald's "Exit," Carman's "Low Tide on Grand Pré." It is even more striking when Carman or Roberts writes a long metrical gabble that occasionally drops into poetry, like Silas Wegg, as it is almost invariably this mood that it drops into. Thus in Roberts' "The Great and the Little Weavers":

> The cloud-rose dies into shadow,
> The earth-rose dies into dust.

---

[3]Wilson Macdonald (1880-1967), was a minor but popular poet best known for his romantic, elegantly executed lyrics. His simple vision of life made him unpopular among Modernists of the A. J. M. Smith and F. R. Scott generation.

The "great gray shape with the paleolithic face" of Pratt's *Titanic* and the glacier of Birney's *David* are in much the same tradition as the gloomy and unresponsive nature of *Jephthah's Daughter*. In fact the tragic features in Pratt mainly derive from his more complex view of the situation of Heavysege's poem. Man is also a child of nature, in whom the mindlessness of the animal has developed into cruelty and malice. He sees two men glare in hatred at one another on the street, and his mind goes away back before the emergence of fur or feather, back to the unvocal sea and down deep where the darkness spills its wash on the threshold of light, where the lids never close upon the eyes, where the inhabitants slay in silence and are as silently slain. From the very beginning, in *Newfoundland Verse,* Pratt was fascinated by the relentless pounding of waves on the rocks, a movement which strangely seems to combine a purpose with a lack of it. This rhythm recurs several times in Pratt's work: in the charge of the swordfish in *The Witches' Brew;* in the "queries rained upon the iron plate" of *The Iron Door;* in the torpedo launched from "The Submarine;" in the sinking of the Titanic itself, this disaster being caused by a vainglorious hubris which in a sense deliberately aimed at the iceberg. In *Brébeuf* the same theme comes into focus as the half-mindless, half-demonic curiosity which drives the Iroquois on through torture after torture to find the secret of a spiritual reality that keeps eluding them.

It is Pratt who has expressed in *Towards the Last Spike* the central comic theme, and in *Brébeuf* the central tragic theme, of the Canadian imagination, and it is Pratt who combines the two in "The Truant," which is in my anthology because it is the greatest poem in Canadian literature. In it the representative of mankind confronts a "great Panjandrum," a demon of the mathematical order of nature of a type often confused with God. In the dialectic of their conflict it becomes clear that the great Panjandrum of nature is fundamentally death, and that the intelligence that fights him, comprehends him, harnesses him, and yet finally yields to his power is the ultimate principle of life, and capable of the comedy of achievement only because capable also of the tragedy of enduring him:

> We who have learned to clench
> Our fists and raise our lightless sockets
> To morning skies after the midnight raids,
> Yet cocked our ears to bugles on the barricades,
> And in cathedral rubble found a way to quench
> A dying thirst within a Galilean valley —
> No! by the Rood, we will not join your ballet.

We spoke at the beginning of certain principles that become important in the study of Canadian poetry. One of these is the fact that while literature may have life, reality, experience, nature or what you will for its content, the forms of literature cannot exist outside literature, just as the forms of sonata and fuge cannot exist outside music. When a poet is confronted with a new life or environment, the new life may suggest a new content, but obviously cannot provide him with a new form. The forms of poetry can be derived only from other poems, the forms of novels from other novels. The imaginative content of Canadian poetry, which is often primitive, frequently makes extraordinary demands on forms derived from romantic or later traditions. Duncan Campbell Scott, for instance, lived in Ottawa as a civil servant in the Department of Indian Affairs, between a modern city and the Ungava wilderness. He has a poem on the music of Debussy and he has a poem on a starving squaw trying to catch fish for her child and having nothing but her own flesh to bait the hook with. To find anything like such incongruity in English life we have to go clear back to Anglo-Saxon times. If we think of an English poet, with his head full of ancient battles and myths of dragon-fights, in the position of having to write for the sophisticated audience of Rome and Byzantium, we shall have some parallel to the technical problems faced by a Lampman or a Scott who had only the elaborate conventions of Tennysonian romanticism to contain his imaginative experience. Pratt's attempt to introduce the imagery of dragon-killing into a poem about the Canadian Pacific Railway is another good example; and I have much sympathy for the student who informed me in the examinations last May that Pratt had written a poem called Beowulf and his Brothers.

I think it is partly an obscure feeling for more primitive forms that accounts for the large number of narratives in Canadian poetry. I am aware, of course, that the narrative was a favourite romantic form, but the themes of Canadian narrative, the sacrifice of Jephthah's daughter, the catching of Isabella Crawford's Max in a log jam, Dominique de Gourges's quest for vengeance in D. C. Scott, the death of Birney's David on the glacier, have a primeval grimness about them that is not romantic or even modern fashion. Pratt has also turned to older and more primitive types of narrative: Chaucerian beast-fable in the "Pliocena Armageddon" and "The Fable of the Goats," saint's legend in *Brébeuf*, heroic rescue in *The Roosevelt and the Antinoe.*

It is more common for a Canadian poet to solve his problem of form by some kind of erudite parody, using that term, as many critics now do, to mean adaptation in general rather than simply a lampoon, although adaptation usually has humorous overtones. In Charles Mair's "Winter" some wisps of Shakespearean song are delicately echoed in a new context, and Drummond's best poem, "The Wreck of the Julie Plante," is an admirable parody of the ballad, with its tough oblique narration, its moralizing conclusion, and its use of what is called incremental repetition:

> For de win' she blow lak' hurricane,
> Bimeby she blow some more.

According to his own account, Pratt, after his college studies in theology, psychology, literature, and the natural sciences, put everything he knew into his first major poetic effort, an epic named "Clay," which he promptly burnt. Soon afterwards all this erudition went into reverse and came out as the fantasy of *The Witches' Brew*, in which parody has a central place. Since then, we have parody in Anne Wilkinson and Wilfred Watson, who use nursery rhymes and ballads as a basis; Birney's *Trial of a City* is among other things a fine collection of parodied styles; and Klein's devotion to one of the world s greatest parodists, James Joyce, has produced his brilliant bilingual panegyric on Montreal:

> Grand port of navigations, multiple
> The lexicons uncargo'd at your quays,
> Sonnant though strange to me; but chiefest, I,
> Auditor of your music, cherish the
> Joined double-melodied vocabulaire
> Where English vocable and roll Ecossic,
> Mollified by the parle of French
> Bilinguefact your air!

Much of Canada's best poetry is now written by professors or others in close contact with universities. There are disadvantages in this, but one of the advantages is the diversifying of the literary tradition by a number of scholarly interests. Earl Birney's "Anglo-Saxon Street" reminds us that its author is a professor of Anglo-Saxon. Louis MacKay, professor of Classics, confronts an unmistakably Canadian landscape with a myth of Eros derived from Catullus[4]:

---

[4]When Frye reprinted this essay in *The Bush Garden* in 1971, he replaced Catullus with Virgil. He also made some minor editorial changes, mostly by eliding those references that had already been used in other essays, namely "Canada and its Poetry" and "The Narrative Tradition in English-Canadian Poetry."

The hard rock was his mother; he retains
Only her kind, nor answers any sire.
His hand is the black basalt, and his veins
Are rocky veins, ablaze with gold and fire.

Robert Finch, professor of French, carries on the tradition of Mallarmé and other *symbolistes*; one of his most successful poems, "The Peacock and the Nightingale," goes back to the older tradition of the medieval *débat*. Klein, of course, has brought echoes from the Talmud, the Old Testament, and the whole range of Jewish thought and history; and the erudition necessary to read Roy Daniells and Alfred Bailey with full appreciation is little short of formidable. It may be said, however, that echoes and influences are not a virtue in Canadian poetry, but one of its major weaknesses. Canadian poetry may echo Hopkins or Auden today as it echoed Tom Moore a century ago, but in every age Echo is merely the discarded mistress of Narcissus. This question brings up the most hackneyed subject in Canadian literature, which I have left for that reason to the end.

Political and economic units tend to expand as history goes on; cultural units tend to remain decentralized. Culture like wine, seems to need a specific locality, and no major poet has been inspired by an empire, Virgil being, as the *Georgics* show, an exception that proves the rule. In this age of world-states we have two extreme forms of the relationship between culture and politics. When cultural developments follow political ones, we get an anonymous international art, such as we have in many aspects of modern architecture, abstract painting, and twelve-tone music. When a cultural development acquires a political aspect, we frequently get the curious modern phenomenon of the political language, where a minor language normally headed for extinction is deliberately revived for political purposes. Examples are Irish, Norwegian, Hebrew, and Afrikaans, and there are parallel tendencies elsewhere. I understand that there is a school of Australian poets dedicated to putting as many aboriginal words into their poems as possible. As the emotional attachments to political languages are very violent, I shall say here only that this problem has affected the French but not the English part of Canadian culture. As we all know, however, English Canada has escaped the political language only to become involved in a unique problem of self-identification, *vis-à-vis* the British and American poets writing in the same tongue. Hence in every generation there has been the feeling that whether poetry itself needs any defense or manifesto, Canadian poetry certainly does.

The main result of this has been that Canadian poets have been urged in every generation to search for appropriate themes, in other words to look for content. The themes have been characterized as national, international, traditional, experimental, iconic, iconoclastic: in short, as whatever the propounder of them would like to write if he were a poet, or to read if he were a critic. But the poet's quest is for form, not content. The poet who tries to make content the informing principle of his poetry can write only versified rhetoric, and versified rhetoric has a moral but not an imaginative significance: its place is on the social periphery of poetry, not in its articulate centre. The rhetorician, Quintilian tell us, ought be a learned and good man, but the critic is concerned only with poets.

By form I do not of course mean external form, such as the use of a standard metre or conventions. A sonnet has form only if it really is fourteen lines long: a ten-line sonnet padded out to fourteen is still a part of chaos, waiting for the creative word. I mean by form the shaping principle of the individual poem, which is derived from the shaping principles of poetry itself. Of these latter the most important is metaphor, and metaphor, in its radical form, is a statement of identity: this is that, A is B. Metaphor is at its purest and most primitive in myth, where we have immediate and total identifications. Primitive poetry, being mythical, tends to be erudite and allusive, and to the extent that modern poetry takes on the same qualities it becomes primitive too. Here is a poem by Lampman, written in 1894:

So it is with us all; we have our friends
    Who keep the outer chambers, and guard well
Our common path; but there their service ends,
    For far within us lies an iron cell
Soundless and secret, where we laugh or moan
    Beyond all succour, terribly alone.

And here is a poem by E. W. Mandel, published in 1954:

It has been hours in these rooms,
the opening to which, door or sash,
I have lost. I have gone from room to room
asking the janitors who were sweeping up
the brains that lay on the floors,
the bones shining in the wastebaskets,
and once I asked a suit of clothes
that collapsed at my breath and bundled
and crawled on the floor like a coward.
Finally, after several stories,
in the staired and eyed hall,
I came upon a man with the face of a bull.

Lampman's poem is certainly simpler, closer to prose and to direct statement of emotion. All these are characteristics of a highly developed and sophisticated literary tradition. If we ask which is the more primitive, the answer is certainly the second poem, as we can see by turning to the opening pages of the anthology to see what primitive poetry is really like. Here is a Haida song translated by Hermia Fraser:

> I cannot stay, I cannot stay!
> I must take my canoe and fight the waves,
> For the Wanderer spirit is seeking me.
>
> The beating of great, black wings on the sun,
> The Raven has stolen the ball of the sun,
> From the Kingdom of
> Light he has stolen the sun...
>
> The Slave Wife born from the first clam shell
> Is in love with the boy who was stolen away,
> The lovers have taken the Raven's fire.

When we look for the qualities in Canadian poetry that illustrate the poet's response to the specific environment that we call approximately Canada, we are really looking for the mythopeic qualities in the poetry. This is easiest to see, of course, when the poetry is mythical in content as well as form. In the long mythopeic passage from Isabella Crawford's *Malcolm's Katie*, beginning "The South Wind laid his moccasins aside," we see how the poet is, first, taming the landscape imaginatively, as settlement tames it physically, by animating the lifeless scene with humanized figures, and, second, integrating the literary tradition of the country by deliberately re-establishing the broken cultural link with Indian civilization:

> ...for a man
> To stand amid the cloudy roll and moil,
> The phantom waters breaking overhead,
> Shades of vex'd billows bursting on his breast,
> Torn caves of mist wall'd with a sudden gold,
> Reseal'd as swift as seen — broad, shaggy fronts,
> Fire-ey'd and tossing on impatient horns
> The wave impalpable — was but to think
> A dream of phantoms held him as he stood.

And in the mythical figures of Pratt, the snorting iron horses of the railways, the lumbering dinosaurs of *The Great Feud*, the dragon of *Towards the Last Spike*, and above all Tom the Cat from Zanzibar, the

Canadian cousin of Roy Campbell's flaming terrapin, we clearly have other denizens of the monstrous zoo that produced Paul Bunyan's ox Babe, Paul Bunyan himself being perhaps a descendant of the giants who roamed the French countryside and were recorded by the great contemporary of Jacques Cartier, Rabelais.

We are concerned here, however, not so much with mythopeic poetry as with myth as a shaping principle of poetry. Every good lyrical poet has a certain structure of imagery as typical of him as his handwriting, held together by certain recurring metaphors, and sooner or later he will produce one or more poems that seem to be at the centre of that structure. These poems are in the formal sense his mythical poems, and they are for the critic the imaginative keys to his work. The poet himself often recognizes such a poem by making it the title poem of a collection. They are not necessarily his best poems, but they often are, and in a Canadian poet they display those distinctive themes we have been looking for which reveal his reaction to his natural and social environment. Nobody but a genuine poet ever produces such a poem, and they cannot be faked or imitated or voluntarily constructed. My anthology is largely held together by such poems: they start approximately with D. C. Scott's "Piper of Arll," and continue in increasing numbers to our own day. I note among others Leo Kennedy's "Words for a Resurrection," Margaret Avison's "Neverness," Irving Layton's "Cold Green Element," Douglas LePan's "Idyll," Wilfred Watson's "Canticle of Darkness," P. K. Page's "Metal and the Flower," and similar poems forming among a younger group that includes James Reaney, Jay Macpherson, and Daryl Hine. Such poems enrich not only our poetic experience but our cultural knowledge as well, and as time goes on they become increasingly the only form of knowledge that does not date and continues to hold its interest for future generations.

"Preface to an Uncollected Anthology" in: *Studia Varia*, Royal Society of Canada, Literary and Scientific Papers, ed. E. G. D. Murray. Toronto: University of Toronto Press, 1957

Conclusion to a *Literary History of Canada*

Some years ago, a group of editors met to draw up the first tentative plans for a history of English Canadian literature.[1] What we then dreamed of is substantially what we have got, changed very little in essentials. I expressed at the time the hope that such a book would help to broaden the inductive basis on which some writers on Canadian literature were making generalizations that boarded on guesswork. By "some writers" I meant primarily myself. I find, however, that more evidence has in fact tended to confirm most of my intuitions on the subject.

To study Canadian literature properly, one must outgrow the view that evaluation is the end of criticism, instead of its incidental by-product. If evaluation is one's guiding principle, criticism of Canadian literature would become only a debunking project, leaving it a poor naked *alouette* plucked of every feather of decency and dignity. True, what is really remarkable is not how little but how much good writing has been produced in Canada. But this would not affect the rigorous evaluator. The evaluative view is based on the conception of criticism as concerned mainly to define and canonize the genuine classics of literature. And Canada has produced no author who is a classic in the sense of possessing a vision greater in kind than that of his best readers (Canadians themselves might argue about one or two, but in the perspective of the world at large the statement is true). There is no Canadian writer of whom we can say what we can say of the world's major writers, that their readers can grow up inside their work without ever being aware of a circumference. Thus the metaphor of the critic as "judge" holds better for the Canadian critic who is never dealing with the kind of writer who judges him.

This fact about Canadian literature, so widely deplored by Canadians, has one advantage. It is much easier to see what literature is trying to do when we are studying a literature that has not quite done it. If no Canadian author pulls us away from the Canadian context to-

[1]Carl F. Klinck, gen. ed., *Literary History of Canada*. Toronto: University of Toronto Press, 1965, pp. XIV, 945.

ward the centre of literary experience itself, then at every point we remain aware of his social and historical setting. The conception of what is literary has to be greatly broadened for such a literature. The literary, in Canada, is often only an incidental quality of writing which, like those of the many of the early explorers, are as innocent of literary intentions as a mating loon. Even when it is literature in its orthodox genres of poetry and fiction, it is more significantly studied as a part of Canadian life than as a part of an autonomous world of literature.

So far from merely admitting or conceding this, the editors have gone out of their way to emphasize it. We have asked for chapters on political, historical, religious, scholarly, philosophical, scientific, and other non-literary writing, to show how the verbal imagination operates as a ferment in all cultural life. We have included the writings of foreigners, of travellers, of immigrants, of emigrants — even of emigrants whose most articulate literary emotion was their thankfulness at getting the hell out of Canada. The reader of this book, even if he is not Canadian or much interested in Canadian literature as such, may still learn a good deal about the literary imagination as a force and function of life generally. For here another often deplored fact also becomes an advantage: that many Canadian cultural phenomena are not peculiarly Canadian at all, but are typical of their wider North American and Western contexts.

This book is a collection of essays in cultural history, and of the general principles of cultural history we still know relatively little. It is, of course, closely related to political and to economic history, but it is a separate and definable subject in itself. Like other kinds of history, it has its own themes of exploration, settlement, and development, but these themes relate to a social imagination that explores and settles and develops, and the imagination has its own rhythms of growth as well as its own modes of expression. It is obvious that Canadian literature, whatever its inherent merits, is an indispensable aid to the knowledge of Canada. It records what the Canadian imagination has reacted to, and it tells us things about this environment that nothing else will tell us. By examining this imagination as the authors of this book have tried to do, as an ingredient in Canadian verbal culture generally, a relatively small and low-lying cultural development is studied in all its dimensions. There is far too much Canadian writing for this book not to become, in places, something of a catalogue; but the outlines of the structure are clear. Fortunately, the bulk of Canadian non-literary writing, even today, has not yet declined into the state of sodden specialization in which the readable has become the impure.

I stress our ignorance of the laws and conditions of cultural history for an obvious reason. The question: why has there been no Canadian writer of classical proportions? may naturally be asked. At any rate it often has been. Our authors realize that it is better to deal with what is there than to raise speculations about why something else is not there. But it is clear that the question haunts their minds. And we know so little about cultural history that we not only cannot answer such a question, but we do not even know whether or not it is a real question. The notion, doubtless of romantic origin, that "genius" is a certain quantum that an individual is born with, as he might be born with red hair, is still around, but mainly as a folktale motif in fiction, like the story of Finch in the Jalna books.[2] "Genius" is as much, and as essentially, a matter of social context as it is of individual character. We do not know what the social conditions are that produce great literature, or even whether there is any causal relation at all. If there is, there is no reason to suppose that they are good conditions, or conditions that we should try to reproduce. The notion that the literature one admires must have been nourished by something admirable in the social environment is persistent, but has never been justified by evidence. One can still find books on Shakespeare that profess to make his achievement more plausible by talking about a "background" of social euphoria produced by the defeat of the Armada, the discovery of America a century before, and the conviction that Queen Elizabeth was a wonderful woman. There is a general sense of filler about such speculations, and when similar arguments are given in a negative form to explain the absence of a Shakespeare in Canada they are no more convincing. Puritan inhibitions, pioneer life, "an age too late, cold climate, or years" — these may be important as factors or conditions of Canadian culture, helping us to characterize its qualities. To suggest that any of them is a negative cause of its merit is to say much more than anyone knows.

One theme which runs all through this book is the obvious and unquenchable desire of the Canadian cultural public to identify itself through its literature. Canada is not a bad environment for the author, as far as recognition goes: in fact the recognition may even hamper his development by making him prematurely self-conscious. Scholarships, prizes, university posts, await the dedicated writer: there are so many medals offered for literary achievement that a modern Canadian Dryden might well be moved to write a satire on medals, except that if he did he would promptly be awarded the medal for satire and humour. Publishers take an active responsibility for native literature, even po-

[2]The author of *Jalna* (1927), Mazo de la Roche (1879-1961), was a popular romantic fiction writer whose initial success led her to produce fifteen novels in the 'Jalna' series, centered on the Whiteoaks family and their idyllic gentleman farmer's estate near Clarkson, Ontario.

etry; a fair proportion of the books bought by Canadian readers are by Canadian writers; the CBC and other media help to employ some writers and publicize others. The efforts made at intervals to boost or hard-sell Canadian literature, by asserting that it is much better than it actually is, may look silly enough in retrospect, but they were also, in part, efforts to create a cultural community, and the aim deserves more sympathy than the means. Canada has two languages and two literatures, and every statement made in a book like this about "Canadian literature" employs the figure of speech known as synecdoche, putting a part for the whole. Every such statement implies a parallel or contrasting statement about French-Canadian literature. The advantages of having a national culture based on two languages are in some respects very great, but of course they are for the most part potential. The difficulties, if more superficial, are also more actual and more obvious.

Some of the seminal facts about the origins of Canadian culture are set down with great clarity near the beginning of this book. Canada began as an obstacle, blocking the way to the treasures of the East, to be explored only in the hope of finding a passage through it. English Canada continued to be that long after what is now the United States had become a defined part of the Western world. One reason for this is obvious from the map. American culture was, down to about 1900, mainly a culture of the Atlantic seaboard, with a western frontier that moved irregularly but steadily back until it reached the other coast. The Revolution did not essentially change the cultural unity of the English-speaking community of the North Atlantic that had London and Edinburgh on one side of it and Boston and Philadelphia on the other. But Canada has, for all practical purposes, no Atlantic seaboard. The traveller from Europe edges into it like a tiny Jonah entering an inconceivably large whale, slipping past the Straits of Belle Isle into the Gulf of St. Lawrence, where five Canadian provinces surround him, for the most part invisible. Then he goes up the St. Lawrence and the inhabited country comes into view, mainly a French-speaking country, with its own cultural traditions. To enter the United States is a matter of crossing an ocean; to enter Canada is a matter of being silently swallowed by an alien continent.

It is an unforgettable and intimidating experience to enter Canada in this way. But the experience initiates one into that gigantic east-to-west thrust which historians regard as the axis of Canadian development, the "Laurentian" movement that makes the growth of Canada geographically credible. This drive to the west has attracted to itself nearly everything that is heroic and romantic in the Canadian tradition. The original impetus begins in Europe, for English Canada in the British Isles, hence though adventurous it is also a conservative force, and naturally tends to preserve its colonial link with its starting-point. Once the Canadian has settled down in the country, however, he then becomes aware of the longitudinal dimension, the southward pull toward the richer and more glamorous American cities, some of which, such as Boston for the Maratimes and Minneapolis for the eastern prairies, are almost Canadian capitals. This is the axis of another kind of Canadian mentality, more critical and analytic, more inclined to see Canada as an unnatural and politically quixotic aggregate of disparate northern extensions of American culture — "seven fishing-rods tied together by the ends," as Goldwin Smith put it.

The simultaneous influence of two larger nations speaking the same language has been practically beneficial to English Canada, but theoretically confusing. It is often suggested that Canada's identity is to be found in some *via media*, or *via mediocris,* between the other two. This has the disadvantage that the British and American cultures have to be defined as extremes. Haliburton[3] seems to have believed that the ideal for Nova Scotia would be a combination of American energy and British social structure, but such a chimera, or synthetic monster, is hard to achieve in practice. It is simpler merely to notice the alternating current in the Canadian mind, as reflected in its writing, between two moods, one romantic, traditional and idealistic, the other shrewd, observant and humorous. Canada in its attitude to Britain tends to be more royalist than the Queen, in the sense that it is more attracted to it as a symbol of tradition than as a fellow-nation. The Canadian attitude to the United States is typically that of a smaller country to a much bigger neighbour, sharing in its material civilization but anxious to keep clear of the huge mass movements that drive a great imperial power. The United States, being founded on a revolution and a written constitution, has introduced a deductive or *a priori* pattern into its cultural life that tends to define an American way of life and mark it off from anti-American heresies. Canada, having a seat on the sidelines of the American Revolution, adheres to the inductive and the expedient. The Canadian genius for compromise is reflected in the existence of Canada itself.

The most obvious tension in the Canadian literary situation is in the use of language. Here, first of all, a traditional standard English collides with the need for a North American vocabulary and phrasing.

---

[3]Thomas Chandler Haliburton (1796-1865) was a Supreme Court judge of Nova Scotia, a prominent politician and a man of letters. Today he is remembered primarily for his satirical sketches of life in the colony of Nova Scotia, first published in *The Novascotian* and later as *The Clockmaker; or the Sayings and Doings of Samuel Slick, of Slickville,* 1836.

As long as the North American speaker feels that he belongs in a minority, the European speech will impose a standard of correctness. This is to a considerable extent still true of French in Canada, with its campaigns against "joual" and the like. But as the Americans began to outnumber the British, Canada tended in practice to fall in with the American developments, though a good deal of Canadian theory is still Anglophile. A much more complicated cultural tension arises from the impact of the sophisticated on the primitive, and vice versa. The most dramatic example, and one I have given elsewhere, is that of Duncan Campbell Scott, working in the Department of Indian Affairs in Ottawa. He writes of a starving squaw baiting a fish-hook with her own flesh, and he writes of the music of Debussy and the poetry of Henry Vaughan. In English literature we have to go back to Anglo-Saxon times to encounter so incongruous a collision of cultures.

Cultural history, we said, has its own rhythms. It is possible that one of these rhythms is very like an organic rhythm: that there must be a period, of a certain magnitude, as Aristotle would say, in which a social imagination can take root and establish a tradition. American literature had this period, in the north-eastern part of the country, between the Revolution and the Civil War. Canada has never had it. English Canada was first a part of the wilderness, then a part of North America and the British Empire, then a part of the world. But it has gone through these revolutions too quickly for a tradition of writing to be founded on any one of them. Canadian writers are, even now, still trying to assimilate a Canadian environment at a time when new techniques of communication, many of which, like television, constitute a verbal market, are annihilating the boundaries of that environment. This foreshortening of Canadian history, if it really does have any relevance to Canadian culture, would account for many features of it: its fixation on its own past, its penchant for old-fashioned literary techniques, its preoccupation with the theme of strangled articulateness. It seems to me that Canadian sensibility has been profoundly disturbed, not so much by our famous problem of identity, important as that is, as by a series of paradoxes in what confronts that identity. It is less perplexed by the question "Who am I?" than by some such riddle as "Where is here?"

We are obviously not to read the "mystique of Canadianism" back into the pre-Confederation period. Haliburton, for instance, was a Nova Scotian, a Bluenose: the word "Canadian" to him would have summoned up the figure of someone who spoke mainly French and whose enthusiasm for Haliburton's own political ideals would have been extremely tepid. The mistique of Canadianism was specifically the cultural accompaniment of Confederation and the imperialistic mood that followed it. But it came so suddenly after the pioneer period that it was still full of wilderness. To feel "Canadian" was to feel part of a no-man's land with huge rivers, lakes, and islands that very few Canadians had ever seen. "From sea to sea, and from the river onto the ends of the earth" — if Canada is not an island, the phrasing is still in the etymological sense isolating. One wonders if any other national consciousness has had so large an amount of the unknown, the unrealized, the humanly undigested, so built into it. Rupert Brooke[4] speaks of the "unseizable virginity" of the Canadian landscape. What is important here, for our purpose, is the position of the frontier in the Canadian imagination. In the United States one could choose to move out of the frontier or to retreat from it back to the seaboard. The tension built up by such migrations have fascinated many American novelists and historians. In the Canadas, even in the Maratimes, the frontier was all around one, a part and a condition of one's whole imaginative being. The frontier was primarily what separated the Canadian, physically or mentally, from Great Britain, from the United States, and even more important, from other Canadian communities. Such a frontier was the immediate datum of his imagination, the thing that had to be dealt with first.

After the Northwest passage failed to materialize, Canada became a colony in the mercantilist sense, treated by others less like a society than as a place to look for things. French, English, Americans plunged into it to carry off its supplies of furs, minerals, and pulpwood, aware only of their immediate objectives. From time to time recruiting officers searched the farms and villages to carry young men off to death in a European dynastic quarrel. Travellers visit Canada much as they would visit a zoo: even when their eyes momentarily focus on the natives they are still thinking primarily of how their own sensibility is going to react to what it sees. A feature of Canadian life that has been noted by writers from Susanna Moodie onward is the paradox of vast empty spaces and lack of privacy, with no defenses against the prying or avaricious eye. The resentment expressed against this in Canada seems to have taken political rather than literary forms: this may be partly because Canadians have learned from their imaginative experience to look at each other in much the same way: "as objects, even as obstacles," as one writer says.

---

[4]Rupert Brooke (1887-1915), English poet remembered for his wartime sonnet-series, *1914*, 1915. His travelogue, *Letters from America,* 1916, which includes a section describing his journey through Canada, is considered one of the best books written on the subject.

It is not much wonder if Canada developed with the bewilderment of a neglected child, preoccupied with trying to define its own identity, alternately bumptious and diffident about its own achievements. Adolescent dreams of glory haunt the Canadian consciousness (and unconsciousness), some naive and some sophisticated. In the naive area are the predictions that the twentieth century belongs to Canada, that our cities will become much bigger than they ought to be, or, like Edmonton and Vancouver, "gateways" to somewhere else, reconstructed Northwest passages. The more sophisticated usually take the form of a Messianic complex about Canadian culture, for Canadian culture, no less than Alberta, has always been "next year country." The myth of the hero brought up in the forest retreat, awaiting the moment when his giant strength will be fully grown and he can emerge into the world, informs a good deal of Canadian criticism down to our own time.

Certain features of life in a new country that are bound to handicap its writers are obvious enough. In drama, which depends on a theatre and consequently on a highly organized urban life, the foreshortening of historical development has been particularly cruel, as drama was strangled by the movie just as it was getting started as a popular medium. Other literary genres have similar difficulties. Culture is born in leisure and an awareness of standards, and pioneer conditions tend to make energetic and uncritical work an end in itself, to preach a gospel of social unconsciousness, which lingers long after the pioneer conditions have disappeared. The impressive achievements of such a society are likely to be technological. It is the inarticulate part of communication, railways and bridges and canals and highways, that Canada, one of whose symbols is the taciturn beaver, has shown its real strength. Again, Canadian culture, and literature in particular, has felt the force of what may be called Emerson's law. Emerson remarks in his journals that in a provincial society it is extremely easy to reach the highest level of cultivation, extremely difficult to take one step beyond that. In surveying Canadian poetry and fiction, we feel constantly that all the energy has been absorbed in meeting a standard, a self-defeating enterprise because real standards can only be established, not met. Such writing is academic in the pejorative sense of that term, an imitation of a prescribed model, second-rate in conception, not merely in execution. It is natural that academic writing of this kind should develop where literature is a social prestige symbol. However, it is not the handicaps of Canadian writers but the distinctive features that appear in spite of them which are the main concern of this book, and so of its conclusion.

II

The sense of probing into the distance, of fixing the eyes on the skyline, is something that the Canadian sensibility had inherited from the *voyageurs.* It comes into Canadian painting a good deal, in Thomson whose focus is so often farthest back in the picture, where a river or a gorge in the hills twists elusively out of sight, in Emily Carr whose vision is always, in the title of a compatriot's book of poems, "deeper into the forest." Even in the Maritimes, where the feeling of linear distance is less urgent, Roberts contemplates the Tantramar marshes in the same way, the refrain of "miles and miles" having clearly some incantatory power for him. It would be interesting to know how many Canadian novels associate nobility of character with a faraway look, or base their perorations on a long-range perspective. This might be only a *cliché,* except that it is often found in sharply observed and distinctively written books. Here, as a random example, is the last sentence of W. O. Mitchell's *Who Has Seen the Wind*: "The wind turns in silent frenzy upon itself, whirling into a smoking funnel, breathing up top soil and tumbleweed skeletons to carry them on its spinning way over the prairie, out and out to the far line of the sky."

A vast country sparsely inhabited naturally depends on its modes of transportation, whether canoe, railway, or the driving and riding "circuits" of the judge, the Methodist preacher, or the Yankee peddler. The feeling of nomadic movement over great distances persists even into the age of the aeroplane, in a country where writers can hardly meet one other without a social organization that provides travel grants. Pratt's poetry is full of his fascination with means of communication, not simply the physical means of great ships and locomotives, though he is one of the best of all poets on such subjects, but with communication as message, with radar and asdic and wireless signals, and, in his war poems, with the power of rhetoric over fighting men. What is perhaps the most comprehensive structure of ideas yet made by a Canadian thinker, the structure embodied in Innis's[5] *The Bias of Communication,* is concerned with the same theme, and a disciple of Innis, Marshall McLuhan, continues to emphasize the unity of communication, as a complex containing both verbal and non-verbal factors, and warns us against making unreal divisions within it. Perhaps it is not too fanciful

---

[5]Harold Adams Innis (1894-1952) was one of Canada's most influential modern thinkers. A political scientist and economist, he studied the influence of communication on the development of Canada as a nation. His two seminal works are *Empire and Communications,* 1946, and *The Bias of Communication,* 1951.

to see this need for continuity in the Canadian attitude to time as well as space, in its preoccupation with its own history, its relentless cultural stock-takings and self-inventories. The Burke sense of society as a continuum — consistent with the pragmatic and conservative outlook of Canadians — is strong and begins early. As I write, the centennial of Confederation in 1967 looms up before the country with the moral urgency of a Day of Atonement: I use a Jewish metaphor because there is something Hebraic about the Canadian tendency to read its conquest of a promised land, its Maccabean victories of 1812, its struggle for the central fortress on the hill at Quebec, as oracles of a future. It is doubtless only on accident that the theme of one of the most passionate and intense of all Canadian novels, A. M. Klein's *The Second Scroll*, is Zionism.

Civilization in Canada, as elsewhere, has advanced geometrically across the country, throwing down the long parallel lines of the railways, dividing up the farm lands into chessboards of square-mile sections and concession-line roads. There is little adaptation to nature: in both architecture and arrangement, Canadian cities and villages express rather an arrogant abstraction, the conquest of nature by an intelligence that does not love it. The word conquest suggests something military, as it should — one thinks of General Braddock,[6] preferring to have his army annihilated rather than fight the natural man on his own asymmetrical ground. There are some features of this generally North American phenomenon that have a particular emphasis in Canada. It has often been remarked that Canadian expansion westward had a tight grip of authority over it that American expansion, with its outlaws and sherrifs and vigilantes and the like, did not have in the same measure. America moved from the back country to the wild west; Canada moved from a New France held down by British military occupation to a northwest patrolled by mounted police. Canada has not had, strictly speaking, an Indian war: there has been much less of the "another redskin bit the dust" feeling in our historical imagination, and only Riel[7] remains to haunt the later period of it, though he is a formidable figure enough, rather like what a combination of John

[6]Edward Braddock (1695-1755), British commander-in-chief in North America during an early phase of French and Indian Wars.

[7]Louis Riel (1844-1885) led the North West Rebellion of 1885 in which the Métis attempted to redress their grievances. Riel was eventually captured, tried, convicted and hanged in Regina in 1885. Many Canadians, especially French-Canadians, regard Riel a hero and a patriot who fought for the rights of his people.

Brown[8] and Vanzetti[9] would be in the American conscience. Otherwise, the conquest, for the last two centuries, has been mainly of the unconscious forces of nature, personified by the dragon of the Lake Superior rocks in Pratt's *Towards the Last Spike*:

> On the North Shore a reptile lay asleep —
> A hybrid that the myths might have conceived,
> But not delivered.

Yet the conquest of nature has its own perils for the imagination, in a country where the winters are so cold and where conditions of life have so often been bleak and comfortless, where even the mosquitoes have been described as "mementoes of the fall." I have long been impressed in Canadian poetry by a tone of deep terror in regard to nature, a theme to which we shall return. It is not a terror of the dangers or discomforts or even the mysteries of nature, but a terror of the soul at something that these things manifest. The human mind has nothing but human and moral values to cling to if it is to preserve its integrity or even its sanity, yet the vast unconsciousness of nature in front of it seems an unanswerable denial of those values. I notice that a sharp-witted Methodist circuit rider speaks of the "shutting out of the whole moral creation" in the loneliness of the forest.

If we put together a few of these impressions, we may get some approach to characterizing the way in which the Canadian imagination has developed in its literature. Small and isolated communities surrounded with a physical or psychological "frontier," separated from one another and from their American and British cultural sources: communities that provide all that their members have in the way of distinctively human values, and that are compelled to feel a great respect for the law and order that holds them together, yet confronted with a huge, unthinking, menacing, and formidable physical setting — such communities are bound to develop what we may provisionally call a garrison mentality. In the earliest maps of the country the only inhab-

---

[8]John Brown (1800-1859), American abolitionist, convicted of treason and conspiracy and executed for having taken direct action to free slaves by force.

[9]Bartolomeo Vanzetti, fish-peddler, and Nicola Sacco, shoemaker, were executed in Massachusetts in 1925 for holdup murders in 1920. The case generated a great deal of interest in the United States and elsewhere because it was suspected that the two had been accused and convicted not on evidence but because of their unpopular political, social and religious views. It was believed in many camps that Sacco and Vanzetti were victims of a widespread xenophobic and anti-radical hysteria that swept the United States in the early 1920s.

ited centres are forts, and that remains true of the cultural maps for a much later time. Frances Brook, in her eighteenth-century *History of Emily Montague*, wrote of what was literary a garrison; novelists of our day studying the impact of Montreal on Westmount write of a psychological one.

A garrison is a closely knit and beleaguered society, and its moral and social values are unquestionable. In a perilous enterprise one does not discuss causes or motives: one is either a fighter or a deserter. Here again we may turn to Pratt, with his infallible instinct for what is central in the Canadian imagination. The societies in Pratt's poems are always tense and tight groups engaged in war, rescue, martyrdom, or crisis, and the moral values expressed are simply those of that group. In such a society the terror is not for the common enemy, even when the enemy is or seems victorious, as in the extermination of the Jesuit missionaries or the crew of Franklin (a great Canadian theme that Pratt pondered but never completed). The real terror comes when the individual feels himself becoming an individual, pulling away from the group, loosing the sense of driving power that the group gives him, aware of a conflict within himself far subtler than the struggle of morality against evil. It is much easier to multiply garrisons, and when that happens, something anti-cultural comes into Canadian life, a dominating herd-mind in which nothing original can grow. The intensity of the sectarian divisiveness in Canadian towns, both religious and political, is an example: what such groups represent, of course, *vis-à-vis* one another, is "two solitudes," the death of communication and dialogue. Separatism, whether English or French, is culturally the most sterile of all creeds. But at present I am concerned rather with a more creative side of garrison mentality, one that has positive effects on our intellectual life.

Earlier Canadian writers were certain of their moral values: right was white, wrong black, and nothing else counted or even existed. Such certainty invariably produces a sub-literary rhetoric. Or, as Yeats would say, we make rhetoric out of quarrels with one another, poetry out of the quarrel with ourselves. To use words, for any other purpose than straight description or command, is a form of play, a manifestation of *homo ludens*. But there are two forms of play, the contest and the construct. The editorial writer attacking the Family Compact,[10] the preacher demolishing imaginary atheists with the argument of design, are using words aggressively, in theses that imply antithesis. Ideas are weapons: one seeks the verbal *coup de grâce*, the irrefutable refutation.

---

[10]The Family Compact, a Tory oligarchy in nineteenth-century Ontario which provoked the 1837 rebellion.

Such a use of words is congenial enough to the earlier Canadian community: all the evidence, including the evidence of this book, points to a highly articulate and argumentative society in nineteenth-century Canada. We notice that scholarship in Canada has so often been written with more conviction and authority, and has attracted wider recognition, than the literature itself. There are historical reasons for this, apart from the fact, which will become clearer as we go on, that scholarly writing is more easily attached to its central tradition.

Leacock has a story which I often turn to because the particular aspect of Canadian culture it reflects has never been more accurately caught. He tells us of the rivalry in an Ontario town between two preachers, one Anglican and the other Presbyterian. The latter taught ethics in the local college on weekdays — without salary — and preached on Sundays. He gave his students, says Leacock, three parts Hegel and two parts St. Paul, and on Sunday he reversed the dose and gave his parishioners three parts St. Paul and two parts Hegel. Religion has been a major — perhaps the major — cultural force in Canada, at least down to the last generation or two. The churches not only influenced the cultural climate but took an active part in the production of poetry and fiction, as the popularity of Ralph Connor[11] reminds us. But the effective religious factors in Canada were doctrinal and evangelical, those that stressed the arguments of religion at the expense of its imagery.

Such a reliance on the arguing intellect was encouraged by the philosophers, who in the nineteenth century were invariably idealists with a strong religious bias. One writer quotes the Canadian philosopher George[12] as saying that civilization consists "in the conscience and intellect" of a cultivated people, and Watson[13] as asserting that

---

[11]'Ralph Connor,' pseudonym for Charles William Gordon (1860-1937). Ordained Presbyterian minister and Doctor of Divinity, Gordon was a passionate missionary and one of Canada's first best-selling novelists. Among his numerous novels, all of which celebrate the triumphant goodness of a Christian hero, the best known are *The Man from Glengarry*, 1901, and *Glengarry School Days*, 1902.

[12]James George (1818-70) was a colourful and controversial professor of philosophy at Queen's University under whose chairmanship philosophy became recognized as a subject distinct from theology.

[13]John Watson (1847-1939) was the first Canadian philosopher to achieve an international reputation. He taught for half a century at Queen's University and for two decades was its Vice-Principal. *The Interpretation of Religious Experience*, published in two volumes in 1912, is considered his crowning achievement in the field of idealistic philosophy.

"we are capable of knowing Reality as it actually is... Reality when so known is absolutely rational." An even higher point may have been reached by that triumphant theologian whose book I have not read but whose title I greatly admire: *The Riddle of the Universe Solved.* Naturally sophisticated intelligence of this kind was the normal means of contact with literature. We are told that James Cappon judged poetry according to whether it had a "rationalized concept" or not — this would have been a very common critical assumption. Sara Jeannette Duncan shows us a clergyman borrowing a copy of Browning's *Sordello,* no easy reading, and returning it with original suggestions for interpretation. Such an interest in ideas is not merely cultivated but exuberant.

But using language as one would use an axe, formulating arguments with sharp cutting edges that will help to clarify one's view of the landscape, remains a rhetorical and not a poetic achievement. To quote Yeats again, one can refute Hegel (perhaps even St. Paul) but not the "Song of Sixpence." To create a disinterested structure of words, in poetry or in fiction, is a very different achievement, and it is clear that an intelligent and able rhetorician finds it particularly hard to understand how different it is. A rhetorician practicing poetry is apt to express himself in spectral arguments, generalizations that escape the feeling of possible refutation only by being vast enough to contain it, or vaporous enough to elude it. The mystique of Canadianism was accompanied by an intellectual tendency of this kind. World-views that avoided dialectic, of a theosophical or transcendentalist cast, became popular among the Canadian poets of that time, Roberts and Carman particularly, and later among painters, as the reminiscences of the Group of Seven make clear. Bucke's[14] *Cosmic Consciousness,* though not mentioned by any of our authors so far as I remember, is an influential Canadian book in this area. When minor rhetorically-minded poets sought what Samuel Johnson calls, though in a very different context, the "grandeur of generality," the result is what has been well described as "jejune chatter about infinity," and the like.

The literature of protest illustrates another rhetorical tradition. In the nineteenth century the common assumption that nature had revealed the truth of progress, and that it was the duty of reason to accommodate that truth to mankind, could be either a conservative or a radical view. But in either case it was a revolutionary doctrine, intro-

---

[14]Richard Maurice Bucke (1837-1902) was a world-renowned authority on mental and nervous diseases. He was also an impassioned mystic whose work in this field was influenced by the poetry of Walt Whitman. His *Cosmic Consciousness: A Study of Evolution of the Human Mind,* 1901, is considered a major contribution to the study of mysticism.

ducing the conception of change as the key to the social process. In the proletarian social Darwinists, who represented "the fusion of secularism, science and social discontent," there was a strong tendency to regard literature as a product and a symbol of a ruling-class mentality, with, as we have tried to indicate, some justification. Hence radicals tended either to hope that "the literature of the future will be the powerful ally of Democracy and Labour Reform," or to assume that serious thought and action would bypass the creative writer entirely, building a scientific socialism and leaving him to his Utopian dreams.

The radicalism of the period up to the Russian Revolution was, from a later point of view, largely undifferentiated. A labour magazine could regard Ignatius Donnelly, with his anti-Semitic and other crank views, as an advanced thinker equally with William Morris and Edward Bellamy. Similarly, even today, in Western Canadian elections, a protest vote may go Social Credit or NDP without much regard to the difference in political philosophy between these parties. The depression introduced a dialectic into Canadian social thought which profoundly affected its literature. In one writer's striking phrase, "the Depression was like an intense magnetic field that deflected the course of all the poets who went through it." In this period there were, of course, the inevitable Marxist manifestos, assuring the writer that only social significance, as understood by Marxism, would bring vitality to his work. The *New Frontier,* a far-left journal of that period shows an uneasy sense on the part of its contributors that this literary elixir of youth might have to be mixed with various other potions, not all favourable to the creative process: attending endless meetings, organizing, agitating, marching, demonstrating, or joining the Spanish Loyalists. It is easy for the critic to point out the fallacy of judging the merit of literature by its subject-matter, but these arguments over the role of "propaganda" were genuine and serious moral conflicts. Besides helping to shape the argument of such novels as Grove's *The Master of the Mill* and Callaghan's[15] *They Shall Inherit the Earth,* they raised the fundamental issue of the role of the creative mind in society, and by doing so helped to give maturity and depth to Canadian writing which is a permanent part of its heritage.

It is not surprising, given this background, that the belief in the inspiration of literature by social significance continued to be an active force long after it had ceased to be attached to any specifically Marxist

---

[15]Morley Callaghan (1903-90) one of Canada's first major writers of realistic fiction. Author of numerous novels, including *Strange Fugitive,* 1928; *More Joy in Heaven,* 1937; and *A Passion in Rome,* 1961. His short stories appeared in *Morley Callaghan's Stories,* 1951, and in *Lost and Found Stories,* 1985.

or other political programmes. It is still strong in the *Preview*[16] group in the forties, and in their immediate successors, though the best of them have developed in different directions. The theme of social realism is at its most attractive, and least theoretical, in the poetry of Raymond Souster. The existentialist movement, with its emphasis on the self-determination of social attitudes, seems to have had very little direct influence in Canada: the absence of the existential in Pratt suggests that this lack of influence may be significant.

During the last decade or so a kind of social Freudianism has been taking shape, mainly in the United States, as a democratic counterpart of Marxism. Here society is seen as controlled by certain anxieties, real or imaginary, which are designed to repress or sublimate human impulses toward a greater freedom. These impulses include the creative and the sexual, which are closely linked. The enemy of the poet is not the capitalist but the "square," or representative of repressive morality. The advantage of this attitude is that it preserves the position of rebellion against society for the poet, without imposing on him any specific social obligations. This movement has had a rather limited development in Canada, somewhat surprisingly considering how easy a target the square is in Canada: it has influenced Layton and many younger Montreal poets, but has not affected fiction to any great degree, though there may be something of it in Richler. It ignores the old political alignments: the Communists are usually regarded as Puritanic and repressive equally with the bourgeoisie, and a recent poem of Layton's contrasts the social hypocrisy in Canada with contemporary Spain. Thus it represents to some extent a return to the undifferentiated radicalism of a century before, though no longer in a political context.

As the centre of Canadian life moves from the fortress to the metropolis, the garrison mentality changes correspondingly. It begins as an expression of the moral values generally accepted in the group as a whole, and then, as society gets more complicated and more in control of its environment, it becomes more of a revolutionary garrison within a metropolitan society. But though it changes from a defense of to an attack on what society accepts as conventional standards, the literature it produces, at every stage, tends to be rhetorical, an illustration or allegory of certain social attitudes. These attitudes help to unify the mind of the writer by externalizing his enemy, the enemy being the anti-creative elements in life as he sees life. To approach these ele-

---

[16]This group was named after a Montreal-based periodical *Preview*, 1942-5, which featured poetry, short stories and articles and was known for its sophistication and cosmopolitanism. Its editors included F. R. Scott, P. K. Page and A. M. Klein.

ments in a less rhetorical way would introduce the theme of self-conflict, a more perilous but ultimately more rewarding theme. The conflict involved is between the poetic impulse to construct and the rhetorical impulse to assert, and the victory of the former is the sign of the maturing of the writer.

III

There is of course nothing in all this that differentiates Canadian from other related cultural developments. The nineteenth-century Canadian reliance on the conceptual was not different in kind from that of the Victorian readers described by Douglas Bush, who thought they were reading poetry when they were really only looking for Great Thoughts. But if the tendency was not different in kind, it was more intense in degree. Here we need another seminal fact, one that we have stumbled over already: the fact that the Canadian literary mind, beginning as it did so late in the cultural history of the West, was established on a basis, not of myth, but of history. The conceptual emphasis in Canadian culture we have been speaking of is a consequence, and an essential part, of this historical bias.

Canada, of course, or the place where Canada is, can supply distinctive settings and props to a writer who is looking for local colour. Tourist-writing has its own importance (e.g., *Maria Chapdelaine*), as has the use of Canadian history for purposes of romance, of which more later. But it would be an obvious fallacy to claim that the setting provided anything more than novelty. When Canadian writers are urged to use distinctively Canadian themes, the fallacy is less obvious, but still there. The forms of literature are autonomous: they exist within literature itself, and cannot be derived from any experience outside literature. What the Canadian writer finds in his experience and environment may be new, but it will be new only as content: the form of his expression of it can take shape only from what he has read, not from what he has experienced. The great technical experiments of Joyce and Proust in fiction, of Eliot and Hopkins in poetry, have resulted partly from profound literary scholarship, from seeing the formal possibilities inherent in the literature they have studied. A writer who is or who feels removed from his literary tradition tends rather to take over forms already in existence. We noticed how often critics of Canadian fiction have occasion to remark that a novel contains a good deal of sincere feeling and accurate observation, but that it is spoiled by an unconvincing plot, usually one too violent or dependent on coincidence for such material. What has happened is that the author felt he could make a novel out of his knowledge and observation, but had no story in particular to tell. His material did not come to him in the form of a story, but as a consolidated chunk of experience, reflection, and sensibility. He had to invent a plot to put this material in causal shape (for writing, as Kafka says, is an art of causality), to pour the new wine of content into the old bottles of form. Even Grove works in this way, though Grove, by sheer dogged persistence, does get his action powerfully if ponderously moving.

Literature is conscious mythology: as society develops, its mythical stories become structural principles of storytelling, its mythical concepts, sun-gods and the like, become habits of metaphorical thought. In a fully mature literary tradition the writer enters into a structure of traditional stories and images. He often has the feeling, and says so, that he is not actively shaping his material at all, but is rather a place where a verbal structure is taking its own shape. If a novelist, he starts with a story-telling impetus; if a poet, with a metaphor-crystallizing impetus. Down to the beginning of the twentieth century at least, the Canadian who wanted to write started with a feeling of detachment from his literary tradition, which existed for him mainly in his school books. He had probably, as said above, been educated in a way that heavily stressed the conceptual and argumentative use of language. We have been shown how the Indians began with a mythology which included all the main elements of our own. It was, of course, impossible for Canadians to establish any real continuity with it: Indians, like the rest of the country, were seen as nineteenth-century literary conventions. Certain elements in Canadian culture, too, such as the Protestant revolutionary view of history, may have minimized the importance of the oral tradition in ballad and folk song, which seems to have survived best in Catholic communities. In Canada the mythical was simply the "prehistoric" (this word, we are told, is a Canadian coinage), and the writer had to attach himself to his literary tradition deliberately and voluntarily. And though this may be no longer true or necessary, attitudes surviving from an earlier period of isolation still have influence.

The separation of subject and object is the primary fact of consciousness, for anyone so situated and so educated. Writing for him does not start with a rhythmical movement, or an impetus caught from or encouraged by a group of contemporaries: it starts with reportage, a single mind reacting to what is set over against it. Such a writer does not naturally think metaphorically but descriptively; it seems obvious to him that writing is a form of self-expression dependent on the gathering of a certain amount of experience, granted some inborn sensitivity toward that experience. We note how many Canadian novelists have written only one novel, or only one good novel, how many Canadian poets have written only one good book of poems, generally their first. Even the dream of "the great Canadian novel," the feeling that somebody some day will write a Canadian fictional classic, assumes that whoever does it will do it only once. This is a characteristic of writers dominated by the conception of writing up experiences or observations: nobody has enough experience to keep on writing about it, unless his writing is an incidental commentary on a non-literary career.

The Canadian writers who have overcome these difficulties and have found their way back to the real headwaters of inspiration are heroic explorers. There are a good many of them, and enough of them to say that the Canadian imagination has passed the stage of exploration and has embarked on that of settlement. But it is of course full of the failures as well as the successes of exploration, imaginative voyages to Golconda[17] that froze in the ice, and we can learn something from them too. Why do Canadians write so many historical romances, of what has been called the rut and thrust variety? One can understand it in the early period: the tendency to melodrama in romance makes it part of a central convention of that time. But romances are still going strong in the twentieth century and if anything even stronger in our own day. They get a little sexier and more violent as they go on, but the formula remains much the same: so much love-making, so much "research" about antiquities and costume copied off filing cards, more love-making, more filing cards. There is clearly a steady market for this, but the number of writers engaged in it suggests other answers. There is also a related fact, the unusually large number of Canadian popular best-selling fiction-writers, from Agnes Fleming through Gilbert Parker to Mazo de la Roche.

In nineteenth-century Canadian literature not all the fiction is romance, but nearly all of it is formula-writing. In the books of this type that I have read I remember much honest and competent work. Some of them did a good deal to form my own infantile imagination, and I could well have fared worse. What there is not, of course, is a recreated view of life, or anything to detach the mind from its customary attitudes. In the early twentieth century we begin to notice a more consistent distinction between the romancer, who stays with established values and usually chooses a subject remote in time from himself, and the realist, who deals with contemporary life, and therefore — it appears to be a therefore — is more serious in intention, more concerned to unsettle a stock response. One tendency culminates in Mazo de la Roche, the other in Mor-

---

[17]Golconda, an ancient city in India, famous for diamond cutting — a place of great riches.

ley Callaghan, both professional writers and born story-tellers, though of very different kinds. By our own time the two tendencies have more widely diverged. One is mainly romance dealing with Canada's past, the other is contemporary realism dealing with what is common to Canada and the rest of the world, like antique and modern furniture stores. One can see something similar in the poetry, a contrast between a romantic tradition closely associated with patriotic and idealistic themes, and a more intellectualized one with a more cosmopolitan bias. This contrast is prominently featured in the first edition of A. J. M. Smith's anthology, *Book of Canadian Poetry* (1943).

This contrast of the romantic and the realistic, the latter having a moral dignity that the former lacks, reflects the social and conceptual approach to literature already mentioned. Here we are looking at the same question from a different point of view. Literature, we said, is conscious mythology: it creates an autonomous world that gives us an imaginative perspective on the actual one. But there is another kind of mythology, one produced by society itself, the object of which is to persuade us to accept existing social values. "Popular" literature, the kind that is read for relaxation and the quieting of the mind, expresses the social mythology. We all feel a general difference between serious and soothing literature, though I know of no critical rule for distinguishing them, nor is there likely to be one. The same work may belong to both mythologies at once, and in fact the separation between them is largely a perspective of our own revolutionary age.

In many popular novels, especially in the nineteenth century, we feel how strong the desire is on the part of the author to work out his situation within a framework of established social values. In the success-story formula frequent in such fiction the success is usually "emotional," i. e, the individual fulfills himself within his community. There is nothing hypocritical or cynical about this: the author usually believes very deeply in his values. Moral earnestness and the posing of serious problems are by no means excluded from popular literature, any more than serious literature is excused from the necessity of being entertaining. The difference is in the position of the reader's mind at the end, in whether he is being encouraged to remain within his habitual social responses or whether he is being prodded into making the steep and lonely climb into the imaginative world. This distinction in itself is familiar enough, and all I am suggesting here is that what I have called the garrison mentality is highly favourable to the growth of popular literature in this sense. The role of romance and melodrama in consolidating a social mythology is also not hard to see. In romance the characters tend to be psychological projections, heroes, heroines, villains, father-figures, comic-relief caricatures. The popular romance operates on Freudian principles, releasing sexual and power fantasies without disturbing the anxieties of the superego. The language of melodrama, at once violent and morally conventional, is the appropriate language for this. A subliminal sense of the erotic release in romance may have inspired some of the distrust of novels in nineteenth-century pietistic homes. But even those who preferred stories of real life did not want "realism": that, we learn, was denounced on all sides during the nineteenth century as nasty, prurient, morbid, and foreign. The garrison mentality is that of its officers: it can tolerate only the conservative idealism of its ruling class, which for Canada means the moral and propertied middle class.

The total effect of Canadian popular fiction, whatever incidental merits in it there may be, is that of a murmuring and echoing literary collective unconscious, the rippling of a watery Narcissus world reflecting the imaginative patterns above it. Robertson Davies' *Tempest Tost* is a sardonic study of the triumph of a social mythology over the imaginative one symbolized by Shakespeare's play. Maturity and individualization, in such a body of writing, are almost the same process. Occasionally a writer is individualized by accident. Thus Susanna Moodie in the Peterborough bush, surrounded by a half-comic, half-sinister rabble that she thinks of indifferently as Yankee, Irish, native, republican, and lower class, is a British army of occupation in herself, a one-woman garrison. We often find too, as in Leacock, a spirit of criticism, even of satire, that is the complementary half of a strong attachment to the mores that provoke the satire. That is, a good deal of what goes on in Mariposa may look ridiculous, but the norms or standards against which it looks ridiculous are provided by Mariposa itself. In Sara Jeannette Duncan there is something else again, as she watches the garrison parade to church in a small Ontario town: "The repressed magnetic excitement in gatherings of familiar faces, fellow-beings bound by the same convention to the same kind of behaviour, is precious in communities where the human interest is still thin and sparse." Here is a voice of genuine detachment, sympathetic but not defensive either of the group or of herself, concerned primarily to understand and to make the reader see. The social group is becoming external to the writer, but not in a way that isolates her from it.

This razor's edge of detachment is naturally rare in Canadian writing, even in this author, but as the twentieth century advances and Canadian society takes a firmer grip of its environment, it becomes easier to assume the role of an individual separated in standards and attitudes from the community. When this happens, an ironic or realistic literature becomes fully possible. This new kind of detachment of course often means only that the split between subject and object has become identified with a split between the individual and society. This is particularly likely to happen when the separated individual's point of view is also that of the author, as in the stories of misunderstood genius with which many minor authors are fascinated. This convention was frequent in the plays of the twenties, and even more so in the fiction. But some of the most powerful of Canadian novels have been those in which this conflict has been portrayed objectively. Buckler's[18] *The Mountain and the Valley* is a Maratime example, and Sinclair Ross's *As for Me* and *My House* one from the prairies.

The essayist B. K. Sandwell remarks: "I follow it [society] at a respectful distance...far enough away to make it clear that I do not belong to it." It is clear that this is not necessarily any advance on the expression of conventional social values in popular romance. The feeling of detachment from society means only that society has become more complex, and inner tensions have developed in it. We have traced this process already. The question that arises is: once society, along with physical nature, becomes external to the writer, what does he then feel a part of? For rhetorical or assertive writers it is generally a smaller society, the group that agrees with them. But the imaginative writer, though he often begins as a member of a school or group, normally pulls away from it as he develops.

If our general line of thought is sound, the imaginative writer is finding his identity within the world of literature itself. He is withdrawing from what Douglas LePan calls a country without a mythology into the country of mythology, ending where the Indians began. The dramatist John Coulter says of his play, or libretto, *Deirdre of the Sorrows*: "The art of a Canadian remains... the art of the country of his forebears and the old world heritage of myth and legend remains his heritage...though the desk on which he writes be Canadian." But the progress may not be a simple matter of forsaking the Canadian for the international, the province for the capital. It may be that when the Canadian writer attaches himself to the world of literature, he discovers, or rediscovers, by doing so, something in his Canadian environment which is more vital and articulate than a desk.

---

[18]Ernest Buckler (1908-84) was one of Canada's leading fiction writers from Nova Scotia. He is best known for his coming-of-age novel, *The Mountain and the Valley*, 1952.

IV

At the heart of all social mythology lies what may be called, because it usually is called, a pastoral myth, the vision of a social ideal. The pastoral myth in its most common form is associated with childhood, or with some earlier social condition — pioneer life, the small town, the *habitant* rooted to his land — that can be identified with childhood. The nostalgia for a world of peace and protection, with a spontaneous response to the nature around it, with a leisure and composure not to be found today, is particularly strong in Canada. It is overpowering in our popular literature, from *Anne of Green Gables*[19] to Leacock's *Mariposa*,[20] and from *Maria Chapdelaine* to *Jake and the Kid*.[21] It is present in all the fiction that deals with small towns as collections of characters in search of an author. Its influence is strong in the most serious writers: one thinks of Gabrielle Roy, following her *Bonheur d'occasion* with *La poule d'eau*. It is the theme of all the essayists who write of fishing and other forms of the simpler life, especially as lived in the past. We may quote MacMechan[22]: "golden days in memory for the enrichment of less happier times to come." It even comes into our official documents — the *Massey Report*[23] begins, almost as a matter of course, with an idyllic picture of the Canada of fifty years ago, as a point of departure for its investigations. One writer speaks of the eighteenth-century Loyalists as looking "to a past that had never existed for com-

---

[19] *Anne of Green Gables*, by Lucy Maud Montgomery (1874-1942), has been Canada's most enduring contribution to the world of adolescent literature. The book has been translated into numerous languages, made into a feature film, and performed as a musical annually in Charlottetown since 1965.

[20] *Mariposa* is an imaginary small town in Ontario, with close resemblance to Orillia, where Stephen Leacock (1869-1944) set his most popular work, *Sunshine Sketches of a Little Town*, 1912.

[21] Between 1949 and 1957, W. O. Mitchell (1914-) wrote weekly scripts for CBC radio series 'Jake and the Kid,' thirteen of which, originally written as short stories, were published in 1962 in a collection, *Jake and the Kid*. Otherwise, Mitchell's best-known work is *Who Has Seen the Wind*, 1947.

[22] Archibald MacMechan (1862-1933) is principally remembered for his many collections of essays and for his pioneering critical survey of English- and French-Canadian authors, *Headwaters of Canadian Literature*, 1924.

[23] *Massey Report*, is a 1949 document of the Royal Commission on National Development in the Arts, Letters and Sciences recommending the establishment of a National Library and the Canada Council. The report was one of the most important conscious efforts made in Canada to foster Canadian culture.

fort and illumination," which suggests that the pastoral myth has been around for some time.

The Indians have not figured so largely in the myth as one might expect, though in some early fiction and drama the noble savage takes the role, as he does to some extent even in the Gothic hero Wacousta.[24] The popularity of Pauline Johnson[25] and Grey Owl,[26] however, shows that the kind of rapport with nature which the Indian symbolizes is central to it. Another form of pastoral myth is the evocation of an earlier period of history which is made romantic by having a more uninhibited expression of passion or virtue or courage attached to it. This of course links the pastoral myth with the vision of vanished grandeur that comes into the novels about the *ancient régime*. In *The Golden Dog* and *The Seats of the Mighty*[27] the forlorn little fortress of seventeenth-century Quebec, sitting in the middle of what Madame de Pompadour called "a few arpents of snow," acquires a theatrical glamour that would do credit to Renaissance Florence. The two forms of the myth collide on the Plains of Abraham, on the one side a marquis[28], on the other a Hanoverian commoner[29] tearing himself reluctantly from the pages of Gray's *Elegy*.

Close to the centre of the pastoral myth is the sense of kinship with the animal and vegetable world, which is so prominent a part of

---

[24]Wacousta is the protagonist in the 1832 novel of the same name by the first Canadian-born novelist, John Richardson (1796-1852). Wacousta, whose real name was Reginald Morton, is the prototype of a white man reinventing himself as a native American.

[25]Pauline Johnson (1861-1913), daughter of a Mohawk father and an English mother, was the first Native-Canadian poet to achieve national reputation. Her collections include *Canadian Born*, 1903, and *Flint and Feather*, 1912.

[26]Archibald Stansfeld Belaney, alias 'Gray Owl' (1888-1938), writer and conservationist. He left England at seventeen, settled in Northern Ontario, and reinvented himself as a native. His books, extremely popular in England during his lifetime, include *Men of the Last Frontier*, 1931, and *The Adventures of Sajo and Her Beaver People*, 1935.

[27]*Ancient Régime* refers to the period of French-Canadian history prior to the British conquest in 1759, a period depicted in two historical romances, *The Golden Dog*, 1877, by William Kirby (1817-1906), and *The Seats of the Mighty*, 1896, by Gilbert Parker (1862-1932).

[28]Louis-Joseph de Montcalm (1712-59), military commander of French troops in North America, defeated by the British on the Plains of Abraham.

[29]James Wolfe (1727-59), British army officer, commander of the British expedition that took Quebec in 1759. His defeat of Montcalm's army marked the beginning of British rule in Canada.

the Canadian frontier. I think of an image in Mazo de la Roche's *Delight*. Delight Mainprize — I leave it to the connoisseurs of ambiguity to explore the overtones of that name — is said by her creator to be "not much more developed intellectually than the soft-eyed Jersey in the byre." It must be very rarely that a novelist — a wideawake and astute novelist — can call her heroine a cow with such affection, even admiration. But it is consistent with her belief in the superiority of the primitive and the instinctive over the civilized and conventional. The prevalence in Canada of animal stories, in which animals are closely assimilated to human behaviour and emotions, illustrates the same point. Conversely, the killing of an animal, as a tragic or ironic symbol, has a peculiar resonance in Canadian poetry, from the moose in Lampman's Long Sault poem to the Christmas slaughter of geese which is the informing theme of James Reaney's *A Suit of Nettles*. More complicated pastoral motifs are conspicuous in Morley Callaghan, who turns continually to the theme of betrayed or victorious innocence — the former in *The Loved and the Lost*, the latter in *Such is My Beloved*. The Peggy of *The Loved and the Lost*, whose spontaneous affection for Negroes is inspired by a childhood experience and symbolized by a child's toy, is particularly close to our theme.

The theme of Grove's *A Search for America* is the narrator's search for a North American pastoral myth in its genuinely imaginative form, as distinct from its sentimental or socially stereotyped form. The narrator, adrift in the New World without means of support, has a few grotesque collisions with the hustling mercantilism of American life — selling encyclopedias and the like — and gets badly bruised in spirit. He becomes convinced that this America is a false social development which has grown over and concealed the real American social ideal, and tries to grasp the form of this buried society. In our terms, he is trying to grasp something of the myth of America, the essential imaginative idea it embodies. He meets, but irritably brushes away, the tawdry and sentimentalized versions of this myth — the cottage away from it all, happy days on the farm, the great open spaces of the west. He goes straight to the really powerful and effective versions: Thoreau's *Walden*, the personality of Lincoln, Huckleberry Finn drifting down the great river. The America that he searches for, he feels, has something to do with these things, though it is not defined much more closely than this.

Grove drops a hint in a footnote near the end that what his narrator is looking for has been abandoned in the United States but perhaps not yet in Canada. This is not our present moral: pastoral myths, even in their genuine forms, do not exist as places. They exist rather in such things as the loving delicacy of perception in Grove's own *Over Prairie*

Trails and *The Turn of the Year*. Still, the remark has some importance because it indicates that the conception of "Canada" can also become a pastoral myth in certain circumstances. One writer, speaking of the nineteenth-century mystique of Canadianism, says: "A world is created, its centre in the Canadian home, its middle distance the loved landscape of Canada, its protecting wall the circle of British institutions... a world as centripetal as that of Sherlock Holmes and as little liable to be shaken by irruptions of evil." The myth suggested here is somewhat Virgilian in shape, pastoral serenity serving as a prologue to the swelling act of the imperial theme. Nobody who saw it in that way was a Virgil, however, and it has been of minor literary significance.

We have said that literature creates a detached and autonomous mythology, and that society itself produces a corresponding mythology, to which a good deal of literature belongs. We have found the pastoral myth, in its popular and sentimental social form, to be an idealization of memory, especially childhood memory. But we have also suggested that the same myth exists in a genuinely imaginative form, and have found its influence in some of the best Canadian writers. Our present problem is to see if we can take a step beyond Grove and attempt some characterization of the myth he was looking for, a myth which would naturally have an American context but a particular reference to Canada. The sentimental nostalgic pastoral myth increases the feeling of separation between subject and object by withdrawing the subject into a fantasy world. The genuine myth, then, would result from reversing this process. Myth starts with the identifying of subject and object, the primary imaginative act of literary creation. It is therefore the most explicitly mythopeic aspect of Canadian literature that we have to turn to, and we shall find this centred in the poetry rather than the fiction. There are many reasons for this: one is that in poetry there is no mass market to encourage the writer to seek refuge in conventional social formulas.

A striking fact about Canadian poetry is the number of poets who have turned to narrative forms (including closet drama) rather than lyrical ones. The anthologist who confines himself wholly to the lyric will give the impression that Canadian poetry really began with Roberts's "Orion" in 1880. Actually there was a tradition of narrative poetry well established before that (Sangster, Heavysege, Howe, and several others), which continues into the post-Confederation period (Mair, Isabella Crawford, Duvar, besides important narrative works by Lampman and D. C. Scott). It is clear that Pratt's devotion to the narrative represents a deep affinity with the Canadian tradition, although so far as I know (and I think I do know) the affinity was entirely unconscious on his part. I have written about the importance of narrative poetry in Canada elsewhere, and have little new to add here. It has two characteristics that account for its being especially important in Canadian literature. In the first place, it is impersonal. The bald and dry statement is the most effective medium for its treatment of action, and the author, as in the folk song and ballad, is able to keep out of sight or speak as one of a group. In the second place, the natural affinities of poetic narrative are with tragic and ironic themes, not with the more manipulated comic and romantic formulas of prose fiction. Consistently with its impersonal form, tragedy and irony are expressed in the action of the poem rather than in its moods or in the poet's own comment.

We hardly expect the earlier narratives to be successful all through, but if we read them with sympathy and historical imagination, we can see how the Canadian environment has exerted its influence on the poet. The environment, in nineteenth-century Canada, is terrifyingly cold, empty and vast, where the obvious and immediate sense of nature is the late Romantic one, increasingly affected by Darwinism, of nature red in tooth and claw. We notice the recurrence of such episodes as shipwreck, Indian massacres, human sacrifices, lumbermen mangled in log-jams, mountain climbers crippled on glaciers, animals screaming in traps, the agonies of starvation and solitude — in short, the "shutting out of the whole moral creation." Human suffering, in such an environment, is a by-product of a massive indifference which, whatever else it may be, is not morally explicable. What confronts the poet is a moral silence deeper than any physical silence, though the latter frequently symbolizes the former, as in the poem of Pratt that is explicitly called "Silences."

The nineteenth-century Canadian poet can hardly help being preoccupied with physical nature; the nature confronting him presents him with the riddle of unconsciousness, and the riddle of unconsciousness in nature is the riddle of death in man. Hence his central emotional reaction is bound to be elegiac and sombre, full of loneliness and fear, or at least wistful and nostalgic, hugging, like Roberts, a "darling illusion." In Carman, Roberts, and D. C. Scott there is a rhetorical strain that speaks in a confident, radio-announcer's voice about the destiny of Canada, the call of the open road, or the onward and upward march of progress. As none of their memorable poetry was written in this voice, we may suspect that they turned to it partly for reassurance. The riddle of unconsciousness in nature is one that no moralizing or intellectualizing can answer. More important, it is one that irony cannot answer:

> The gray shape with the paleolithic face
> Was still the master of the longitudes.

The conclusion of Pratt's *Titanic* is almost documentary: it is as stripped of irony as it is of moralizing. The elimination of irony from the poet's view of nature makes that view pastoral — a cold pastoral, but still a pastoral. We have only physical nature and a rudimentary human society, not strong enough yet to impose the human forms of tragedy and irony on experience.

The same elegiac and lonely tone continues to haunt the later poetry. Those who in the twenties showed the influence of the death-and-resurrection myth of Eliot, notably Leo Kennedy and A. J. M. Smith, were also keeping to the centre of a native tradition. The use of the Eliot myth was sometimes regarded as a discovery myth, but of course the earlier poets had not only used the same myth, but were equally aware of its origins in Classical poetry, as Carman's *Sappho* indicates. The riddle of the unconscious may be expressed by a symbol such as the agonies of a dying animal, or it may be treated simply as an irreducible fact of existence. But it meets us everywhere: I pick up Margaret Avison and there it is, in a poem called "Identity":

> But on this sheet of beryl, this high sea,
> Scalded by the white unremembering glaze,
> No wisps disperse. This is the icy pole.
> The presence here is single, worse than soul,
> Pried loose forever out of nights and days
> And birth and death
> And all the covering wings.

In such an environment, we may well wonder how the sentimental pastoral myth ever developed at all. But of course there are the summer months, and a growing settlement of the country that eventually began to absorb at least eastern Canada into the north temperate zone. Pratt's Newfoundland background helped to keep his centre of gravity in the elegiac, but when he began to write the feeling of the mindless hostility of nature had largely retreated to the prairies, where a fictional realism developed, closely related to this feeling in mood and imagery. The Wordsworthian sense of nature as a teacher is apparent as early as Mrs. Traill,[30] in whom we note a somewhat selective approach to the subject reminiscent of Miss Muffet. As the sentimental pastoral myth takes shape, its imaginative counterpart takes shape

---

[30]Catharine Parr Traill (1802-99) is chiefly remembered today for her semi-autobiographical and documentary book, *The Backwoods of Canada*, 1836, written from her experience as a pioneer woman living in the Peterborough area of Ontario in the early part of the nineteenth century.

too, the other, gentler, more idyllic half of the myth that has made the pastoral itself a central literary convention. In this version nature, though still full of awfulness and mystery, is the visible representative of an order that man has violated, a spiritual unity that the intellect murders to dissect. This form of the myth is more characteristic of the second phase of Canadian social development, when the conflict of man and nature is expanding into a triangular conflict of nature, society, and individual. Here the individual tends to ally himself with nature against society. A very direct and haunting statement of this attitude occurs in John Robins's *Incomplete Anglers:* "I can approach a solitary tree with pleasure, a cluster of trees with joy, and a forest with rapture; I must approach a solitary man with caution, a group of men with trepidation, and a nation of men with terror." The same theme also forms part of the final cadences of Hugh MacLennan's *The Watch That Ends the Night:* "In the early October of that year, in the cathedral hush of a Quebec Indian summer with the lake drawing into its mirror the fire of the maples, it came to me that to be able to love the mystery surrounding us is the final and only sanction of human existence."

It is the appearance of this theme in D. C. Scott which makes him one of the ancestral voices of the Canadian imagination. It is much stronger and more continuous in Lampman, who talks less than his contemporaries and strives harder for the uniting of subject and object in the imaginative experience. This union takes place in the contact of individual poet and a landscape uninhabited except for Wordsworth's "huge and mighty forms" that are manifested by the union:

> Nay more, I think some blessèd power
> Hath brought me wandering idly here.

Again as in Wordsworth, this uniting of individual mind and nature is an experience from which human society, as such, is excluded. Thus when the poet finds a "blessed power" in nature it is the society he leaves behind that tends to become the God-forsaken wilderness. Usually this society is merely trivial or boring; once, in the unforgettable "The City of the End of Things," it becomes demonic.

The two aspects of the pastoral tradition we have been tracing are not inconsistent with each other; they are rather complementary. At one pole of experience there is a fusion of human life and the life in nature; at the opposite pole is the identity of the sinister and terrible elements in nature with the death-wish in man. In Pratt's "The Truant" the "genus *homo*" confronts the "great Panjandrum" of nature who is also his own death-wish: the great Panjandrum is the destructive force in the Nazis and in the Indians who martyred Brébeuf, the capacity in man that enables him to be deliberately cruel. Irving Layton shows us not only the cruelty but the vulgarity of the death-wish consciousness; as it has no innocence, it cannot suffer with dignity, as animals can; it loses its own imaginary soul by despising the body:

> Listen: for all his careful fuss,
> Will this cold one ever deceive us?
> Self-hating, he rivets a glittering wall;
> Impairs it by a single pebble
> And loves himself for that concession.

We spoke earlier of a civilization conquering the landscape and imposing an alien and abstract pattern on it. As this process goes on, the writers, the poets especially, tend increasingly to see much of this process as something that is human but still dehumanized, leaving man's real humanity a part of the nature that he continually violates but is still inviolate.

Reading through any good collection of modern Canadian poems or stories, we find every variety of tone, mood, attitude, technique, and setting. But there is a certain unity of impression one gets from it, an impression of gentleness and reasonableness, seldom difficult or greatly daring in its imaginative flights, the passion, whether of love or anger, held in check by something meditative. It is not easy to put the feeling in words, but if we turn to the issue of the *Tamarack Review* that was devoted to West Indian literature, or to Hungarian poems translated by Canadians in the collection *The Plough and the Pen*, we can see by contrast something of both the strength and the limitations of the Canadian writers. They too have lived, if not in Arcadia, at any rate in a land where empty space and the pervasiveness of physical nature have impressed a pastoral quality on their minds. From the deer and fish in Isabella Crawford's "The Canoe" to the frogs and toads in Layton, from the white narcissus of Knister[31] to the night-blooming cereus of Reaney, everything that is central in Canadian writing seems to be marked by the imminence of the natural world. The sense of this imminence organizes the mythology of Jay Macpherson; it is the sign in which Canadian soldiers conquer Italy in Douglas LePan's *The Net and the Sword;* it may be in the foreground, as in *Alden Nowlan*, or in the background, as in *Birney*; but it is always there.

---

[31]Raymond Knister (1899-1932) was one of Canada's first Modernists. He wrote stories, posthumously edited by Michael Gnarowski as *Selected Stories of Raymond Knister*, 1977, and a novel, *White Narcissus*, 1929. He also edited an important book of stories, *Canadian Short Stories*, 1928.

To go on with this absorbing subject would take us into another book: *A Literary Criticism of Canada*, let us say. Here we can only sum up the present argument emblematically, with two famous primitive American paintings. One is "Historical Monument of the American Republic," by Erastus Salisbury Field. Painted in 1876 for the centennial of the Revolution, it is an encyclopaedic portrayal of events in American history, against a background of soaring towers, with clouds around the spires, and connected by railway bridges. It is a prophetic vision of the skyscraper cities of the future, of the tremendous technological will to power of our time and the civilization it has built, a civilization now gradually imposing a uniformity of culture and habits of life all over the globe. Because the United States is the most powerful centre of this civilization, we often say, when referring to its uniformity, that the world is becoming Americanized. But of course America itself is being Americanized in this sense, and the uniformity imposed on New Delhi and Singapore, or on Toronto and Vancouver, is no greater than that imposed on New Orleans or Baltimore. A nation so huge and so productive, however, is deeply committed to this growing technological uniformity, even though many tendencies may pull in other directions. Canada has participated to the full in the wars, economic expansions, technological achievements, and internal stresses of the modern world. Canadians seem well adjusted to the new world of technology and very efficient at handling it. Yet in the Canadian imagination there are deep reservations to this world as an end of life in itself, and the political separation of Canada has helped to emphasize these reservations in its literature.

English Canada began with the influx of defeated Tories after the American Revolution, and so, in its literature, with a strong anti-revolutionary bias. The Canadian radicalism that developed in opposition to Loyalism was not a revival of the American revolutionary spirit, but a quite different movement, which had something in common with the Toryism it opposed: one thinks of the Tory and radical elements in the social vision of William Cobbett,[32] who also finds a place in the Canadian record. A revolutionary tradition is liable to two defects: to an undervaluing of history and an impatience with law, and we have seen how unusually strong the Canadian attachment to law and history has been. The attitude to things American represented by Haliburton is not, on the whole, hostile: it would be better described as non-committal, as when Sam Slick speaks of a Fourth of July as "a splendid specta-

[32]William Cobbett (1766-1835) wrote vivid sketches of late eighteen-century life in the Maritimes, collected in *The Life and Adventures of Peter Porcupine*, 1796, and in *Advice to Young Men*, 1830.

cle: fifteen millions of freemen and three millions of slaves a-celebratin' the birthday of liberty." The strong romantic tradition in Canadian literature has much to do with its original conservatism. When more radical expressions begin to creep into Canadian writing, as in the poetry of Alexander McLachlan, there is still much less of the assumption that freedom and national independence are the same thing, or that the mercantilist Whiggery which won the American Revolution is necessary the only emancipating force in the world. In some Canadian writers of our own time — I think particularly of Earle Birney's *Trial of a City* and the poetry of F. R. Scott — there is an opposition, not to the democratic but to the oligarchic tendencies in North American civilization, not to liberal but to laissez-faire political doctrine. Perhaps it is a little easier to see these distinctions from the vantage-point of a smaller country, even one which has, in its material culture, made the "American way of life" its own.

The other painting is the much earlier "The Peaceable Kingdom," by Edward Hicks, painted around 1830. Here, in the background, is a treaty between the Indians and the Quaker settlers under Penn. In the foreground is a group of animals, lions, tigers, bears, oxen, illustrating the prophecy of Isaiah about the recovery of innocence in nature. Like the animals of the Douanier Rousseau, they stare past us with a serenity that transcends consciousness. It is the pictorial emblem of what Grove's narrator was trying to find under the surface of America: the reconciliation of man with man and of man with nature: the mood of Thoreau's Walden retreat, of Emily Dickinson's garden, of Huckleberry Finn's raft, of the elegies of Whitman. This mood is closer to the haunting vision of a serenity that is both human and natural which we have been struggling to identify in the Canadian tradition. If we had to characterize a distinctive emphasis in that tradition, we might call it a quest for the peaceable kingdom.

The writers of the last decade, at least, have begun to write in a world which is post-Canadian, as it is post-American, post-British, and post everything except the world itself. There are no provinces in the empire of aeroplane and television, and no physical separation from the centres of culture, such as they are. Sensibility is no longer dependent on a specific environment or even on sense experience itself. A remark of one critic about Robert Finch illustrates a tendency which is affecting literature as well as painting: "the interplay of sense impressions is so complicated, and so exhilarating, that the reader receives no sense impression at all." Marshall McLuhan speaks of the world as reduced to a single gigantic primitive village, where everything has the same kind of immediacy. He speaks of the fears that so many intellectuals have of such a world, and remarks amiably: "Terror is the normal state of any oral society, for in it everything affects everything all the time." The Canadian spirit, to personify it as a single being dwelling in the country from the early voyages to the present, might well, reading this sentence, feel that this was where he came in. In other words, new conditions give the old ones a new importance, as what vanishes in one form reappears in another. The moment that the peaceable kingdom has been completely obliterated by its rival is the moment when it comes into the foreground again, as the eternal frontier, the first thing that the writer's imagination must deal with. Pratt's "The Truant," already referred to, foreshadows the poetry of the future, when physical nature has retreated to outer space and only individual and society are left as effective factors in the imagination. But the central conflict, and the moods in which it is fought out, are still unchanged.

One gets very tired, in old-fashioned biographies, of the dubious embryology that examines a poet's ancestry and wonders if a tendency to fantasy in him could be the result of an Irish great-grandmother. A reader may feel the same unreality in efforts to attach Canadian writers to a tradition made up of earlier writers whom they may not have read or greatly admired. I have felt this myself whenever I have written about Canadian literature. Yet I keep coming back to the feeling that there does seem to be such a thing as an imaginative continuum, and that writers are conditioned in their attitudes by their predecessors, or by the cultural climate of their predecessors, whether there is conscious influence or not. Again, nothing can give a writer's experience and sensitivity any form except the study of literature itself. In this study the great classics, "monuments of its own magnificence," and the best contemporaries have an obvious priority. The more such monuments or such contemporaries there are in a writer's particular cultural tradition, the more fortunate he is; but he needs those traditions in any case. He needs them most of all when what faces him seems so new as to threaten his identity. For present and future writers in Canada and their readers, what is important in Canadian literature, beyond the merits of the individual works in it, is the inheritance of the entire enterprise. The writers of Canada have identified the habits and attitudes of the country, as Fraser and Mackenzie have identified its rivers. They have also left an imaginative legacy of dignity and of high courage.

"Conclusion" in: *Literary History of Canada: Canadian Literature in English.* Edidet by Carl Klinck and others. Toronto: University of Toronto Press, 1965. This slightly edited version was reprinted from *The Bush Garden,* Toronto: House of Anansi Press, 1971.

Conclusion to a *Literary History of Canada*

Second Edition

It is difficult to know what to say, as a general conclusion, to this part of the *Literary History*[1] that is not already said or implied in my previous conclusion. Ten or twelve years is not a generation, much less, even in these future-shock days, an historical period. The logical starting point, I think, has to be the reason for producing a volume of this size so few years after the original one, and the reason is not difficult to grasp. Mr. Cross,[2] writing on history, says that five hundred books in the field were produced during the five of the years he covers; Mr. Woodcock[3] counts over a thousand volumes of verse, excluding anthologies; nearly every contributor says or implies something about the colossal verbal explosion that has taken place in Canada since 1960. Such a quantitative increase eventually makes for a qualitative change: this change cannot, in so short a time, reveal much essentially new to the critical observer, but it does mean that the trends I studied in the previous conclusion have reached something of a crisis since then. All I can do here is to try to characterize that crisis: there can be no question of attempting any rounded general survey of the period.

Our reviewers are comprehensive to the verge of omniscience, and with all their selectivity they have little space to do more than mention a great number of books which are not simply entertaining, interesting, or instructive, but are richly rewarding to read. Such critical comments as they are able to make are often tantalizingly brief, like

---

[1]Carl F. Klinck, ed., *Literary History of Canada* 2nd ed. Toronto: University of Toronto Press, 1976, pp. 318-32, Vol. 3.

[2]Michael S. Cross is Professor of History, Dalhousie University, Halifax, and Editor of the *Canadian Historical Review*. He contributed a chapter, "Canadian History," to *Literary History Canada*, 2nd edition.

[3]George Woodcock (1912-94) wrote numerous books on a wide spectrum of subjects — political science, history, biography, literary criticism — including Canadian Literature. He was the editor of *Canadian Literature* and contributed a chapter, "Poetry," to *Literary History of Canada*, 2nd edition.

Mr. New's[4] remark about the influence of structuralism and linguistics on the prose style of Canadian fiction. The fact that the book is something of a catalogue is nothing against it, but is on the contrary essential to its usefulness. Part of the total verbal explosion is the information explosion, and one of the more efficient ways of trying to cope with that is the "review of recent scholarship" article, a genre which this book closely approximates.

Critical methods, confronting such an avalanche of material, have to become rather more subtle then they were in the old days of collecting Canadians, putting authentic specimens of Loyalist descent (or "stock," in the E. K. Broadus anthology[5]) in the centre of a penumbra of immigrant, expatriate, transient, and tourist writers, some of whom, like Grove or Grey Owl, turned out to be masks of quite different people. The mask in Canadian literature would make a good thesis for somebody, and doubtless has done. Twenty years ago, the Canadian critical scene was full of schools and orthodoxies and heresies and divergencies and conflicting theories, the prevalence of which, in literary criticism no less than in religion or psychology, indicates a general failure to understand what is being talked about. It would be an affectation for me to pretend not to notice that I am extensively featured in this book myself, and among the many things I am grateful for and deeply appreciate, one is the fact that the phrase "the Frye school of mythopoeic poetry" is so briefly dismissed by Mr. Woodcock. There is no Frye school of mythopoeic poetry; criticism and poetry cannot possibly be related in that way; the myth of a poem is the structural principle of the poem, and consequently all poems that make any sense at all are equally mythopoeic, and so on and so on: the phrase, as Borges remarks about something in Fichte, is almost inexhaustibly fallacious. The concreteness of this book, the absence of anxiety and special pleading, the constant awareness of the genuine authority of the literature the reviewer is dealing with, is reflected in the literature itself. Mr. Bissell[6] notes

---

[4]William H. New (1938-) is Professor of English, University of British Columbia. General Editor of *Literary History of Canada*, 2nd edition, Vol. IV, present editor of *Canadian Literature* and author of numerous books, including *Articulating West*, 1972, and *Canadian Short Fiction*, 1986. He contributed a chapter, "Fiction," to *Literary History of Canada*, 2nd edition.

[5]E. K. Broadus (1876-1936), an educational pioneer who founded the University of Alberta. He was also known for his anthology of Canadian writing, *Book of Canadian Prose and Verse*, 1923.

[6]Claude Bissell (1916-), University Professor, University of Toronto and President of the University of Toronto 1958-71. He wrote two books on education and numerous articles on Victorian and Canadian literature. He con-

that a good deal of recent political writing, even strongly partisan, shows a real concern for objectivity and respect for facts; and similarly, the thesis novel, the assertive poem, the rib-nudging allegory, the assumption that literature can be "effective" only when it turns into subliterary rhetoric, seem to be receding from the literary scene.

For well over a century, and years before the satire in *Grip*[7] that Mr. Pacey[8] quotes, discussions about Canadian literature usually took the form of the shopper's dialogue: "Have you any Canadian literature today?" "Well, we re expecting something in very shortly." But that age is over, and writing this conclusion gives me rather the feeling of driving a last spike, of waking up from the National Neurosis. There is much more to come, just as there were all those CPR trains still to come, but Canadian literature is here, perhaps still a minor but certainly no longer a gleam in a paternal critic's eye. It is a typically Canadian irony that such a cataract started pouring out of the presses just before Marshall McLuhan became the most famous of Canadian critics for saying that the book was finished. I doubt if one can find this in McLuhan, except by quoting him irresponsibly out of context, but it is what he was widely believed to have said, and the assertion became very popular, as anything that sounds anti-intellectual always does. Abandoning irony, one may say that a population the size of English-writing Canada, subject to all the handicaps which have been chronicled so often in Canadian criticism, does not produce such a bulk of good writing without an extraordinary vitality and morale behind it. At the same time, to achieve, to bring a future into the present, is also to become finite, and the sense of that is always a little disconcerting, even though becoming finite means becoming genuinely human.

Canadians, as I have implied, have a highly developed sense of irony, but even so, De Gaulle's monumental gaffe of 1967, "vive le Québec libre," is one of the great ironic remarks in Canadian history, because, it was hailing the emergence of precisely the force that Quebec had really got free from. For the Quiet Revolution was as impressive an achievement of imaginative freedom as the contemporary world can

---

tributed a chapter, "Politics and Literature in the 1960s," to Literary History of Canada, 2nd edition.

[7]*Grip* was Canada's first comic cartoon, published weekly from May 1873 to May 1874.

[8]Desmond Pacey (1917-75) was Professor of English at the University of New Brunswick, Fredericton, and a prominent critic of Canadian writing. His publications include *Frederick Philip Grove*, 1945, *Ten Canadian Poets*, 1958 and *Essays in Canadian Criticism*, 1969. He contributed "The Course of Canadian Criticism" to *Literary History of Canada*, 2nd edition.

show: freedom not so much from clerical domination or corrupt politics as from the burden of tradition. The whole *je me souviens* complex in French Canada, the anxiety of resisting change, the strong emotionalism which was, as emotion by itself always is, geared to the past: this was what Quebec had shaken off to such an astonishing degree. It was accompanied, naturally enough, by intense anti-English and separatist feelings, which among the more confused took the form that De Gaulle was interested in, a French neo-colonialism. This last is dead already; separatism is still a strong force, and will doubtless remain one for some time, but one gets the feeling that it is being inexorably bypassed by history, and that even if it achieves its aims it will do so in a historical vacuum. I begin with French Canada because it seems to me that the decisive cultural event in English Canada during the past fifteen years has been the impact of French Canada and its new sense of identity. After so long and so obsessive a preoccupation with the same subject, it took the Quiet Revolution to create a real feeling of identity in English Canada, and to make cultural nationalism, if that is the best phrase, a genuine force in the country, even a bigger and more significant one than economic nationalism, which is, as Mr. Mayo[9] notes, mainly a Central Canadian movement.

The immense power of American penetration into Canada is traditionally thought of as either economic or sub-cultural: Canadians buy American cars and watch American situation comedies on television. Without denying the importance of these phenomena, in the last decade there has been a considerable growth of emphasis on more genuinely cultural aspects. This emphasis has affected Canadian attitudes to the publishing business, to the Canadian editions of *Time* and the *Reader's Digest,* to American television programs brought in, with their advertising, by cable, and to many other things: but perhaps the most widely publicized issue has been that of American appointments to Canadian universities. The reaction to these, proposals for quota systems and the like, may be theoretically untenable and practically impotent, but the kind of problem they try to meet is not unreal one. Academics of course are a conservative breed, and they still try to keep explaining to one another that scholarship knows no boundaries. Scholarship may not, but culture does: and the only reason for having scholarship is that it is necessary to culture.

---

[9]Henry B. Mayo (1911-) is Professor of Political Science, Carlton University, Ottawa. He contributed "Writing in the Social Sciences" to *Literary History of Canada,* 2nd edition, and is the author of *Democracy and Marxism,* 1955 and *Democracy in Canada,* 1975.

I am not a continentalist myself, although I have been called one, and I can see that in the later work of Underhill,[10] for instance, a writer whom of course I deeply respect and have learned much from, a naive admiration for things American amounts almost to a betrayal of his own liberalism. An independent Canada would be much more useful to the United States itself than a dependent or annexed one would be, and it is of great importance to the United States to have a critical view of it centred in Canada, a view which is not hostile but is simply another view. The United States has its share of fools like other countries, and just as fifty years ago senators would propose that Britain hand over Canada in payment of her war debt, so there are senators and others now (see Mr. Chapman's[11] article) who tell us how lovely it would be if we placed all our resources unquestioningly in American hands. Resistance to such things is in the United States' own best interest. The nationalism that has evolved in Canada is on the whole a positive development, in which self-awareness has been far more important than aggressiveness. Perhaps identity only is identity when it becomes, not militant, but a way of defining oneself against something else. In any case problems of culture and of verbal articulation are the primary concerns of this book. I see the kind of creative vitality which this book records as an emerging form of Canadian self-definition, and that involves looking at the difference from the American parallel development. The word "parallel" is important: Canada may be an American colony, as is often said, by me among others, but Canadians have never thought of the United States as a parental figure, like Britain, and analogies of youthful revolt and the like would be absurd.

To begin with a different kind of analogy: in countries were Marxism has not come to power, but where there is a strong Marxist minority, we see what an advantage it is to have a unified conceptual structure that can be applied to practically anything. It may often distort what it is applied to, but that matters less than the tactical advantage of having it. Defenders of more empirical points of view find their battlefronts disintegrating into separate and isolated outposts. They may demonstrate that this or that point is wrong, but such rearguard actions lack glamour. The same principle can be applied to the pragmatic,

---

[10]Frank H. Underhill (1889-1971), author of the 1933 founding manifesto of Canada's first social-democratic party. Although he never wrote a book, his influential historical writing appeared in *In Search of Canadian Liberalism*, 1960.

[11]J. H. Chapman (1940-) is co-author of *Upper Atmosphere and Space Programs in Canada*, 1967. He contributed "The Physical Sciences and Engineering" to *Literary History of Canada*, 2nd edition.

compromising, *ad hoc*, ramshackle Canadian tradition *vis-à-vis* the far more integrated and revolutionary American one. The coherence of the "American way of life" is often underestimated by Americans themselves, because the more thoughtful citizens of any country are likely to be more preoccupied with its anomalies. Hence outsiders, including Canadians, may find the consistency easier to see. De Tocqueville, who didn't like much of what he saw in the United States, wrote his book very largely about that consistency, almost in spite of himself.

As Canada and the United States went their separate ways on the same continent, eventually coming to speak for the most part the same language, their histories took on a strong pattern of contrast. The United States found its identity in the eighteenth century, the age of rationalism and enlightenment. It retains a strong intellectual fascination with the eighteenth century: its founding fathers are still its primary cultural heroes, and the bicentenary celebrations of 1976, from all accounts, will be mainly celebrations of the eighteenth century rather than of the present day. The eighteenth-century cultural pattern took on a revolutionary, and therefore a deductive shape, provided with a manifesto of independence and a written constitution. This in turn developed a rational attitude to the continuity of life in time, and this attitude seems to me the central principle of the American way of life. The best image for it is perhaps that of the express train. It is a conception of progress, but of progress defined by mechanical rather than organic metaphors, and hence the affinity with the eighteenth century is not really historical: it tends in fact to be anti-historical. Washington, Franklin, Jefferson, with their imperturbable common sense, are thought of, in the popular consciousness, more as deceased contemporaries than as ancestors living among different cultural referents. The past is thus assimilated to the present, a series of stations that our express train has stopped at and gone beyond.

In law and politics, new situations are met by reinterpreting, or in the last resort amending, an eighteenth-century document: proceeding, in other words, in a deductive direction, giving priority to the kind of logic which most clearly represents the mechanics of thought. In economics, there has been, and with qualifications there still is, a strong belief in laissez-faire, as a continuous and semi-autonomous process that will work by itself if left alone. The most characteristic American philosophical attitude to education is the pragmatism, so different from Canadian pragmatism, which sees truth as emerging from a course of consistent action. Its most characteristic attitude to education is the anti-contemplative Dewey conception of learning through doing, or, again, through continuous activity. In religion, the real established church in the United States is that of eighteenth-century deism, where God is the umpire behind the competing churches, leaving man to justify himself by the continuity of his good works, which include the separating of church from state and the secularizing of education.

In attempting to characterize such a central driving force, one is bound to oversimplify and ignore powerful counter- forces. The United States is full of people deeply opposed to the attitudes I call characteristic. I see these attitudes, however, as symbols of something which has so far proved flexible enough to contain and absorb those counterforces, greatly modifying itself as it has done so, but becoming stronger in consequence, and hence still in the driver's seat. What I am trying to describe cannot be reduced to a *cliché,* like the "Consciousness One" of *The Greening of America,*[12] or the naive optimism that perished with the 1929 crash, or a simple-minded trust in technology, much less "materialism," or a "worship of the almighty dollar." The traumas of Vietnam and Watergate have another side. The original impulse to go into Vietnam was part of a quite genuine political belief which, as a belief, is still there; and what carried public morale through the sickening revelations of Watergate was a loyalty to the constitutional tradition, which still functions much as the Torah does for Judaism. In the beginning the Americans created America, and America is the beginning of the world. That is, it is the oldest country in the world: no other nation's history goes back so far with less social metamorphosis. Through all the anxieties and doubts of recent years one can still hear the confident tones of its Book of Genesis: "We hold these truths to be self-evident." At least a Canadian can hear them, because nothing has ever been self-evident in Canada.

Canada had no enlightenment, and very little eighteenth century. The British and French spent the eighteenth century in Canada battering down each other's forts, and Canada went directly from the Baroque expansion of the seventeenth century to the Romantic expansion of the nineteenth. The result was the cultural situation that I tried to characterize in my earlier conclusion. Identity in Canada has always had something about it of a centrifugal movement into far distance, of clothes on a growing giant coming apart at the seams, of an elastic about to snap. Stephen Leacock's famous hero who rode off rapidly in all directions was unmistakably a Canadian. This expanding movement has to be counterbalanced by a sense of having constantly to stay together by making tremendous voluntary efforts at intercommunication, whether of building the CPR or of holding federal-provincial conferences.

12*The Greening of America* by C. A. Reich gained the popularity of a cult book in the 1970s.

There is a novel called *Canadian Born*, by Mrs. Humphrey Ward, written about 1908. In the opening pages we meet the heroine, Lady Merton, an Englishwoman whose father is important enough for her to be travelling across Canada in a private railway car. They are held up by a "sink-hole," described as a "place where you can't find no bottom," and which ten train-loads of dumping has failed to fill. Still, Lady Merton is deeply impressed with what she sees of "the march of a new people to its home," especially after she meets an attractive Canadian male, and says to a less enthusiastic Britisher, "Don't you feel that we must get the natives to guide us — to put us in the way? It is only they who can really feel the poetry of it all." She later says: "We see the drama — we feel it — much more than they can who are in it," and quotes Matthew Arnold: "On to the bound of the waste — on to the City of God!"

The author is a keen and intelligent observer, and her view of Canada in 1908 is consistent with many other contemporary views of it. She is also trying hard not to be patronizing. Nevertheless the great march of a new people can be seen better by visitors from higher civilizations, and the natives, poor sods, can only feel (not write) the poetry of it all. They may be headed for the city of God, but it is a very long way to the bound of the waste, and in the meantime there is that sink-hole. She has caught one of the essential Canadian moods, the feeling of apology for being so huge and tedious an obstacle on the way to somewhere more interesting, whether the City of God, the glittering treasures of the Orient, or the opulent United States. It seems to me very characteristic of Canada that its highest Order should have for its motto: "looking for a better country." The quotation is from the New Testament, where the better country really is the City of God, but the feeling it expresses has more mundane contexts.

Such feelings of insecurity and inferiority are still with us: the brain drain has eased considerably, but there is the more serious issue raised in J. J. Brown's *Idea in Exile,*[13] referred to by Mr. Chapman; and we still force pastoral myths on our children designed to reassure their elders, according to Sheila A. Egoff.[14] But transitions to something dif-

[13]J. J. Brown (1916-) described in his important book, *Ideas in Exile: A History of Canadian Invention,* the discrepancy between Canada as a producer of ideas and a place with virtually no native technical industry to use those ideas for invention.

[14]Sheila A. Egoff, Professor, School of Librarianship, University of British Columbia, is the author of *The Republic of Childhood: A Critical Guide To Canadian Children's Literature in English,* 1967. She contributed "Children's Literature" to *Literary History of Canada,* 2nd. edition.

ferent are marked in this book. Some of the articles deal with non-literary subjects, and there, what is important for the present context, is not that many Canadians are distinguished chemists or engineers or whatever, but that all the non-literary subjects have their role to play in creating the imaginative climate that this book is trying to put into isobars. If we look at Mr. Swinton's[15] chapter, for instance, we see that there is no such thing as "Canadian biology": the phrase makes no sense. But the fact that Canada was, a couple of generations ago, regarded as possessed of "unlimited natural resources," and the later pricking of the gaseous balloon, gives biology a distinctive resonance in Canadian cultural life, and helps, for instance, to make Farley Mowat one of our best-known and best-selling authors. Much the same is true of the intense Canadian interest in geology and geophysics, reflected in Mr. Chapman's account of Tuzo Wilson.[16] I have often though that Robert Frost's line, "The land was ours before we were the land's," however appropriate to the United States, does not apply to Canada, where the opposite seems to me to have been true, even in the free land grant days. Canadians were held by the land before they emerged as a people on it, a land with its sinister aspects, or what Warren Tallman, referred to by Mr. Ross,[17] calls the "gray wolf," but with its fostering aspects too, of the kind that come into the phrase of Alice Wilson[18] which one is grateful to Mr. Swinton for quoting: "the earth touches every life."

Many of these themes illustrate the importance in Canada of the theme of survival, the title of Margaret Atwood's very influential book which is, as Mr. Pacey says, a most perceptive essay on an aspect of the Canadian sensibility. Mr. Ross points out some of its limitations: it does not have, and it was clearly not intended to have, the kind of comprehensiveness that a conceptual thesis, like the frontier theory in Ameri-

---

[15]William E. Swinton (1900-1993), Director, Royal Ontario Museum 1963-66, and Professor Emeritus, University of Toronto, is the author of numerous books, including *The Dinosaur,* 1970. He contributed "The Biological Sciences" to *Literary History of Canada,* 2nd edition.

[16]J. Tuzo Wilson (1908-1986), renowned geologist and author of *One Chinese Moon,* 1959 and *Continental Drift,* 1966.

[17]Malcolm Ross (1911-), Professor, Dalhousie University, Halifax, has written extensively on Victorian and Canadian literature. His books include *Milton's Royalism,* 1943, and *Poetry and Dogma,* 1954. Since 1955 he has edited the New Canadian Library. He contributed "Critical Theory: Some Trends" to *Literary History of Canada,* 2nd edition.

[18]Alice Wilson (1881-1964), was Canada's first woman geologist and paleontologist and a distinguished curator of the Royal Ontario Museum.

can history, would need. But it is not simply saying that Canadians are a nation of losers. What the author means by survival comes out more clearly, I think, in her extraordinary novel *Surfacing,* where the heroine is isolated from her small group and finds something very archaic, both inside and outside her, taking over her identity. The word survival implies living through a series of crisis, each one unexpected and different from the others, each one to be met on its own terms. Failure to meet the crisis means that some death principle moves in. From Mr. Goudge[19] we learn that the theme of survival has had some odd extensions in Canadian philosophy: death itself may be simply one more discontinuity in existence.

This discontinuous sense of life is obviously a contrast to the American sense of continuity, and affords more scope for the tragic, as distinct from the ironic, mood in Canadian literature. American fiction is prevailingly ironic for many reasons, but one reason is that irony (as a mode of fiction, not as an attitude) fits the American continuous perspective: it presents life as a horizontal continuum which stops rather than ends, like a car which may or may not go into the ditch but has run out of gas anyway. In tragedy, however dingy the hero may be, there is a fall through time, a polarizing of two levels of existence. They are equally valid forms, but there is a great deal more facile irony than facile tragedy, and the standard ironic formulas, the Slow Strangle, the Ouroboros, or Biting Oneself in the Tail, the Hateful Self-Discovery, are often used rather perfunctorily, as symbols of a serious literary intention. Tragic narratives are more structured, formalized, even contrived, reflecting as they so often do the sense of contrivance in outward circumstances. The affinity with the tragic is part of the affinity with formalism in Canadian writing, and both may be connected with the sense of discontinuity, the feeling for sudden descent or catastrophe, that seems to me to have an unusual emphasis in Canada.

The theme of descent may be as astringent as it is in *Surfacing* or as genial as in Robertson Davies' *Manticore,* where it takes the form of a Jungian analysis followed by images of caves and bears. But in the Zurich clinic, no les than in the Quebec forest, there is still something of the "gray wolf," even of the sink-hole. In the fall of the hero of David Knight's tightly constructed Nigerian story, *Farquharson's Physique,* in the Donnelly massacre at the end of Reaney's trilogy, in

---

[19]Thomas A. Goudge (1910-), Professor of Philosophy, University of Toronto, is the author of numerous books including *The Ascent of Life: Philosophical Study of the Theory of Evolution,* 1961. He was a member of the Editorial Board of *The Encyclopedia of Philosophy,* 1967, and contributed a chapter on philosophical literature to *Literary History of Canada,* 2nd edition.

the writhings of Margaret Laurence's Hagar and Rachel (Mr. New points out the importance of the perspective on time in *The Stone Angel*), we realize that we are still in the country of Grove and Pratt. Some contributors have commented on the tragic tone of George Grant's *Lament for a Nation* and Creighton's *Canada's First Century*[20]: the interest of such books does not end with the issue they deal with, because the tragic is always a major aspect of the human situation. Still, one may hope for a writer of equal power who will see a structure of comedy also in the Canadian story.

If we look at the three eighteenth-century events that defined the future of Canada (as of so much else in the modern world), the Quebec Act, the American Revolution, and the French Revolution, we see the whole range of a political spectrum that still confronts us. The Quebec act came close to an Edmund Burke model: it was an inductive, pragmatic recognition of a *de facto* situation, and the situation was one of those profoundly illogical ones that Burke considered typical of human life generally. The two factors to be taken into account were: (a) the British have conquered the French (b) the British have done nothing of the kind. The only way out of this was a settlement that guaranteed some rights to both parties. The French Revolution, proceeding deductively from general principles, was what Burke condemned so bitterly as "metaphysical," and was also the forerunner of the dialectical Marxist revolutions. The American Revolution came in the middle, a strong contrast to the Canadian settlement, as we have seen, but keeping far more of the broadening-through-precedent British tradition than the French one did.

Hence although the United States itself got started on a revolutionary basis, it was a basis of a kind that made it difficult for that country to come to terms with the later Marxist revolutions. This produced a growing isolation from other revolutionary ideologies and societies, the climax of which was the maintaining, for so many years, of the grotesque fantasy that the refugee army in Formosa was the government of China. At the same time, the "melting pot" assumption of the nineteenth-century United States, the ambition described in the inscription on the Statue of Liberty of making a united democracy out of the most varied social and racial elements, became profoundly modified. The conception of the "hundred per cent American" has been suc-

---

[20]Donald Creighton (1902-79) was a leading Canadian historian and proponent of the Laurentian theory. His major works are: *The Commercial Empire of the St. Lawrence*, 1937; *Dominion of the North*, 1944; *The Road to Confederation: The Emergence of Canada*, 1863-1867, 1964; and *Towards the Discovery of Canada*, 1972.

ceeded by a growing feeling that the various elements in American society can perhaps contribute more to it by retaining something of their original cultural characteristics. Here there is a growing similarity to the Canadian pattern, where the necessity of recognizing two major social elements at the beginning meant that nobody could ever possibly know what a "hundred per cent Canadian" was, and hence led to a much more relaxed ideal of a national "melting pot."

When the last edition of this book was published, the centenary of Canadian Confederation was coming up: the bicentenary of the American Revolution is the corresponding event on the horizon, if an anniversary is an event. It seems to me that a very curious and significant exchange of identities between Canada and the United States has taken place since then. The latter, traditionally so buoyant, extroverted, and forward-looking, appears to be entering a prolonged period of self-examination. I am setting down very subjective impressions here, derived mainly from what little I know of American literature and literary criticism, but I feel that a search for a more genuinely historical dimension of consciousness has been emerging at least since Vietnam turned into a nightmare, and is still continuing. Part of it is a different attitude to the past, a re-examining of it to see what things went wrong when. This is not simply a reversing of the current of continuity, like a psychiatric patient exploring his childhood: there seems to be a growing tendency to think more in terms of inevitable discontinuities. Erik Erikson's[21] book on identity, an attempt to clarify the psychology of the disturbances of a few years ago, is an example.

Another part of the re-examination, and imaginatively perhaps the more significant part, revolves around the question: has the American empire, like the British empire before it, simply passed its climacteric and is it now declining, or at least becoming aware of limits? If so, the past takes on a rise-and-fall parabola shape, not a horizontal line in which the past is on the same plane as the present. This may not sound like much on paper, but changes in central metaphors and conceptual diagrams are symbolic of the most profound disturbances that the human consciousness has to face. After the strident noise and confusion of the later sixties, there was, for all the discussion, an eerie quietness about the response to Watergate, and to the irony of a President's turning into a cleaned-out gambler a few months after getting an over-

[21]Erik Erikson (1902-1944), American psychiatrist noted for introducing the concept of the "identity crisis." His first book, *Childhood and Society,* 1950, is still considered a classic in the field.

whelming mandate. Even the violence of the now almost unmanageable cities seems to have caused less panic than one might reasonably have expected. Perhaps it is not too presumptuous to say, although few non-Canadian readers would understand what was meant, that the American way of life is slowly becoming Canadianized.

Meanwhile, Canada, traditionally so diffident, introverted, past-and-future fixated, incoherent, inarticulate, proceeding by hunch and feeling, seems to be taking on, at least culturally, an inner composure and integration of outlook, even some buoyancy and confidence. The most obvious reasons for this are technological. The airplane and the television set, in particular, have brought a physical simultaneity into the country that has greatly modified the older, and perhaps still underlying, blazed-trail and canoe mentality. As Mr. Cross says, we are now in a post-Laurentian phase of development. In the railway days, being a federal MP from British Columbia or a literary scholar in Alberta required an intense, almost romantic, commitment, because of the investment of time and energy involved in getting from such places to the distant centres that complemented them. Today such things are jobs like other jobs, and the relation to the primary community has assumed a correspondingly greater importance. This is the positive and creative side of the relaxing of centralizing tension in modern society, of which separatism represents a less creative one.

The influence of television is often blamed for violence, and certainly there are television programs that are profoundly distasteful from this point of view. But there is another side to television: bringing the remote into our living room can be a very sobering form of communication, and a genuinely humanizing one. I remember the thirties, when so many "intellectuals" were trying to rationalize or ignore the Stalin massacres or whatever such horrors did not fit their categories, and thinking even then that part of their infantilism was in being men of print: they saw only lines of type on a page, not lines of prisoners shuffling off to death camps. But something of the real evil of the Vietnam war did get on television, and the effect seems to have been on the whole a healthy one. At least the American public came to hate the war, instead of becoming complacent or inured to its atrocities.

Similarly in Canada: Eskimos, blacks, Indians, perhaps even Wasps, cannot go on being comic-strip stereotypes after they have been fully exposed on television. Of course better knowledge can also create dislike and more tension; and when I speak of an exchange of identities I certainly do not mean that Canada will acquire anything of the simplistic optimism of an earlier age in the United States. Television is one of many factors which will make that impossible. Another is the curtailing of resources, already mentioned. Still another is the emergence of chilling technical possibilities in genetics, which raise questions about identity that makes our traditional ones look like learning to spell cat. Another is the geography of the global village. In the nineteenth century the Canadian imagination responded to the Biblical phrase "from the river unto the ends of the earth," and one of the historians referred to by Mr. Cross, W. L. Morton,[22] has written with great sensitivity about the impact, psychological and otherwise, of the northern frontier on the Canadian consciousness. But now Canada has become a kind of global Switzerland, surrounded by the United States on the south, the European common market on the east, the Soviet Union on the north, China and Japan on the west.

In some essays in this book a distinctive Canadian bias shows through that may be culturally significant. The fact that Descartes is a French philosopher is not simply a biographical fact: Descartes is French in the sense that he is a permanent and central part of a tradition that makes France different in its cultural pattern from other countries. Similarly with Locke as a British philosopher, or Kant as a German one, or William James as an American one. Canada seems to have no philosopher of this defining kind: what Canadian philosophy does have is a strong emphasis on religion, so remarkable as to be worth pausing on for a moment.

Mr. Goudge, writing of philosophy, is compelled to deal with religion even though there is a separate chapter on religion; the only cult-philosopher in the country, Bernard Lonergan,[23] referred to by Mr. Grant,[24] is a religious philosopher; much is said in this book and elsewhere about the religious drive in George Grant, in McLuhan, in myself. In Creighton the drive may not be technically religious, but it is certainly prophetic. Here again French Canada established a pattern which English Canada to some degree imitated, of keeping church and state closer together, particularly in education, than was done in the

---

[22]William L. Morton (1908-80), was a follower and expounder of Creighton's Laurentian theory. His books include *The Progressive Party of Canada*, 1950, and *Canadian Identity*, 1961.

[23]Bernard J. F. Lonergan (1904-84), a Roman Catholic theologian of international reputation. He published *Insight*, 1957, *Collection*, 1967 and *Method in Theology*, 1972. A centre for the study of his work has been established at Regis College, Toronto.

[24]Rev. John Webster Grant (1919-), Professor of Church History, Emmanuel College, Victoria University, University of Toronto. His works include *The Canadian Experience of Church Union*, 1967, *The Church in the Canadian Era*, 1972, and *Die Unierte Kirchen*, 1973. He contributed a chapter on religious and theological writing to *Literary History of Canada*, 2nd edition.

United States. Mr. Grant's urbane treatment of ecumenical movements in Canada makes it clear that while religion is ideally a uniting force in society, it is more likely in practice to be a divisive one. Religion in Canada has closely followed the centrifugal and expanding rhythms of Canadian life, spearheaded by missionaries, from the seventeenth-century Jesuits to our own time — even Norman Bethune was a missionary in a sense. As it did so an intensely competitive spirit developed, as we can see if we walk through any Canadian town. The centrifugal movement came to a halt when the population started rolling back into the growing cities, and the urbanizing of Canadian mores greatly weakened the social influence of the Canadian churches, which long remained fixated on the earlier social values. The temperance movement, for example, as we find it in, say, Nellie McClung,[25] was often associated with a very genuine political liberalism, even radicalism, in nineteenth-century Canada, but the growth of cities turned it into a horse-and-buggy phenomenon that could rouse no response except ridicule.

There is nothing here sociologically different from what happened in the United States, but the comparative absence of what I have called American deism may have made the impact of religion on the Canadian consciousness more direct. I remember a *Spring Thaw* skit of some years ago, where a Roman Catholic, an Anglican, and a United Church leader sang a song about charity and brotherly love, then each in turn, after glancing darkly at his confreres, stepped forward and informed the audience that of course *he* was God's accredited spokesman. The audience found the skit very funny, but I recall someone remarking that possibly only a Canadian audience would have done so.

I had long realized that the religious context of so many Canadian intellectuals had something to do with the peripheral situation of Canada, in the way that, for instance, Denmark was an appropriate place for a Kierkegaard in nineteenth-century Europe. Kierkegaard's hostility to what he called "Christendom" had a lot to do with the impact of the mores of bigger countries on his own. When I read Mr. Woodcock on the role of the Canadian poet as a counter-culture hero, something else rang a bell, and enabled me to make a connection with literature.

Canada has always been a cool climate for heroes: Mr. Bissell speaks of the grudging support given to our last three prime ministers, all of whom, whatever one thinks of their policies, have compared

---

[25]Nellie McClung (1873-1951) wrote exclusively about the harsh life of the Prairie homesteaders. She is considered a forerunner of Prairie Realism. Her best-known novels are *Sowing Seeds at Danny*, 1908, and *The Second Chance*, 1910.

very favourably, in intelligence and personal integrity, with some of those who adorned the White House in the same period; and Mrs. Thomas's[26] survey of Canadian biography reveals very little response in Canada to any Carlylean great-man conception of history. It would be interesting, and very typical of Canada, if Canadian literature had found its soul, so to speak, by defining the poet as a counter-hero or anti-hero. Of course this counter-cultural aspect of poetry is true of the United States also; but it seems to me that Canada has been steadily building up something like a North American counter-culture against United States which is now big and complex enough to be examined on its own terms. Once more, "against" simply means differentiation.

It may be the end of the century before any real coherence will emerge from our cultural pattern: so far we are confined to what Eliot would call hints followed by guesses. But some things in the Canadian tradition are beginning to look very international. It seems to me that in the democracies generally today, the dialectical habit of mind is giving way to a tendency to think in containing terms, where the antithesis is included and absorbed instead of being defined by exclusion. This is really a conservative tendency in thought, although not directly connected with political conservatism: Mr. Bissell quotes an example of it from Abraham Rotstein,[27] who is very far from being a right-winger. At the same time, as we can see if we look carefully at what Mr. Cross has to say about W. L. Morton, W. J. Eccles,[28] and Carl Berger[29] in particular, the tendency is conservative, in the sense of revolving around

---

[26]Clara Thomas (1919-), Professor of English, York University, Toronto. She is the author of several books on Canadian biography and criticism, including *Canadian Novelists, 1920-1945*, 1946, *Margaret Laurence*, 1969, *Our Nature: Our Voices*, Vol. I, 1973 and *The Manawaka World of Margaret Laurence*, 1975.

[27]Abraham Rotstein (1929-), Professor of Economics, University of Toronto, is a leading theoretician of left-wing nationalism. Author of *The Precarious Homestead: Essays in Economics, Technology and Nationalism*, 1973, and *Rebuilding from Within: Remedies for Canadian Ailing Economy*, 1984, he has also edited and co-edited numerous books on the subject of Canadian nationalism.

[28]William John Eccles (1917-), Professor of History, University of Toronto, is considered one of the first-rank historiographers of New France in Canada. He is best known for his revisionist biography of Frontenac, *Frontenac: The Courtier Governor*, 1959, for *Canada under Louis XIV, 1663-1701*, 1964, and for *The Canadian Frontier, 1534-1760*, 1969.

[29]Carl Berger (1939-), Professor of History, University of Toronto. Author of *The Sense of Power: Studies in the Ideas of Canadian Imperialism 1867-1914*, 1970 and *The Writing of Canadian History*, 1976.

the question of what it is necessary or important to conserve. As such, it is a tendency that fulfills the tradition of Burke in Canada, in which opposition forms a larger synthesis instead of an apocalyptic separation of sheep and goats. The anti-Marxist attitude of mind suggested here, if I am right about it, is one of crucial importance for literature, in Canada and elsewhere. Marxism is a very remarkable intellectual achievement as well as the dominant moral force in the contemporary world, but, at least wherever it has come to power, it cannot really cope with the humanities or with the place of the arts in modern society.

When I read through the more purely literary chapters of this book, and check them against my own meagre first-hand knowledge, I am struck by a feature of Canadian writing that seems to me a literary parallel to the conservative tendency just spoken of. It might be called formalism or even classicism: I should prefer, however, to call it simply professionalism. Modern society has decreed that very few writers shall live by paper alone, and the great majority of our writers are part-time writers, but that is not what I mean. I mean writing from within literature and within its genres, as opposed to the "I've got something important to say" approach of the amateur, who then looks around for a fictional or poetic vehicle to put his important say into. The professional attitude has affinities, if we like, with the principle that the medium is the message. I should say rather that in fully realized writing there is no difference between structure and content, what is called content being the structure of the individual work, as distinct from the structure of the convention or genre to which it belongs.

Professionalism means technique and craftsmanship, which amateur writers often think of as weakening of the moral fiber. Canadian criticism has been plagued a good deal by the foolish notion that the imagination is a by-product of extremes, specifically emotional extremes. We can't have a great literature in Canada because we are too safe, sane, dull, humdrum — not enough lynchings, one critic suggested. The professional writer discovers from his experience that the imagination is the constructive element in the mind, and that intensity cannot be conveyed except through structure, which includes design, balance, and proportion. Of all genres, this is perhaps most obvious in the drama, where the show has to go over or else, and Mr. Ripley[30] has some trenchant observations about the importance of a professional attitude in the theatre.

---

[30]John Ripley (1940-) is Associate Professor of English, McGill University, Montreal. He contributed a chapter on drama and theater to *Literary History of Canada*, 2nd edition.

Once technique reaches a certain degree of skill, it turns into something that we may darkly suspect to be fun: fun for the writer to display it, fun for the reader to watch it. In the old days we were conditioned to believe that only lowbrows read for fun, and that highbrows read serious literature to improve their minds. The coming of radio did a good deal to help this morbid situation, and television has done something (not enough) more. We now live in a time when Leonard Cohen can start out with an erudite book of poems called *Let Us Compare Mythologies*, the chief mythologies being the Biblical and the Classical, and evolve from there, quite naturally, into a well-known folk singer. Mr. Woodcock points out the immense importance of the revival of the oral tradition, the public speaking of poetry to audiences, often with a background of music, in making the serious poet a genuinely popular figure.

To be popular means having the power to amuse, in a genuine sense, and the power to amuse is, again, dependent on skills and craftsmanship. Woodcock speaks of an element in Earle Birney's poetry that might almost be called stunting, an interest in every variety of technical experiment, as though experiment were an end in itself. This is not a matter of panting to keep up with all the avant-garde movements: Birney is a genuinely contemporary poet, and his versatility expresses a central contemporary interest. Mr. Lane[31] refers to the zany quality in Marshall McCluhan's style that has infuriated some people into calling him a humbug and a charlatan. James Reaney writes plays, sometimes tragic ones, full of the let's-pretend devices of children's games, devices which, if they were described out of their context, might sound like Peter Quince and his wall in *A Midsummer Night's Dream*. The verbal wit that comes through in, say, Leonard Cohen's *Beautiful Losers*, in some of Needham's[32] essays (see Mr. Conron's article), in the concrete poets, is a sign of the presence of seriousness and not the absence of it, the serious being the opposite of the solemn. We are a long way from the days when a bewildered Joyce, confronted with responses to *Finnegan'sWake* which invariably treated it with either awe or ridicule, said: "But why couldn't they see that the book was funny?"

---

[31]Lauriat Lane, JR. (1925-), Professor Emeritus, University of New Brunswick, Fredericton. Editor of *English Studies in Canada*, 1975-, and *Approaches to Walden*, 1961. He contributed a chapter on literary criticism and scholarship to *Literary History of Canada*, 2nd edition.

[32]Richard Needham (1912-96), author and columnist for the *Globe and Mail*, had published *Needham's Inferno*, 1966, *The Garden Needham*, 1968, *Friend in Needham*, 1969 and *Hypodermic Needham*, 1970.

About twenty years ago I started trying to explain that the poet *qua* poet had no notion of life or reality or experience until he had read enough poetry to understand from it how poetry dealt with such things. I was told, in all quarters from Canadian journals (see Mr. Ross's article) to university classrooms, that I was reducing literature to a verbal game. I would not accept the word "reducing," but otherwise the statement was correct enough. Now that the work ethic has settled into a better perspective, the play ethic is also coming into focus, and we can perhaps understand a bit more clearly than we could a century ago why *Othello* and *Macbeth* are called plays. Play is that for the sake of which work is done, the climactic Sabbath vision of mankind.

A book concerned entirely with play in this sense passes over most of what occupies the emotional foreground of our lives at present: inflation, unemployment, violence and crime, and much else. The historian of Elizabethan literature, praising the exuberance and power of that literature, would not necessarily be unaware of the misery, injustice, and savagery that pervaded English life at the time. What seems to come to matter more, eventually, is what man can create in the face of the chaos he also creates. This book is about what has been created, in words and in Canada, during the present age, and the whole body of that creation will be the main reason for whatever interest posterity may take in us.

"Conclusion" in: *Literary History of Canada: Canadian Literature in English,* 2nd ed., in 3 vols. Edited by Carl Klinck and others. Toronto: University of Toronto Press, 1976.

Haunted by Lack of Ghosts

Some Patterns in the Imagery of Canadian Poetry

Very few historical and cultural statements can be made about Canada that do not have obvious counterparts in the United States. At the same time, social developments in a country which has amassed a huge population and has become a great imperial power may have a quite different imaginative resonance in a country with a sparse population and a minor world influence. For example, railways were built across the United States to the Pacific, and the romance of railway-building, along with the accompanying scandals and exploitations, have been factors of unquestionable importance in American culture. But in Canada the building of a single railway line was a matter of life and death to the infant nation, and the completion of it, against almost insuperable obstacles, was not one of many incidents of expansion but a central devouring obsession. Similarly, in the nineteenth century, an American boasting of the great size of America was helping to increase his own feeling of identity with it, whereas in Canada the background of immense rivers, lakes, and islands that very few Canadians had ever seen tended rather to weaken the sense of an identity that was already precarious.

In the United States, expansion into the West brought with it almost everywhere a sense of new opportunities for life in a new land. But while the Canadian expansion into the north looks vast enough on a map, the inference that there is unlimited room for people in Canada is an illusion. As the Canadian historian, W. L. Morton, says in *The Canadian Identity*, "The great staple trades have been extensive, ingathering trades... most of Canada is simply a hinterland extensively exploited from the soil base of the St. Lawrence and Saskatchewan valleys, and from the delta of the Fraser." Increased immigration, in Canada no less than in Australia, means primarily an increase in the population of two or three cities which are already too big. The fact that the country grew up from two peoples speaking different languages meant that nobody could ever know what a "hundred per cent Canadian" was, and hence the population became less homogeneous. An ethnic minority in any case is more conspicuous in a smaller population.

And while we hear a good deal about separatism in Quebec, every part of Canada has strong separatist feelings: the Atlantic Provinces and western Canada also tend to feel that they are, *vis-à-vis* central Canada, in the same mercantile bind that the United States was in before 1776, and that they are forced to export at a lower price, and import at a higher price, than they would do if they had more autonomy.

Canada was first settled, like the United States, in the seventeenth century, but, in striking contrast to the United States, there was nothing culturally distinctive about Canada's eighteenth century, and the country went directly from seventeenth-century Baroque expansiveness to nineteenth-century Romantic expansiveness. There are some curious reversals of American historical movements in Canadian history. The Americans had first a revolutionary war against a European power, followed by a civil war within the country itself. Canada had a civil war first, which was a struggle of European powers on its soil, followed by a war of independence against the United States — at least, so far as the War of 1812 had any meaning at all for Canada, that was its meaning. A generation or two ago, girls in Quebec convent schools were taught that the British conquest was the will of God, saving them from the atheistic horrors of the French Revolution. It might have been added, with some justification, that the British conquest also preserved the French language and culture itself in Canada. The French lost the country primarily because they had very little interest in keeping it, and if they had held it they would doubtless have sold it, as they did Louisiana.

In any case Canada was founded on the Quebec Act of 1774, which recognized the *de facto* situation that while the British were technically the conquerors, the country could not survive as a British possession unless a settlement was made which guaranteed rights to the French. The Quebec Act was a conservative measure, conforming to Edmund Burke's principle of a synthesis containing opposed principles, in contrast to the revolutionary, and therefore more dialectical, attitude established by the victorious Whigs in the United States. Its revolutionary basis, along with the written constitution which was an integral part of that basis, makes for a deductive and continuous pattern in American life, as the constitution is reinterpreted or, in the last resort, amended. In Canada a discontinuous, *ad hoc*, illogical series of bargains and compromises succeeded the Quebec Act. Margaret Atwood's book on the spirit of Canadian literature, *Survival*, has become very influential partly through its inspired choice of a title: the word "survival" in itself implies a discontinuous series of crisis, each to be met on its own terms, each having to face the imminent threat of not surviving.

For all its centrifugal expansion, the American consciousness revolves around one or two centripetal symbols of the nation as a whole, notably the President and the flag. In Canada the parliamentary system of election places much less emphasis on the party leader as a personality, and it is even more significant that Canada had no official flag of its own until the middle of the twentieth century. Francis Sparshott, in a poem called "Episode in Frederick, Md.," muses obliquely about this:

"Spare, if you must, this old grey head,
But shoot your country's flag!" she said.
"You got it wrong, you stupid bag.
You mean, —`Don't shoot your country's flag.'"
"Yes, yes, young man, that's what I said:
Shoot if you must this old grey head."
"Pardon me, lady, that is not
What you first said you wanted shot."
Then down the street the General came,
His sword unsheathed, his eyes aflame.
"Sergeant! Don't contradict the lady.
Holes in the head she's got already;
Six more won't make no never mind.
Present!... Aim!... FIRE:"
Still down the wind
Streams the bright symbol of her honour,
But Mrs. Fritchie is a goner.
So now the Yanks have both a flag
And a distinctive national hag.

The author tells me that he was not aware, in writing the last line, that Canada also has had, in a sense, a distinctive national hag. No genuine portrait of English Canada's best-known heroine, Laura Secord, exists, and the deficiency is made up for by a grisly reproduction of a male elder statesman, with the beard removed and a shawl put over the head, purporting to represent her in old age. I mention this because it illustrates so clearly the perennial Canadian problems of publicizing the heroes of a country which has manifested a great deal of remarkable courage but has never responded with much warmth to charismatic leadership. Canadian heroes include such ambiguous figures as William Lyon Mackenzie, leader of the 1837 rebellion against the "Family Compact" (the Tory establishment in nineteenth-century Ontario), whose role became very unheroic when the shooting started, but who nonetheless still stands for the nonconformist conscience of Canada, an unwillingness to knuckle under to any kind of foreign or domestic domination. Thus Dennis Lee, in a poem called "1838":

The British want the country
For the Empire and the view.
The Yankees want the country for
A yankee barbecue.
The Compact want the country
For their merrie green domain.
They'll all play finders-keepers till
Mackenzie, come again.

Mackenzie was a crazy man,
He wore his wig askew,
He donned three bulky overcoats
In case the bullets flew.
Mackenzie talked of fighting
While the fight went down the drain.
But who will speak for Canada?
Mackenzie, come again.

Seventeenth-century Europe brought three cultural imports into the New World of North America. One was the revolutionary monotheism of Christianity, with its horror of "idolatry," that is, the sense of the numinous in nature. For Christianity, the gods that had been discovered in nature were all devils: man could raise his consciousness toward the divine only through human institutions. It followed that a natural religion like that of the Indians simply had to be extirpated if the Indians were to realize their human potential. The second was the Baroque sense of the power of mathematics, the results of which can still be seen in the grid patterns of our cities, in the concession lines in the rural areas, and in the great burden of geometry that North American life in particular carries. The third was the Cartesian egocentric consciousness, the feeling that man's essential humanity was in his power of reasoning, and that the nature outside human consciousness was pure extension: a turning away from nature so complete that it became a kind of idolatry in reverse.

A friend of mine watching two Western farmers driving fence stakes and hearing one say to the other, "Put'er in coupla inches west," remarked that a consciousness as closely geared to the points of the compass as that was obviously in intimate touch with the land. I was inclined to disagree, feeling that it was a consciousness of nature as a territory but not as a home. It goes with the feeling that improved human communications means a straighter and therefore less interesting path through nature, until with the airplane the sense of travelling through nature itself disappears. I said in an earlier article on Canadian literature that the Canadian problem of identity seemed to me primarily connected with locale, less a matter of "Who am I?" than of "Where is here?" Another friend, commenting on this, told me a story about a doctor from the south (that is, from one of the Canadian cities) travelling on the Arctic tundra with an Eskimo guide. A blizzard blew up, and they had to bivouac for the night. What with the cold, the storm, and the loneliness, the doctor panicked and began shouting "We are lost!" The Eskimo looked at him thoughtfully and said, "We are not lost. We are here." A vast gulf between an indigenous and an immigrant mentality opened at that point; the possibility of eventually closing this gulf is the main theme of what follows.

Yeats speaks in one of his prose works of the Port Royal logicians,[1] followers of Descartes, who cut up animals alive because everything outside man was a machine to them and they simply could not believe that anything without human consciousness could feel pain. The attitude of the Canadian fur trade, spreading traps over the north to catch animals, was not very different: for it, the mink, the beaver, and the silver fox were not living creatures but only potential fur coats. A growing sense of guilt about this attitude gives a peculiarly haunting resonance to the theme of the death of an animal in Canadian literature. (See, for example, Al Purdy's "The Death of Animals" in *Poems for All the Annettes* [1962], a poem too long to quote and too intricate to quote from.) Similarly, the destruction of the native culture, more particularly of its religion, leaves us with the feeling well described by the philosopher George Grant in *Technology and Empire* (1969):

> That conquering relation to place has left its mark within us. When we go into the Rockies we may have the sense that gods are there. But if so, they cannot manifest themselves to us as ours. They are the gods of another race, and we cannot know them because of what we are, and what we did. There can be nothing immemorial for us except the environment as object.

Much the same thing is said in poetry by Douglas LaPan, in a poem significantly called "A Country without a Mythology":

---

[1] Port Royal Logicians included such prominent thinkers as Antoine Arnauld (1612-1694) and Pierre Nicole (1625-1695) whose book *The Port-Royal Logic (Logique on l'art de penser)*, 1662, was extremely influential to the development of the eighteenth-century Cartesian scholarship.

> No monuments or landmarks guide the stranger
> Going among this savage people...
>
> And not a sign, no emblem in the sky
> Or boughs to friend him as he goes; for who
> Will stop where, clumsily contrived, daubed
> With war-paint, teeters some lust-red manitou?

A parenthetical remark in Leonard Cohen's novel *Beautiful Losers* links a similar feeling of guilt to the colonial mentality of Canadians:

> Some part of the Canadian Catholic mind is not certain of the Church's victory over the Medicine Man. No wonder the forests of Quebec are mutilated and sold to America.

From my study of Canadian literature, in particular, I have found much evidence for the critical principle of the fallacy of imaginative projection, that is, the notion that a poet can confront some impressive object like Niagara Falls or Lake Louise and become "inspired" by it. An egocentric consciousness, Pascal's thinking reed, in the centre of a country as huge and unresponsive as Canada finds the environment less impressive than oppressive. It is not only that nature is so big and the winters so cold, but also that there is a lurking feeling that if anything did speak to the poet from nature it would speak only to condemn. That is why I have adopted for my title the last line of Earle Birney's poem "Can. Lit.": "It's only by our lack of ghosts we're haunted." There are gods here, and we have offended them. They are not ghosts: we are the ghosts, Cartesian ghosts caught in the machine that we have assumed nature to be. Hence the characteristic Canadian feeling noted by the scholar and critic Robert McDougall:

> In our literature, heroic action remains possible, but becomes so deeply tinged with futility that withdrawal becomes a more characteristic response than commitment. The representative images are those of denial and defeat rather than fulfillment and victory.

One obvious corollary of this feeling is the sense that "civilized" man, with his economy of waste, his relentless plundering of a nature which he thinks is there only to be exploited by him, his infinite capacity to litter his surroundings with every conceivable variety of excrement is the essential principle of pollution in nature, a monstrous deformation or cancer that nature itself has produced by mistake. Thus Margaret Atwood, in a poem called "Backdrop Addresses Cowboy," where the cowboy is perhaps less a cowboy than a symbol of the more fatuous forms of mass culture:

> I am also what surrounds you:
> my brain
> scattered with your
> tincans, bones, empty shells
> the litter of your invasions.

James Reaney, studying "Winnipeg Seen as a Body of Time and Space," makes an explicit contrast with the native relation to nature:

> Winnipeg, what once were you? You were,
> Your hair was grass by the river ten feet tall,
> Your arms were burr oaks and ash leaf maples,
> Your backbone was a crooked silver muddy river,
> Your thoughts were ravens in flocks, your bones were snow,
> Your legs were trails and your blood was a people
> Who did what the stars did and the sun...
>
> Then on top of you fell
> A Boneyard wrecked auto gent, his hair
> Made of rusted car door handles, his fingernails
> Of red Snowflake Pastry signs, his belly
> Of buildings downtown; his arms of sewers,
> His nerves electric wires, his mouth a telephone,
> His backbone — a cracked cement street. His heart
> An orange pendulum bus crawling with the human fleas.
> Of a so-so civilization — half gadget, half flesh
> I don't know what I would have instead
> And they did what they did more or less.

The phenomenon described is hardly peculiar to Canada, but again it has a distinctive resonance in a country where there is so much nature that ought to be unspoiled. The theme celebrated in science fiction, of nature's eventual revenge, seems to be less frequent in Canadian poetry, although E. J. Pratt, in a late poem called "The Good Earth," notices in passing that the death wish in man himself is partly a form of that revenge:

> Hold that synthetic seed, for underneath
> Deep down she'll answer to your horticulture:
> She has a way of germinating teeth
> And yielding crops of carrion for the vulture.

A curious schizophrenia can be seen in a good deal of nineteenth-century Canadian poetry, the sense of loneliness and alienation urgently demanding expression along with a good deal of prefabricated rhetoric about the challenge of a new land and the energetic optimism demanded to meet it. The latter mood often attempts to suppress or, failing that, to outshout the former one, but with little consistent success. Again, Margaret Atwood, who has inherited Pratt's instinct for what is imaginatively central in Canadian sensibility, studies this split consciousness in her *Journals of Susanna Moodie*. This book of poems follows the life of the redoubtable Susanna Strickland, who after her marriage came out to Ontario in the eighteen-thirties and wrote *Roughing It in the Bush*. Toward the end of the sequence, in a poem called: "Thoughts from Underground," the poet describes the conflict in her heroine's mind between her very real hatred for the country that had caused her so much suffering and the rhetoric that she thought she ought to be producing about its material progress and cultural enlightenment:

> Then we were made successful
> and I felt I ought to love
> this country.
> I said I loved it
> and my mind saw double.
>
> I began to forget myself
> in the middle
> of sentences. Events
> were split apart.

A similar rhetorical epilepsy may be observed in some of the semiofficial poets of the confederation period and later, notably Charles G. D. Roberts and Bliss Carman. Roberts begins a poem called "Canada" thus:

> O Child of Nations, giant-limbed,
>   Who stand'st among the nations now
> Unheeded, unadorned, unhymned,
>   With unanointed brow, —

This apostrophe is also an invocation, not a genuine invocation, such as Homer would make to a Muse or some shaping spirit of poetry asking it to take over the poem, but one addressed to Roberts himself and intended to help him work himself into the proper emotional state for a sublime ode. The rest of the poem illustrates the principle that evocations addressed to oneself are seldom answered. Here is Bliss Carman, at the close of a poem which has become perhaps less celebrated than notorious in Canadian literature:

> Only make me over, April,
> When the sap begins to stir!
> Make me man or make me woman,
> Make me oaf or ape or human,
> Cup of flower or cone of fir;
> Make me anything but neuter
> When the sap begins to stir!

The critic E. K. Brown remarks on this passage that the tone is "jaunty" and that the jaunty cannot also be poetic. I think myself that Carman has fallen foul of another well-known literary principle, the positive force of the negative statement. One who says "the day was not hot and stifling" has said something much hotter than he means; and when Carman prays to be made "anything but neuter" he is sowing a doubt in his reader's mind whether, when the sap rises in spring, the poet will be able to rise with it. Both poets, especially Carman, wrote a good deal of verse dedicated to the power of positive thinking, but the tone is almost invariably forced, and invites Emily Dickinson's dry comment on Joaquin Miller, "Transport is not urged." Yet both Roberts and Carman could be haunting and eloquent poets as long as their tone was nostalgic, elegiac, or plangent: Carman's "Low Tide on Grand Pré" is a fine example. So the question naturally comes to mind: why were these poets so much better at whimpering than at banging?

The answer has already been implied: the nostalgic and elegiac are the inevitable emotional responses of an egocentric consciousness locked into a demythologized environment. Wherever reason is regarded as the distinctively human element in consciousness, the impulse to write poetry remains rhetorical (in the sense of oratorical), preoccupied with versifying prose statements and talking about emotional attitudes instead of presenting them. Eventually it becomes clear that the focus of such a response, in such conditions, is the moment of death. Death is the one point at which man and nature really become identified; it is also, in a sense, the only event in which the genuinely heroic aspect of human life emerges. A life in which energy is expended in subduing a tiny fraction of space has little room for the heroic, until death rounds off the total effort and gives it another dimension. Without death, the struggle would seem only unending and hopeless. John McCrae, the author of "In Flanders Fields," was a poet much possessed by death, and he has a poem called "The Unconquered Dead" in which one chilling phrase identifies the heroic with the ability to die:

> We might have yielded, even we, but death
> Came for our helper.

In such a setting the Indian appears as a noble savage in the sense that his life is so largely one of stoically enduring both the suffering imposed by nature and those he inflicts on himself and others. In Duncan Campbell Scott's "The Forsaken," an Indian woman, trying to get food for her baby in winter, baits a fishhook with her own flesh. Later, as an old woman whom the tribe can no longer afford to feed, she is abandoned and left to lie down in the snow to die. Similarly, in Pratt's *Brébeuf and His Brethren*, the martyrdom of the Jesuit missionaries is nothing that they are seeking for itself, but it is the one real triumph of their service of Christ.

While some nineteenth- and the early twentieth-century Canadian poets were rhetoricians, others understood better that the central poetic impulse is imaginative and not rhetorical, and that its most direct product is mythology, which is essentially the humanizing of nature. Charles Mair, author of *Tecumseh*, produced in 1901 a rather maundering poem called "Summer," of this general texture:

> Or, if Fancy still would trace
> Forms ideal, forms of grace,
> Still would haunt, in dreamy trance,
> Kindred regions of Romance,
> Let her now recall the sweet
> Image of lorn Marguerite.

What is interesting about this poem is that it is a completely rewritten version of a poem written in 1868, which was both explicitly mythological and very much livelier:

> And let nymph-attended Pan
> Come in habit of a man,
> Singing songs of reeds and rushes,
> Elder brakes and hazel bushes.
> See him swing and jig about,
> Whilst the merry, rabble rout
> Chases round with joined hands,
> Twitching slily, when he stands,
> At his back, his garments tearing,
> All his swart, brute-buttocks baring.

Mair eventually came to realize that his 1868 muse was the authentic one, and her genteel 1901 sister a phony. In Isabella Crawford's extraordinary narrative poem *Malcolm's Katie* (1884), there is an explicitly mythical section beginning "The South Wind laid his moccasins aside," which contains the following passage:

> In this shrill moon the scouts of winter ran
> From the ice-belted north, and whistling shafts
> Struck maple and struck sumach — and a blaze
> Ran swift from leaf to leaf, from bough to bough;
> Till round the forest flash'd a belt of flame
> In this shrill moon the scouts of winter ran
> And inward lick'd its tongues of red and gold
> To the deep, tranced, inmost heart of all.
> Rous'd the still heart — but all too late, too late.
> Too late, the branches welded fast with leaves,
> Toss'd loosen'd to the winds — too late the sun
> Pour'd his last vigor to the deep, dark cells
> Of the dim wood. The keen two-bladed Moon
> Of Falling Leaves roll'd up on crested mists
> And where the lush, rank boughs had foil'd the sun
> In his red prime, her pale, sharp fingers crept
> After the wind and felt about the moss,
> And seem'd to pluck from shrinking twig and stem
> The burning leaves — while groan'd the shudd'ring wood.

There are several things to notice here. In the first place, the progression of seasons, with its great cycle of colour that emerges in spring, bursts into flame in the fall, and dies out in the winter, is seen as a kind of battle of Titans. Nature here is not a Cartesian extension in space, but a field of conflicting energies which are seemingly just about to take on the forms of mythological beings. Second, for all the riot of colour, the "inmost heart of all" does not quite come to life: something makes that "too late," and we are pulled around to death and winter again. The process is almost an allegory of the Canadian poetic imagination, making a tremendous effort to rouse itself and create a reborn mythology out of the abandoned Indian one, an effort still premature and collapsing before its fulfillment, but indicating that something new is on the way. The direct vision of nature in this passage is equally remarkable. Isabella Crawford has done in words much what the painter Tom Thomson was later to do in his art: evoking a dissonance of colour that seems like an autonomous force of life itself bursting through the tree trunks, the sumac, and the sky.

Speaking of painting, the British painter and writer Wyndham Lewis, who spent some years in Canada during the Second World War, makes this comment about A. Y. Jackson, one of the twentieth-century Group of Seven landscape painters, perhaps with an underlying allusion to the Carman poem already cited:

> Jackson is no man to go gathering nuts in May. He has no wish to be seduced every spring when the sap rises — neither he nor nature are often shown in these compromising moods. There is something of Ahab in him; the long white contours of the Laurentian Mountains in mid-winter are his elusive leviathan.

The leviathan also recurs in Wilfred Watson's fine poem on another Canadian painter, the British Columbian Emily Carr:

> Like Jonah in the green belly of the whale
> Overwhelmed by Leviathan's lights and liver
> Imprisoned and appalled by the belly's wall
> Yet inscribing and scoring the uprush
> Sink vault and arch of that monstrous cathedral,
> Its living bone and its green pulsing flesh —
> Old woman, of your three days' anatomy
> Leviathan sickened and spewed you forth
> In a great vomit on coasts of eternity.

The image of being swallowed by the leviathan is an almost inevitable one for Canada: the whole process of coming to the country by ship from Europe, through the Strait of Belle Isle and the Gulf of Saint Lawrence and then up the great river, suggests it, again a marked contrast to the United States, with its relatively straight north-south coastline. In Pratt's narrative poem on the building of the Canadian Pacific Railway, *Towards the Last Spike,* the dragon image appears, the symbol of a nature so totally indifferent to man and his concerns that it is irrelevant to wonder whether it is dead or alive:

> On the North Shore a reptile lay asleep
> A hybrid that the myths have conceived,
> But not delivered, as progenitor
> Of crawling, gliding things upon the earth...
> This folded reptile was asleep or dead:
> So motionless, she seemed stone dead — just seemed:
> She was too old for death, too old for life...
> Ice-ages had passed by and over her,

But these, for all their motion, had but sheared
Her spotty carboniferous hair or made
Her ridges stand out like the spikes of molochs...
Was this the thing Van Horne set out
To conquer?

Van Horne was the builder of the Canadian Pacific Railway, and the stretch of Precambrian shield in northern Ontario was one of his most formidable obstacles.

In the Bible, of course, the leviathan swallows Jonah, a prototype not only of Emily Carr but of the Jesus who descended to the world of death and hell for three days. In the closely related myth of Saint George and the dragon, Saint George dies along with the dragon he kills, and has to be separately brought to life. What such myths appear to be telling us is that the leviathan is the monster of indefinite time and space surrounding us on all sides: we are all born inside his belly, and we never escape from it; he is the body of death from which we cannot be delivered. The Christian, Baroque, Cartesian attitude that the white invaders brought from Europe helped to insure that in Canada the sense of being imprisoned in the belly of a mindless emptiness would be at its bleakest and most uncompromising. As we have seen the ego's one moment of genuine dignity in such a situation is the moment either of death or of some equally final alienation. Among the poets of the generation of Roberts, Carman, and D. C. Scott, Archibald Lampman achieved the highest consistent level of poetry, partly because he was prudent enough to stick to elegiac moods. His poems are almost invariably those of a solitary watcher of the nature around him: the idiom is strongly Wordsworthian, but the greater sense of indifference in the landscape makes him more conscious of his solitude than Wordsworth:

I sat in the midst of a plain on my snowshoes with bended knee
Where the thin wind stung my cheeks,
And the hard snow ran in little ripples and peaks,
Like the fretted floor of a white and petrified sea.

And a strange peace gathered about my soul and shone,
As I sat reflecting there,
In a world so mystically fair,
So deathly silent — I so utterly alone.

The poem called "Winter Solitude," expresses a kind of serenity that Lampman constantly sought. Margaret Avison presents us with a similar landscape but a different response to it:

But on this sheet of beryl, this high sea,
Scalded by the white unremembering glaze,
No wisps disperse. This is the icy pole.
The presence here is single, worse than soul,
Pried loose forever out of nights and days
And birth and death
And all the covering wings.

I have quoted this passage elsewhere, but keep returning to it because, apart from its great eloquence, the poem from which it comes is called "Identity," and what it shows us is an identity driven into a last stand of such total isolation that it can define itself only by extinction, unless it can make some effort of rebirth.

I earlier quoted George Grant as saying that the gods of the Rockies are the gods of another race, and that we can make no contact with them because of what we are, and what we did. The statement sounds irrefutable, at least in prose, but it is not what the present generation of poets is saying. John Newlove, for example, in a poem called "The Pride," says,

not this handful
of fragments, as the indians
are not composed of
the romantic stories
about them, or of the stories
they tell only, but
still ride the soil
in us, dry bones a part
of the dust in our eyes,
needed and troubling
in the glare, in
our breath, in our
ears, in our mouths,
in our bodies entire, in our minds,
until at last we become them

in our desires, our desires,
mirages, mirrors, that are theirs, hard-
riding desires, and they
become our true forebears, moulded
by the same wind or rain,
and in this land we
are their people, come
back to life.

In this poem the Indians symbolize a primitive mythological imagination which is being reborn in us: in other words, the white Canadians, in their imaginations, are no longer immigrants but are becoming indigenous, recreating the kind of attitudes appropriate to people who really belong here. We may remember that "primitive" poetry, which is created in a society where the poets are the custodians of culture and learning, is very direct in its impact, sometimes needing footnotes for those outside its orbit of allusions, but not at all inclined to talk around or avoid its subject. Thus a Haida song as translated, or adapted, by Hermia Fraser:

> I cannot stay, I cannot stay!
> The Raven has stolen the Child of the Chief,
> Of the Highest Chief in the Kingdom of Light.
>
> The Slave Wife born from the first clam shell
> Is in love with the boy who was stolen away,
> The lovers have taken the Raven's fire.
>
> The Slave who was born from the first clam shell
> Has made love to the wife who was born from the shell,
> This Slave man has stolen her treasures away.

The Haida lived on the Queen Charlotte Islands off the coast of British Columbia. Living there now is the extraordinary poet Susan Musgrave, who has produced four volumes of verse in the first twenty-five years of her life, and who shows throughout them strong imaginative links with a people whom she clearly thinks as poetically her ancestors. In a poem called "Witchery Way" the sense of an indigenous creative power reforming in the present and immediate future seems indicated in the phrase about "the dark seed of their coming":

> Sometimes an old man
> crouches at the river —
> sometimes he is someone
> whose bones are not formed.
>
> Sometimes an old woman
> with fisher-skin quiver,
> sometimes on the low banks
> hungry after blood...
>
> Sometimes an old man
> whispers down the smoke hole,

sometimes an old woman
furrows in the wind.
My skin is thick
with the dark seed
of their coming —
the blade of a fine axe
wedged between my eyes.

It should go without saying that I am not speaking of the content or subject matter of such poems, but of the imaginative attitude that produces their structures.

A poetic consciousness formed within the leviathan of Canadian nature, feeling that it belongs there and can no longer think of itself as a swallowed outsider, would naturally be preoccupied with two themes in particular: the theme of descent into the self and the theme of forming, within that self, an imaginative counterpart of what is outside it. The sense of a responding imagination which is part of its surroundings, and not a detached consciousness rolling over it like so much tumbleweed, already appears in Lampman and is in fact the reason why so much of his work is focused on the theme of serenity. Thus in a poem called "Storm":

O Wind, wild-voicèd brother, in your northern cave,
  My spirit also being so beset
With pride and pain, I heard you beat and rave,
  Grinding your chains with furious howl and fret,
Knowing full well that all earth's moving things inherit
  The same chained might and madness of the spirit,
That none may quite forget.

The same kind of microcosmic imagery continues in Irving Layton's "The Cold Green Element" and in A. M. Klein's very central poem, "Portrait of the Poet as Landscape," which concludes:

Therefore he seeds illusions. Look, he is
the nth Adam taking a green inventory
in the world but scarcely uttered, naming, praising...
For to praise

the world — he, solitary man — is breath
to him...

These are not mean ambitions. It is already something
merely to entertain them. Meanwhile he

> makes of his status as zero a rich garland,
> a halo of his anonymity,
> and lives alone, and in his secret shines
> like phosphorus. At the bottom of the sea.

The closing lines echo Eliot on the poet as catalyst and Keats on the poet's lack of identity, but the final phrase comes out of the belly of the Canadian leviathan, for the leviathan, as no one knew better than Klein, is a sea monster.

Earlier Canadian poetry was full of solitude and loneliness, of the hostility or indifference of nature, of the fragility of human life and values in such an environment. Contemporary Canadian poetry seems to think rather of this outer leviathan as a kind of objective correlative of some Minotaur that we find in our own mental labyrinths. The mind has become a dark chamber, or *camera obscura*, and its pictures are reflections of what is at once physical and human nature. A poem of Gwendolyn MacEwen, "Dark Pines under Water," explicitly links the poetic consciousness with reflection and descent:

> This land like a mirror turns you inward
> And you become a forest in a furtive lake;
> The dark pines of your mind reach downward...
>
> There is something down there and you want it told.

Similar themes of descent are in Margaret Atwood's work, especially *Procedures for Underground*, in Eli Mandel's *Fuseli Poems*, and, very remarkably, in Jay Macpherson's *Welcoming Disaster*, a sequence in which the sections have such titles as "The Way Down" and "The Dark Side." The imagery of this book, of a perilous descent into a world which is at once a world of fear and a world of love, of horror and of creation, recurs in Alden Nowlan's "Geneaology of Morals":

> Take any child dreaming of pickled bones
> shelved in a coal-dark cellar understairs
> (we are all children when we dream) the stones
> red-black with blood from severed jugulars.
>
> Child Francis, Child Gilles went down those stairs,
> returned sides, hands and ankles dripping blood,
> Bluebeard and gentlest saint. The same nightmares
> instruct the evil, as inform the good.

The conception of nature as a mechanism, which began to take its modern form in the seventeenth century, meant, of course, that Western man was developing an increasingly mechanistic civilization. Canada was opened up by technology of navigation and surveying and held together by the technology of transportation, which has left its mark in the great bridges and railways and seaports and in the network of canals in southern Ontario. Up to, say, the Second World War, the inarticulate aspect of communication was the one that had top priority. Pratt's fascination with the rumbling and creaking of machinery, his constant awareness of the throbbing engines at the heart of the ship, indicated that poetry had with him become sufficiently aware of its surroundings to make poetic imagery out of technology. The development of technology makes for a growing introversion in life, with the high-rise apartments and office buildings, the superhighways, where falling asleep is one of the hazards, the tunnel-like streets, with pedestrians hustled out of the way of motor traffic as peasants used to be on the approach of nobility. Even in Pratt, society is held together only by the emergencies of "survival."

Culturally, this introversion reached its height with the blind man's medium of the radio and the deaf man's medium of the silent movie, the latter being a close relative of the puppet show. The television set is technically even more introverted, setting up a round-the-clock fantasy world that we can stay in without even making the effort of joining an audience. And yet the centering on both sound and vision sets limits to the introversion. Turn off the sound, and we are in the world of the puppet show again, totally uninvolved; turn off the screen and listen to the sound track, and a similar detachment occurs. But in the fully centered medium, for all the avoiding of reality, we are occasionally compelled to see glimpses of an actual and very human world. Whether cabinet ministers or Eskimos, people are ultimately compelled to look like people on television, instead of like abstractions of charisma or legend. The television set seems to me to provide an analogue, in the mass media, to the imagery of descent that I have been trying to trace in poetry, which ends not in introversion but in an intensely centered vision.

Besides television, the airplane is a technological development which has begun to make more human sense of the colossal space of Canada. Nature as seen from a plane forms patterns reminding us of the more abstract painters, Borduas[2] and Pellan[3] and Harold Town, who

---

[2]Paul-Émile Borduas (1905-60), the leader of the Mouvement Automatistes, exerted a profound influence on the subsequent generation of Canadian artists. In

have succeeded the Group of Seven, but it figures less in the imagery of poetry, poets being, for the most part, children of the earth mother rather than the sky father. An analogy to the aerial perspective, which I think may be something more than an analogy, is the attitude to tradition in contemporary Canadian poetry. Tradition is usually thought of as linear, and as forming a series of conventions which continually go out of date, so that a poet has to be careful not to become associated with an obsolete fashion. In Canada tradition has become, in the last generation or so at least, a much more simultaneous and kaleidoscopic affair, reminding us perhaps of the welter of historical allusions in the costumes of young people. The echoes of Spenser in James Reaney's *A Suit of Nettles,* of descent themes from Ishtar to Boris Karloff movies in Macpherson's *Welcoming Disaster*, of prosodic devices from Old English to concrete poetry in Earle Birney, while they certainly assume a cultivated reader, are both unforced and unpedantic, and illustrate very clearly the advantage, for a Canadian poet, of being able to look down on tradition all at once, instead of being pushed ahead of it like a terminal moraine of a glacier. In the words of the critic Milton Wilson:

> But one of the advantages of a poetry less than a hundred years old is that all the things that couldn't happen when they should have happened keep happening all the time... Having begun a millennium too late, there is not much point being correctly fashionable.

Canadian literature has always been thought of as having its centre of gravity in the future. Now that it has come into the present also, it may, by being where it is as well as what it is, help to make its own contribution to the future that we all hope for — not apocalyptic futures of fantasy and nightmare, but a future in which Western man has come home from his exile in the land of unlikeness and has become something better than the ghost of an ego haunting himself.

"Haunted by Lack of Ghosts: Some Patterns in the Imagery of Canadian Poetry" in: *The Canadian Imagination: Dimensions of a Literary Culture*. Edited by David Staines. Cambridge: Harvard University Press, 1977

---

the movement's manifesto, *Réfus Global,* he denounced the authority of establishment, proclaiming the artist's right to total freedom of expression.

[3]Alfred Pellam (1906-88) was the first Canadian painter to have a solo exhibition in Paris at the Musée national d'arte moderne, 1955. Pellam's paintings are known for cubist and surrealistic representations of reality.

Culture as Interpenetration

As long as I have been a literary critic, I have been interested in the relations between a culture and the social conditions under which it is produced. It has always puzzled me why so little seems to be known about this, when so much work, even so much first-rate work, has been done in what seems to be all the relevant areas. I have also been watching the Canadian cultural scene for about forty years, and I feel that Canada is perhaps as interesting and valuable a place as any to study such a question. What follows is a series of observations that might conceivably lead to some more general principles on the subject. I am confining the term culture, because of limited space, to the creative arts, and to painting and literature within those arts.

There is an aged and now somewhat infirm joke to the effect that the United States has passed from barbarism to decadence without an intervening period of civilization. A parallel and possibly more accurate statement might be made of Canada: that it has passed from a pre-national to a post-national phase without ever having become a nation. It very nearly became one in the two decades following the second World War, when it took an active part in international politics, acquired a national flag, and was for a time a perceptible military and naval power. But it never shook off its role as an American satellite sufficiently to be taken very seriously as a distinctive political presence even then. As third-world nations began to emerge in Africa and Asia, Canada's much more low-keyed nationalism became increasingly inaudible, like a lute in a brass band. Two books with highly significant titles appeared at the beginning and end respectively of this period: A. R. M. Lower's *Colony to Nation* in 1946 and George Grant's *Lament for a Nation* in 1965. When Trudeau became prime minister and adopted Marshall McLuhan as one of his advisors, Canada reverted to tribalism.

The settlement of America was a centrifugal movement out from Britain and France, and to centralize is to create hierarchy. The top of the hierarchy is the central city, London or Paris, which is where all the cultural action is. In Elizabethan England, for example, literary culture was a London culture. If a writer were upper class, he would write Petrarchan love lyrics and send them around to his friends in manuscript, prior to arranging for a publisher to steal them. If he were a middle class, he would turn to the theatre or to pamphleteering. But *qua* writer he could hardly live or work for long outside London: one thinks of Herrick, for instance, a parson stuck in Devonshire, writing nostalgically of jewelry, perfume, women's clothes, and his happy times with the "tribe of Ben." This situation lasted until late in the eighteenth century. Wordsworth was the first major English writer to set up his headquarters outside London, and of course by Victorian times, with the rise of the great Midland cities, the cultural picture was quite different. In France, with its more limited industrial development, culture remained fixated on Paris for a much longer time. As late as my own student days, I remember seeing in Paris an exhibition of a sculptor who lived in (I think) Dijon, advertised under the slogan "France is not Paris."

Discussions about Canadian literature began, in English Canada, about a hundred years ago, when it was still uncertain whether the condition was one of genuine pregnancy or merely wind. At that time the commonest argument advanced was that in a young and newly settled country the priorities were material ones, and that literature and the other arts would come along when economic conditions were more advanced. This argument makes very little sense: in a genuinely primitive community, like that of the Eskimos, where food and shelter are requirements that have constantly to be met, poetry (and other arts, such as carving) leaps into the foreground as one of the really essential elements of life. Something similar may be true of new societies that are not primitive: seventeenth-century Puritans in Massachusetts wrote poetry and carried on with their pamphlet war against the Anglican establishment. It is also possible, in modern times, for the centrifugal movement from the main centres to reverse itself, for works of culture to be export goods coming out of a small community. One thinks of the amount of Anglo-Irish literature produced in the last century, which was certainly never intended for the Dublin market.

No: Canadian assumption about the low and late priority of creative activity were mercantilist assumptions, and signified the acquiescence by Canadians in their role as producers of raw materials for manufacturing centres outside Canada. What got the priority were the engineering modes of communication, the fantastically long and expensive railways, bridges and canals that sprouted out of the nineteenth-century Canadian landscape. It was no more natural for Canada to produce such things than to produce major developments in literature or painting, but they were produced because they fitted the premises of Canadian mythology at the time. But while the prevailing mood was one of expansion into a bountiful future, other directions were indicated by the turn of the century, when the Boer War was fought. In the first World War there was a patriotic picture called "Canada's Answer," depicting battleships on the ocean. The point of the picture was, of course, Canada's willingness to defend the mother country by sending soldiers over the sea. But the subject of the picture was again an engineering mode of communication, except that this time it was associated with a feeling that the noblest destiny for a human Canadian life was to become a sacrificial object in a European war. The assumptions here are getting a little more sinister than the purely mercantilist ones, and need more looking into.

One of the most remarkable works of fiction in our time, Thomas Pynchon's *Gravity's Rainbow,* suggests that the human instinct to see humanly intelligible pattern and design in nature is a form of paranoia. That is, man cannot endure the thought of an environment that was not made primarily for his benefit, or, at any rate, made without reference to his own need to see order in it. Man describes his total environment as a "universe," something that all turns around one centre, though often mentally suppressing the fact that that centre is himself. He clings to the argument of design as long as he can, projecting the notion of a man-related universe on God: when he is forced to give that up, he plunges into a mathematical order, the animated algebra of technology. As he goes on, it becomes increasingly clear that his "rage for order," in Stevens' phrase, is linked to a death-wish — Pynchon's symbol for it is the V-2 rocket bomb of the second World War.

However, to live without the sense of a need for order, Pynchon suggests, requires an inhuman detachment that is not possible nor perhaps desirable. What fights effectively against the destructive impulse can only be a "counterforce" or creative paranoia, a unifying power that works towards life and the fulfillment of desire instead of towards death. Such a creative force would naturally be closely allied to the work of the dream. Freud, in the *Traumdeutung,* remarks more than once on the curious compulsion in the dream work to unify a great variety of disparate experiences and themes. For Pynchon the opposite of this creative drama, the anti-dream, so to speak, is Kekulé's famous dream of ouroboros that turned into the benzene rings, and thereby inaugurated a new and deadly era of technology. There are other vivid episodes in the book making the same point. We are told of a madman who exterminated the dodoes in Mauritius because, being awkward and unadaptable, they seemed to him an offense against the argument for design. This modulates to a hideous picture of the formerly German colony of Southwest Africa, where the native population was slaughtered to the verge of extinction out of the bloodthirsty superstition known as social Darwinism, the belief that some people are better fitted to survive than others because they possess greater power of destruction. It seems to me that this argument in *Gravity's Rainbow* affords an instructive parallel to some of the social conditions underlying Canadian literature.

New France and New England were colonized in the Baroque phase of European development. Certain religious and philosophical assumptions that they brought with them explain a good many features of the colonization. Let us take the religious ones first. Christianity is a revolutionary and urban religion, and, like Marxism in our day, it started with all the revolutionary characteristics: the belief in a specific historical revelation, a canon of sacred texts, an obsession with the danger of heresy, and, above all, a dialectical habit of mind, a tendency to polarize everything into the for and the against. Such an attitude is by no means essential to a religion. When Buddhism came to Japan it collided with the indigenous Shinto cult, and after a good deal of tension, a Buddhist theologian suggested that the *kami*, the gods and nature-spirits of Shinto, could be thought of as emanations of the Buddha: in short, that Shintoism could be regarded as a positive analogy of Buddhism. As a result the two religions have co-existed in Japan ever since. But for Christianity, as for Islam and Marxism later, nothing will go right until the entire world is united in the right creed, and whatever place there might be in Christian thought for natural religion, no non-Christian faith can ever be anything but a negative analogy, a demonic parody, of Christianity. And when even saints and martyrs firmly believe that the only good heathenism is a dead heathenism, it becomes very easy for others to infer that the only good heathen is a dead heathen. What is particularly horrifying about the extinction of, say, Beothuks in Newfoundland is the casualness with which it was done, the ability to murder people of a different ethnical group without loosing five minutes' sleep over it. It is rather curious that the Eichmann trial of a few years ago should have come to so many people as a shocking discovery.

The difference between the Puritan Protestantism of New England and the Jansenist Catholicism of New France are of very little importance here. Both felt equally that there could be no truck with any nature-spirits or with any sense of identity between human and animal life, such as we have in some aspects of totemism. The horror of idolatry, the feeling that there could be nothing numinous in nature and that all the spiritual beings man had discovered in nature were really devils, was deeply rooted in Christianity, as was the feeling that man had to depend solely on human and social institutions for any improvements in his status. Nature became therefore an unrestricted area for human exploitation. God had said to Noah after the flood, at the very beginning of history: "The fear of you and the dread of you shall be upon every beast of the earth... into your hands are they delivered." Hence the savage and superstitious custom of apologizing to the spirit of the fish or the deer and explaining that the human hunters were taking only enough for their food was replaced by the enlightened and civilized custom of slaughtering everything in sight until one species after another disappeared from the earth forever.

Such traditional tendencies had been increased by the Baroque sense, most articulate in Descartes, that the consciousness of man created an immense gap between him and all other living creatures, who belonged primarily in a world of mechanism. The newly discovered power of mathematics, too, was at its clearest at the exploring and pioneering periphery of Baroque culture, in the astrolabes and compasses that guided the explorer, in the grid-patterns that eventually were imposed on city and country alike. Every "improvement" in communication since then, in railway, highway, or airway, has meant a shorter and straighter path through nature until, with the plane, the sense of moving through nature practically disappears. What does not disappear is the attitude of arrogant ascendancy over nature. For the white conquerors of this continent, creation does not begin with an earth-mother who is the womb and tomb of all created things, but with a sky-father who planned and ordered and made the world, in a *tour de force* of technology. The despoiling of nature has now reached the point at which the white settlement of America begins to look like a very clear example of what Pynchon means by his death-wish paranoia, a destructiveness increasing in efficiency and ferocity until it finally began to turn on itself.

Baroque Christianity still maintained the rigidly authoritarian world-picture inherited from medieval times, in which there is a downward movement from God to man and an upward movement from man towards God. For natural religion like that of most of the native peoples, evil, suffering and above all death do not cause a problem: death belongs in the cycle of nature from the beginning. But for a religion thinking in terms of an omniscient God planning and making the world, the world as originally made could not have had any evil or death in it, and hence a myth of fall was necessary to account for the contrast between the model world that God must have made and the actual world that surrounds us. The gap caused by the fall was closed by the Incarnation, when a principle of authority descended from the divine world to the human one. This principle of authority continues in the church and in the secular power focused in the monarchy. Man's response to divine authority is to raise his status from the lower nature into which he fell to the higher nature symbolized by the garden of

Eden. But he can do this only through answering obedience to the sacraments of the church, the principles of morality, and the canons of secular law. Once again, there is no significant difference on this point between the Quebec Catholic and the Massachusetts Puritan. The Puritans were revolutionaries, but not for liberal and democratic reasons: they looked forward to a rule of the elect in which, to paraphrase Paul, the powers that be would not be ordained of God for man's sins, but ordained *by* God for his redemption.

The first white man to write poetry in what is now Canada, Marc Lescarbot, wrote a poem in 1606 addressed to some Frenchmen returning to France from Port Royal. He says (in F. R. Scott's translation):

> It is you who go to see congenial friends
> In language, habits, customs and religion
> And all the lovely scenes of your own nation,
> While we among the savages are lost
> And dwell bewildered on this clammy coast.

Then he pulls himself together and speaks of what may yet be made of the country, after, perhaps, missionaries will have come

> And bring conversion to this savage nation
> That has no God, no laws and no religion.

Lescarbot thus defines a kind of cultural primal scene for Canada. In front of him, as he gazes wistfully at it, is the ship going back to rejoin the centre of culture and good life in France. Behind him is the great gap in existence, like one of the black holes of modern astronomy, created by the indigenous people — that is, of course, created by his view of them. We notice how the cultural situation exactly fits the religious and political one. In culture, as in religion and politics, the homeland is the source of authority, and the first duty of a colonial culture is to respond to it.

Lescarbot's verses inaugurate the first period of Canadian culture, the uncomplicated provincial or colonial period. One may distinguish three main phases in its development. In the first phase the provincial culture tends to imitate externally rather than by absorption, accepting certain standards and trying to meet them. It confines its attention to what is established in the homeland and has become a principle of cultural authority there. It is obvious that cultural lag is built in to such a process. In poetry of the Confederation period and earlier, while the ostensible echoes may be from Tennyson or Victor Hugo, the actual texture of the verse is usually closer to James Thomson or Béranger. Such external imitation is a self-defeating enterprise because a writer cannot meet external standards, but can only establish his own. Gradually, however, the first phase evolves into the second phase. The more mature colonial writing gets, the more contemporary the influences become: the writer has got out of the schoolroom and has joined a community. It is still a mercantilist situation, but some initiative has gone into the provincial manufacturers.

These two phases represent different and contrasting ways of dealing with a sense of urgency connected with content, with a need to grapple directly with the new stimuli and situations encountered in a new land. Content is often regarded, even by artists themselves, as dictating its own forms, but this is an elementary fallacy: the forms of every art are generated from within the art. In the first phase it is obscurely felt that the more traditional the form, the better adapted it is to containing the new experience. The second phase swings to the opposite extreme and assumes that only the latest models are equipped to do the same job.

Poetry in Canada did not fare very well under these imitative phases, although naturally we can see a steady maturing process going on as, in English, pre-Raphealite formulas are replaced by the influence of Eliot and the later Yeats, and, in French, a good deal of yawny verse about the *terroir* gives way to livelier echoes of Paul Fort and Claudel. Fiction was even more retarded. Painting is by far the most interesting art in Canada up to about 1960. Here the urgency of new content could find its place in a remarkable documentary development, which begins with the military and exploring painting of the age of Paul Kane[1] and Thomas Davies[2] and continues through Thomson and the Group of Seven in Ontario, along with Emily Carr in British Columbia and a number of painters in Quebec. It is often said that these later groups broke with stale pictorial conventions and began to look directly at the country in front of them. There clearly must be some truth in this, as I have said it myself: however, the fallacy of content shaping form lurks within it. The lapse of time brings with it a decreasing attention to subject-matter and an increasing awareness of convention. It is this lapse of time that makes us more conscious of the Barba-

---

[1]Paul Kane (1810-71), was one of Canada's leading artist-explorers. He is best known for his sketches of Native Canadians which he produced on his various trips across the country.

[2]Thomas (Davis) Davies (1737-1812) was a soldier and artist whose paintings are some of the earliest pictorial documents of colonial life in Canada.

zon[3] and Dutch pastoral influences on the older landscape painters, and the continuing of the lapse that turns our interest from the "solemn land" of northern Ontario as painted by Thomson and MacDonald[4] towards the *fauve* and *art nouveau* conventions that controlled their vision of it.

The final phase, in which provincial culture becomes fully mature, occurs when the artist enters into the cultural heritage that his predecessors have drawn from, and paints or writes without any sense of criterion external to himself and his public. Here the anxieties about meeting proper standards or being up to date or expressing a distinctive subject-matter with enough emphasis (or what was once called, in connection with Hemingway, false hair on the chest) have all disappeared. While I was reviewing English Canadian poetry during the fifties,[5] I noticed how many of the best people were turning erudite, allusive, even academic. I felt that this indicated the growth of an unforced and relaxed sense of a cultural tradition, one which could now be absorbed instead of merely imitated or echoed. Of course all the anxieties listed above were still in the air, and I was widely regarded as encouraging a new form of inhibited provincialism. But what I saw in, for example, Leonard Cohen's *Let us Compare Mythologies*, Jay Macpherson's *The Boatman*, Margaret Avison's *Winter Sun*, James Reaney's *Suit of Nettles* seemed to me an attitude to cultural tradition that looked forward rather than back.

In 1952 some people in a small town in Ontario, simply because it was called Stratford, decided to put on some Shakespeare, and a Shakespeare festival began there the next year. The director was Tyrone Guthrie and the leading actors were Alec Guinnes and Irene Worth — not precisely what the CRTC would call Canadian content. Those who think in pigeonholes could hardly point to anything more obvi-

---

[3]Barbazon Painters, a group of mid-nineteenth-century French artists, most of whom were landscapists. The group was influenced by the Dutch masters of the seventeenth century and included such men as Camille Corot and Jean-Francois Millet.

[4]J. E. H. MacDonald (1873-1932), painter and founder of the Group of Seven. He decorated St. Anne's Church, Toronto, 1923, and taught at the Ontario College of Art.

[5]In 1950 Frye was asked by J. R. MacGillvray, editor of the *University of Toronto Quarterly*, to take over the annual survey of Canadian poetry in its "Letters in Canada" issue, which had been conceived and carried out by the late E. K. Brown. Through the decade, Frye regularly assessed the evolution and growth of Canadian poetry, and he considered this reviewing as important "field work" in developing his theory of literature.

ously parochial and colonial. Yet there are three factors to be considered. First, the beginning of the Shakespeare festival at Stratford turned out to be a very important event in the history of Canadian drama: it helped to foster a school of Canadian actors, and the lift in morale it represented fostered Canadian playwriting as well. Second, it represented an extraordinary recreation of the power and freshness of Shakespeare himself: one almost felt sorry for the British, who, having no Stratford except the one that had actually produced Shakespeare, would find it harder to make this kind of rediscovery of him. And third, Shakespeare at Stratford does not stand alone, because Molière played a very similar role in the development of French Canadian drama, at roughly the same time.

In proportion as Canada shook off its external and subordinating assumptions about its English and French cultural heritages, the genuine form of cultural development became more obvious. This genuine form is what I mean by interpenetration. As Shelley demonstrated in his *Defense of Poetry,* the language of the creative imagination is a language that cannot argue: it is not based on propositions that do battle with their implied opposites. What it does is to create a vision that becomes a focus for a community. This means that it has, at least at the beginning, a limited range. Shelley himself, writing in a culture that had been London-dominated for a thousand years, suggests (in his preface to *Prometheus Unbound*) that for the best future developments in culture England should break down into about forty republics, each with a central city about the size of Periclean Athens or Medicean Florence.

Shelly was writing at a time when there was a strong liberal sympathy with self-determinism of nations as opposed to empires, with Italy against the Austrian empire, with Greece against the Turkish one. Since then it has become increasingly obvious that political and economic organization tends to centralize and unify. But Shelley seems to be right about cultural matters. Literature and painting do appear to depend on decentralization in a very subtle way. The artist seems to draw strength from a very limited community: American writers, for instance, generally turn out, under closer analysis, to be southern writers, New England writers, expatriate writers, New York writers, and so on. They need a certain cultural coherence within their community, but the community itself is not their market. This is where the principle of interpenetration operates: the more intensely Faulkner concentrates on his unpronounceable county in Mississippi, the more intelligible he becomes to readers all over the world.

We are back to the question of the challenge of content. Contemporary painting and writing, whatever the language, speaks an international idiom, and the capitals where that idiom is established are still, as they have always been, the big centres, London, Paris, New York. Trying to ignore this international idiom is, experience suggests, futile, and leads only to a kind of archaism. The general principle appears to be that a painter or writer who is self-conscious about his immediate context will be likely to sound provincial, whereas a painter or writer who accepts a provincial milieu, in, say, Newfoundland or southern British Columbia, will be much less likely to do so. A Canadian artist may leave Canada to live and work in one of the big centres, like the painter Riopelle,[6] but this does not affect the matter. Within the last twenty years we have been seeing more and more areas of this huge and sparsely settled country become culturally visible through painters and writers who belong, as creative people, less to Canada than to the prairies, the Pacific coast, the Atlantic coast, southern Ontario or Quebec. The process has been aided by Canada's more relaxed attitude to ethnical groups: there is no such thing as a hundred per cent Canadian, and the homogenizing of immigrants has been less intense than in the United States. But if we look at the pictures of Kurelek[7] on the prairies or Jack Chambres in Ontario, or read Buckler on the Maritimes or Rudy Wiebe on Alberta Mennonites, we can see the "provincial" aspect of Canadian culture going into reverse, from inarticulate form to articulate content.

"Culture as Interpenetration" in: *Divisions on a Ground: Essays on Canadian Culture.* Edited by James Polk. Toronto: House of Anansi Press, 1982.

[6]Jean-Paul Riopelle (1923-) has been painting in Paris since 1947 and is Canada's most internationally acclaimed canvas painter.

7William Kurelek (1927-1977), painter and writer, best known for his symbolic and religious paintings often exploring the life of his prairie Ukrainian roots, and for his children's books, including *A Prairie Boy's Winter*, 1973, and *Lumberjack*, 1974.

National Consciousness in Canadian Culture

A year or two ago I was present at a public hearing of the Canadian Radio and Television Commission, when leaders of the Cree Indian and Eskimo peoples in the far north were protesting against the destroying of their cultures by the mass media. One of them said that the overwhelming impression made on them by the media was that life in the south was "soft, violent, and sick." Some months later I was present at another CRTC[1] hearing, on violence in television. There it was said that violence was an American phenomenon, being a cheap way of producing programmes for a huge mass market, and not a problem in Canada, except as a result of importing American programmes into Canada by cable. The conclusion of the second hearing was oddly similar to that of the first. There is no question of one group of people being inherently less violent than another: the principle involved is simply the elementary arithmetic of original sin. More people are always worse than fewer people.

At the same time more people are more aggressive and highly organized, and can force that organization on less populous communities. It seems doubtful at present that much of what is distinctive about the indigenous cultures of the north will long survive. One of their spokesmen asked us on the CRTC if we realized what an in-joke such a program as *All in the Family*[2] seemed in Frobisher or Aklavik. But probably, before long, that unpleasant family will become part of their family too. Similarly, our undefended border is very effectively defended on one side, the United States being a highly protectionist country in culture as in other aspects of life, and the Canadian instinct for compromise has to make the best of it. If a Canadian novelist writes about

[1] CRTC (Canadian Radio-television and Telecommunication Commission). The Broadcasting Act, 1967-68, established the Canadian Radio-television Commission to regulate and supervise all aspects of the Canadian Broadcasting system. The CRTC decides on the issuance and renewal of licences for all broadcasting undertakings.

[2] *All in the Family* was a popular television series in the 70s and the 80s, depicting a dysfunctional American working-class family.

people in Manitoba and wishes to find an American publisher, it is relatively easy for him (or her: I am thinking particularly of the ill-starred career of Martha Ostenso)[3] to push them over the border into North Dakota, in deference to the publisher's conviction that his readers will have a nervous breakdown if they pick up a novel with a Canadian setting. Some of Stephen Leacock's most unmistakably Canadian vignettes, in *Arcadian Adventures with the Idle Rich* and elsewhere, have American setting for the same reason. Again, if Canadian university graduates are excluded from the American job markets and the Canadian universities are full of Americans who make no concessions to their Canadian environment, it is easy for Canadians to rationalize the situation by saying that scholarship, like Canada, has no defended boundaries. Perhaps only intellectuals worry about cultural distinctiveness, and perhaps only because they have invented most of it themselves. The CRTC has constantly been reminded, first by broadcasters and later by cable operators, that the majority of Canadians prefer American programmes, including the brutal ones.

And yet this represents a temptation to be fought against. I detected a certain desperation in the statements of the Cree and Eskimo leaders, a feeling which was more than simply a fear that their cultures were being exterminated by the high-powered death-wish of southern civilization. It was rather a feeling that their own people might not care very much if they did lose their distinctive identity and simply merge into the Canadian mass. There would be strong economic arguments for their doing so, if not cultural ones. One hears the same tone among French-speaking Canadians, opposing the way that Canadian French so often breaks down into an English dialect, or the way that so many ambitious young Francophones accept English as their career language. One hears it among spokesmen for ethnical minorities, including Jewish leaders who seem almost to regret the decline of anti-Semitism, and of course among English-speaking Canadians where the threat to distinctiveness is regularly associated with America. But when we look at the United States itself, we can see that there is nothing American in the debasing of standards: that is simply human inertia, and such inertia destroys everything distinctive in American life equally with Canada.

The fight for cultural distinctiveness, from this point of view, is a fight for human dignity itself, for the variety in life that nothing but

---

[3]Martha Ostenso (1900-63), a native of Manitoba and author of over a dozen volumes of fiction and a collection of poetry, is primarily remembered for her `realistic' novel, *Wild Geese*.

genuine culture can ever produce, for the unity that is at the opposite pole from uniformity. Many years ago Toynbee[4] defined one of the central problems of society as the need to foster what he called creative minorities without allowing the emergence of what he called a dominant minority. Our current struggles for "affirmative action," our repudiation of "elitism," and the like, get this issue very confused at times, but it remains a genuine issue, especially when it is not recognized to be one, as is so often true of the United States *vis-à-vis* Canada. And to distinguish what is creative in a minority from what attempts to dominate, we have to distinguish between cultural issues, which are inherently decentralizing ones, and political and economic issues, which tend to centralization and hierarchy.

It is easy for those outside Canada to exaggerate the influence and persistence of the British connection on Canadian cultural development. It often comes as a surprise to my American friends that Canadians need passports to enter Great Britain, even though when they get there they go through a special door marked "Commonwealth." The British connection in Canada was culturally most important in the period between Confederation and the First World War. At that time Canada was trying to think of itself as a single nation extending "from sea to sea." As there was so much empty space in between, the Canadian consciousness could hardly match the American sense of a vast society slowly pushing a frontier westward until it reached the Pacific. Canada had to think of itself rather as part of a world-circling empire, its railways filling the gap in communication between Europe and the East, its natural resources contributing to a global technology, its young men taking part in the only social activity they were really wanted for outside Canada, imperial wars. As Charles G. D. Roberts says:

> And some Canadian lips are dumb
> Beneath Egyptian sands.

The American influence on Canadian literature in English has always been at least as direct and immediate as the British influence, and often more so. Cultural connections with Britain were of course close all through the nineteenth century, but they were no closer than those in the New England of Emerson and Henry James. In fact Canadians felt

---

[4]Arnold Toynbee (1889-1975), English historian who rejected Spengler's biological concept of civilization as an organism with a life span of 1,000 years. Toynbee explained civilizations' decline in terms of moral transgression. His numerous books include *America and the World Revolution*, 1962, and *Cities on the Move*, 1970.

that there was far less attention paid to them in Great Britain than they would have got if they had come from a sovereign state. There is a story, recorded in Smollett's[5] *Humphrey Clinker*, of the delight of George II on being told that a rumor that the French had marched on Louisburg from Acadia must have been false, because Cape Breton is an island. This story symbolizes much in the British connection that still rankles in the Canadian consciousness. I have elsewhere made the obvious but often overlooked observation that the French lost Canada mainly because they had very little interest in holding it, and that if they had held it they might well have sold it as they did Louisiana. The British took a less parochial view of their empire, but still their flaccid attitude to Canadian interests, from the Treaty of Ghent in 1814 through all the nineteenth-century boundary disputes, gave Canada a strong sense of not getting the support it needed for its unusually difficult problem of identity. Nobody has much use for a colony, apparently, or at least for the human part of it.

It is a standard practice of universities in settled areas, like Harvard or Yale or Toronto, to send its graduates out to civilize the boondocks and then recall them when they have become "established" scholars with nothing much more to say. This is the situation that looms large in the writings of Haliburton, early in the nineteenth century. For all his commitment to the colonial position, Haliburton felt that it developed laziness and overdependence on the mother country, and he thought that his Yankee peddler Sam Slick was a model of what greater energy could do for Nova Scotia, however detached a view he took of Sam Slick's opinions and language. But the greatest energy would be useless unless it coincided with a more actively concerned response from Britain, and Haliburton felt that Britain should be much more active and discriminating in rewarding outstanding service to the colonies, beginning with him. Of the Church of England, for example, he makes Sam Slick say:

> Remove the restrictions on colonial clergy, so that if they deserve promotion in the church to Britain, they needn't be shut out among big bogs, black logs, and thick fogs, for ever and ever.

---

[5]Tobias George Smollett (1721-72), English author best remembered for his picaresque novels, which include such popular titles as *Adventures of Roderick Random*, 1748, and *The Adventures of Sir Lancelot Greaves*, 1762.

In other words, the colonies are essentially penal settlements, and should be regarded as, at least for the well-meaning and deserving, a purgatory rather than a hell.

Another passage in the same paper, from *The Attaché,* is even more striking. At the end of his life Haliburton went to Britain and entered politics there, joining the Conservative party because he thought it was conservative, though by his Bluenose standards of conservatism it was practically a Communist front. We may remember the book called *White Niggers of America,*[6] a manifesto of radical French Canadian protest. It is interesting that identically the same metaphor had been used over a century earlier by the deeply conservative Haliburton to describe the English-speaking colonists in British North America:

> The slave is a slave, and that's his condition. Now the English have two sorts of niggers — American colonists, who are free white niggers; and manufactures laborers' at home, and they are white slave niggers... A colonist and a free nigger don't differ in anythin' but color: both have naked rights, but they have no power given' em to clothe those rights, and that's the naked truth.

It seems to me better to think of Canada, not simply as British America, but as culturally descended from the Tory opposition to the Whig triumph at the time of the Revolutionary War. This is a view of it that would, *mutatis mutandis,* include French Canada, which still flies the pre-revolutionary flag of the lilies. The American assumption that freedom and national independence were inseparable never took as deep a root in Canada, and the uninhibited American development of entrepreneur capitalism was hardly possible in a country equally large but so sparsely populated. Hence it was natural for Canada to combine Tory attitudes with radical ones, just as it was possible, in fact necessary, for it to achieve a fairly high degree of socialization. Most Canadian politicians, whatever their parties or personal beliefs, are compelled to be middle-of-the-road trimmers, for obvious reasons we do not need to go into. But many leading Canadian intellectuals, English or French, could be described as one form or other of Tory radicals.

The distinctive is not unique: what is distinctive is an emphasis, a special proportioning of elements that other societies may have in different proportions. I see something distinctive, in this sense, in the re-

---

[6] *White Niggers of America: The Precocious Autobiography of a Quebec 'Terrorist,'* 1968, English translation 1971, was written by Pierre Vallières (1938-). The book discusses the conflict between Quebec and English Canada in racial terms.

mark of R. H. Bonnycastle, writing in 1841, when he speaks of "the United States, where from the great mixture of races, British feelings and British connection have given way before a flood of undefinable notions about liberty and equality, mixed with aristocratic wealth, slavery, and bigotry in religion." I am quoting this not for its insight but for its commonplaceness. What the writer dislikes is not only American democracy but American oligarchy, the inequalities of wealth and opportunity. The criticism attacks from both sides of the Whig establishment. In the literature of social protest in Canada we find, over and over, a kind of radicalism that seems closer to Tom Paine than Jefferson, often because, like Paine, it has immediate British roots.

Similarly in Susanna Moodie's *Roughing it in the Bush* (1852), the positive virtue of what I have elsewhere called a garrison society show up with great clarity: the constant fight to be clean, fully clothed, disciplined in speech and manner, to maintain any number of standards that we may think unnecessary even though now they would be easy to maintain, emerges with a singular intensity of dedication. Susanna Moodie's effort to remain a gentlewoman in the backwoods makes her the exact opposite of what Carlyle means by an unworking aristocracy. She felt that she belonged to the gentry, and devoted all her waking moments to dramatize her social status. But to do so she was often forced to accept conditions of life that were primitive to the point of squalor. It is no good saying that she had servants to help her put on her show: servants were the most disheartening of all her problems.

A culture founded on a revolutionary tradition, like that of the United States, is bound to show very different assumptions and imaginative patterns from those of a culture that rejects or distrusts revolution. First, an underlying assumption of a successful revolution is "violence pays," and the violence in American life, through the opening of the West to the gangsterism in the immense cities, is part of its revolutionary heritage. In Canada, developing as it did through a series of military occupations, where the red-coated "Mountie," half-policeman and half-soldier, has become a national symbol, the violence has been mainly repressive violence. This means that nine-tenths of it never gets beyond the individual himself, or at most his immediate family. For details of how this self-destructive violence operates, see Canadian fiction, more or less passim: Margaret Atwood's lively book, *Survival,* is written largely about these indecisive "victor-victim" conflicts in Canadian novels. Such a mood, so largely disseminated through society, does not always make for colourful history. Dennis Lee, in his *Civil Elegies,* studies the curious paralyses of the 1837 rebellion, which took the form of:

... the first
spontaneous mutual retreat in the history of warfare

because the rebels did not believe in the logic of rebellion, and their opponents did not believe in the logic of repression. And today, when not only Quebec but Western and Eastern Canada have strong separatist sentiments, separatism is neutralized by a feeling, affecting separatists and federalists alike, that the issue is not really important enough to go beyond the stage of symbolism. Even symbolism has had a curiously muted life in Canada. Older cultural nationalists, for example, warned us against the danger of "flag-waving," disregarding the fact that Canada at the time had no flag to wave. A Newfoundler told me once that he thought that his people had most in common with the Poles, and like them tended to celebrate defeats rather than victories. This was some years before the publication of Ray Smith's story, "Cape Breton is the Thought Control Centre of Canada," which makes the same point for Canada generally. Certainly Canada has been quite as persistently partitioned throughout most of its history: the penalty it pays for having natural resources.

Then again, a revolutionary tradition is a deductive one: it implies a written constitution, which has to be reinterpreted or amended as time goes on, with major premises about human rights, the sense of a break with the past and of continuity with the future. The United States was fortunate in achieving this articulating process in the eighteenth century, perhaps the only time in Western history when reason looked reasonable. The contemporary Quebec Act was the opposite of all this: it consolidated the past, recognized de facto equality of two groups of people divided by language, legal tradition, and very largely by religion, and made an *ad hoc* settlement on the basis later developed theoretically by Burke, of resolving a conflict by recognizing some of the interests on both sides. It provided no blueprint for an indefinite future: it merely solved one crisis with some hope that it would last until the next one. The two countries, with their national birthdays only two days apart, were born under much the same stars, but have reacted to them very differently. In the United States there has been, until recently, a sense of progressive and linear advance, a progress like that of an express train into a future logically related to the past. Everyone quotes the penultimate sentence in *Huckleberry Finn* about lighting out for the Territory, but less attention is paid to the even more significant last sentence: "I been there before." There can be no creative return to the past: the past is absorbed into the future, or, as Whitman says:

> As a projectile form'd, impell'd, passing a certain line, still keeps on,
> So the present, utterly form 'd, impell'd by the past.

This sense of progress derives from a society which has defined its aims and is aware of its assumptions, and the individual defines himself against that society, usually as some kind of explorer or pioneer, whether the frontier implied is physical or cultural. Canada never defined itself as a unified society in this way: there is no Canadian way of life, no hundred per cent Canadian, no ancestral figures corresponding to Washington or Franklin or Jefferson, no eighteenth-century self-evident certainties about human rights, no symmetrically laid out country. Washington became a capital because it was in the logical place for one, between the north and the south: Ottawa became a capital because it was not Montreal or Kingston. A sardonic commentator, writing in 1868, remarks that its name was obviously derived from "Hoot awa," or out of the way. The Canadian sense of the future tends to be apocalyptic: Laurier's *dictum* that the twentieth century would belong to Canada was, even then, implying a most improbable and discontinuous future. The past in Canada, on the other hand, is, like the past of a psychiatric patient, something of a problem to be resolved: it is rather like what the past would be in the United States if it had started with the Civil War instead of the Revolutionary War.

American culture has followed the western pattern, which grew out of the Biblical rejection of what it called "idolatry," that is, the belief that there was something numinous or potentially divine in the natural world. For the Western tradition, man must seek his God or his ideals through his social institutions. Nature is not to be worshiped or even loved: it is to be dominated. Canada tried hard to follow the same pattern, but its society has been less cohesive, and the individual poet or painter finds that it keeps disintegrating: it is hard for him to visualize either the audience in front of him that he is trying to reach or the audience behind him out of which his imagination has grown. In this situation the natural world keeps pushing insistently through the gaps in the mental society. I see constantly in Canadian culture, more particularly in its poetry, a sense of meditative shock produced by the intrusion of the natural world into the imagination. I say intrusion, because it so often looms up with a greater urgency than the poet's social, political or religious outlook is prepared to allow for.

I imagine that W. L. Morton is right in connecting this sense in Canada with the role of the northern frontier in the Canadian imagination. An American who had never seen the Mississippi would not be regarded as a widely travelled man, at least in his own country; but few

Canadians have ever seen the largest river in Canada, the Mackenzie, and the existence of a vast hinterland which is both a part of us and yet not a part of us creates something curiously self-alienating. Morton says:

> And because of this separate origin in the northern frontier, economy, and approach, Canadian life to this day is marked by a northern quality, the strong seasonal rhythm which still governs even academic sessions... The line which marks off the frontier from the farmstead, the wilderness from the baseland, the hinterland from the metropolis, runs through every Canadian psyche.

The last sentence might be equally true of the psyches in Colorado or Arkansas or Oregon: what is different is that in the United States wilderness and baseland can be assimilated by a uniting consciousness. In Canada the wilderness, symbolized by the north, creates a kind of doppelganger figure who is oneself and yet the opposite of oneself. I remember being at a "church supper" in a rural area of Saskatchewan, and hearing one woman say to another: "you know, this last rain wasn't necessary, in the least." It nearly split my own Canadian psyche to hear, in so middle-class a gathering, the murmur of a timeless peasantry scolding its household gods. But such sudden atavisms are almost a commonplace in Canadian literature, whether the setting is rural or urban.

I have often spoken of the presbyopic sense in Canadian culture, the vast distances of river and sky that confer nobility on faraway looks. Donald Creighton, a great master of Canadian rhetoric, ends the first volume of his biography of John A. MacDonald with this sentence:

> They [the parliament buildings] stood out boldly against the sky; and far behind them, hidden in darkness were the ridges of the Laurentians, stretching away, mile after mile, towards the north-west.

The last sentence of the second volume reads:

> Beyond the dock lay the harbour and the islands which marked the end of the lowest of the Great Lakes; and beyond the islands the St. Lawrence River began its long journey to the sea.

I have previously noted the same perspective in Canadian painters, notably Tom Thomson's canoeist's eye that is continually scanning the horizon for some break into still greater distance. The tree in the centre of Thomson's "West Wind" seems deliberately out of visual focus: the eye is led to something behind it. Yet it seems also to be saying: "Look, I belong here: I'm not just an obstacle on the way to the horizon." It is an emblem of Canada itself, so long apologetic for being so big an obstacle on the way to somewhere more interesting, yet slowly becoming a visible object in its own right.

At the very beginning of Canadian literature in English, we have Frances Brooke's *The History of Emily Montague* (1769), in which the narrator remarks:

> Nothing is, in my opinion, so favourable to the display of beauty as a ball. A state of rest is ungraceful... never any human being had such an aversion to still life as I have.

A very innocent and light-hearted remark; but a great deal of Canadian cultural history is summed up in it: the obsession with movement and transportation, the eye that passes over the foreground object, the restlessness that solves all social difficulties by moving somewhere else, the commitment to a society that involves constant movement up and down an immensely long and narrow corridor. Two centuries later than Emily's proclamation of her aversion to still life, E. J. Pratt wrote a poem called "Still Life" which uses the phrase as a term of contempt for poets who do not deal with the great moving issues of society. It is the only poem of his I know with a real tone of hostility in it. Still later we have Gwendolyn MacEwen, in a poem called "The Portage," commenting on the same feature in the Canadian sensibility:

> But now we fear movement
> and now we dread stillness;
> we suspect it was the land
> that always moved, not our ships...

I spoke of Susanna Moodie and her struggle to maintain the social perspective to which she had become accustomed in the unrelenting surroundings of the Canadian bush. Her sister Catharine Parr Traill is, at least superficially, a more attractive personality, making the best of her hardship and cultivating an interest in the nature around her that makes her a kind of miniature Thoreau, especially in her studies of flowers. She says: "To the person who is capable of looking abroad into the beauties of nature, and adoring the Creator through his glorious works, are opened stores of unmixed pleasure, which will not permit her to be dull or unhappy in the loneliest part of our Western Wilderness." The word "her" is worth pausing on for a moment: it seems to be assumed that a woman's life, however arduous the conditions, will show a relatively civilized balance between work and leisure, whereas the male, whether hunter or fisherman or farmer, will merely oscillate between work and idleness. As an early (1818) writer in Newfoundland remarks: "all ranks of society appear to consider debauchery as the only antidote to the *taedium vitae* which prevails between the month of December and the recommencement of the fishery in the May following." Perhaps we have a clue here to the large proportion of women among the best Canadian writers. Mrs. Traill's capacity for detailed attention to "still life" is exceptional, if not unique, in early Canadian writing: at the same time she sometimes gives the impression of having too fixed a smile, too determined a cheerfulness, too resolute to exclude many things she doesn't want yet knows to be there. One suspects that the two qualities are psychologically close together.

What I mean by a meditative shock produced by the natural world in Canadian poetry is not easy to explain, but some examples may clarify it. Let us first take a passage in Isabella Valancy Crawford's *Malcolm's Katie* (1884) that rather upset E. K. Brown, in his pioneering study of Canadian poetry:

> And Max car'd little for the blotted sun,
> And nothing for the startl'd, outshone stars;
> For Love, once set within a lover's breast,
> Has its own Sun — its own peculiar sky,
> All one great daffodil — on which do lie
> The sun, the moon, the stars — all seen at once...

The metamorphosis of distant nature into a single "great daffodil" inside the mind is a kind of imaginative explosion, in which the overlooked and peripheral suddenly turns into something overmastering and central. Or take Frederick Philip Grove's description of a July storm on the prairies in *The Turn of the Year.* There is a flash of lighting followed by thunder, as there so often is in thunderstorms: nothing really happens, and a minute later a "little girl comes out, barefooted, to splash in the pools." What is left in the narrator's mind is very curious:

> Like a desert of barren snow is my mind, a white blank, stunned into unconsciousness of all things about me. But like a scarlet patch of blood shed on a real snowfield there lies on the white impassive background of my vision the memory of that frightful clap of wrath.

The image has nothing clearly to do with summer storms: it is the central image of Canadian fear and guilt: the blank world of white snow stained with the blood of murdered animals. In Irving Layton's "A Tall Man Executes a Jig," a man watches a wounded grass snake "that lugged / Its intestine like a small red valise." It finally dies, and there follows an extraordinary conclusion:

> Meanwhile the green snake crept upon the sky,
> Huge, his mailed coat glittering with stars that made
> The night bright, and blowing thin wreaths of cloud
> Athwart the moon; and as the weary man
> Stood up, coiled above his head, transforming all.

A poem of James Reaney, "The Heart and the Sun," describes a love affair in which the heart swallows the sun but then dies, the sun escaping with the final remark:

> "Alas my love, it is your fate and mine
> That I someday smother whom I kindle
> And give birth to those I'll someday kill."

In these passages something casual and expected in nature goes through a vortex or gyre into the mind, and creates there a riddle of experience which cannot be assimilated to any set of human and social values. Like the gods of polytheism, it is neither good nor evil, but may be either or both. It is usually an object of involuntary contemplation, something that the mind has not consciously attended to but has forced its way in anyhow. It looks almost as though the fear of still life in the Canadian imagination were a fear of, so to speak, catching Nature's eye, as seen not merely in the eye of a dying animal but in the autumnal blaze of a dying leaf, or even, in Pratt's *Towards the Last Spike,* in the glitter of metals blasted by dynamite out of the pre-Cambrian shield.

The unbroken violation of nature in Canada, the economy founded on the trapping and mutilating of animals, the destroying of trees, the drying up of rivers and the polluting of lakes, began inspiring guilt and uneasiness long before the contemporary ecology movement. In Canadian poetry there is a special pathos in dying animals and falling trees, and in many tragic narratives, such as Duncan Campbell Scott's "At the Cedars" and Birney's *David,* where people are killed in log jams or on glaciers, there is a lurking sense not only of the indifference of nature to man, but almost of its exasperation with this parasite of humanity that has settled on it. In one of Ernest Thompson Seton's[7] stories, a hunter is obsessed with the desire to kill a great mountain ram, simply because it is the most beautiful thing he has ever seen. He finally shoots it; reaction sets in; he cuts the head off and puts it on the wall of his cabin with a curtain over it and sits down to wait for the ram, as he says, to get even. Eventually a landslide buries him and his cabin. Modern ecology-conscious writing like that of Farley Mowat merely puts this conception of the nemesis of nature on a less fanciful basis.

We may also notice how often contemporary poets take the traditional Canadian theme of the identity of the hunter and the hunted, and turn it into the theme of metamorphosis, where the victorious human actually becomes the defeated animal, as in the story of Actaeon. We find this in Margaret Atwood's book of verse, *You Are Happy*, especially in the sequence called "Songs of the Transformed," and the series of "Circe/Mud" poems which follows it. It is also prominent in Gwendolyn MacEwan's *Magic Animals*, in Susan Musgrave's Haida poems, and in the many poems about the descent to the darker levels of one's own consciousness, as in Jay Macpherson's *Welcoming Disaster* and Eli Mandel's Minotaur poems. Every so often this theme manifests the split within the psyche that Morton mentions. The poet becomes both a daylight consciousness and a dark shadow of that consciousness which identifies, very often, with a continuously martyred nature. In Francis Sparshott's remarkable long poem, *Rhetoric for a Divided Voice*, we have a dialogue between two halves of the same person, one questioning, the other more elusive and yet more certain of its knowledge. The part called "Half" says:

> I challenge your world to atone
> For my unmerited pain

and the "Other Half" answers:

> Breath is the wraith of frost,
> And breath drawn into hold
> In the temple of the ghost

---

[7]Ernest Thompson Seton (1860-1946) was a self-educated naturalist respected for his meticulous records on the behaviour of animals and birds. He was also an accomplished illustrator and painter and a writer of animal stories. His numerous works of fiction include the following: *Wild Animals I Have Known*, 1898; *Wild Animal Ways*, 1916; and *Johnny Bear and Other Stories*, 1927.

The marriage of dark and cold.
Deep over hands and head
Welcoming snow is thrown;
Deep over head and hands
To the levelling of broken lands,
To the burial of the dead.

It is perhaps worth noticing that the best piece of science fiction in Canadian literature, James de Mille's *A Strange Manuscript Found in a Copper Cylinder*, not published until 1888 but written much earlier, describes a society dedicated to the opposite of all normal human ideals, to darkness, death, poverty and pain.

One could go on with many other examples, but these should make the point. The Tory opposition to the American way of life, which spoke as often from the left of it as from the right, was a strangled and muted voice as long as the United States was progressing, like Whitman's projectile, in more or less a straight line. Now the United States seems to be entering a period of self-examination of taking a more retrospective look at its past and its traditional assumptions. It is even possible that American development has reached a climax and will see its past and future as more of a parabola. There are of course, many movements of imaginative opposition within American literature itself paralleling the Canadian one. But simultaneously with the growth of a new feeling in the United States, there has been in English-speaking Canada, since about 1960, a great upsurge of creative power, both within the conventional forms of poetry and fiction and outside them. In French Canada the parallel upsurge, though equally remarkable, has taken more explicitly political forms. The Canadian recurring themes of self-conflict, of the violating of nature, of individuals uncertain of their social context, of dark, repressed, oracular doubles concealed within each of us, are now more communicable outside Canada in the new mood of the world. The assumption that exploiting nature is the only way to human advancement has lost much of its authority, and so has the geometry, reflected in the grid patterns of our cities and the like, that has ordered so much of our lives since the eighteenth century. Around 1900 the word "square" was a general term of approval: today it means something we are trying to get away from. I imagine that in another ten years there will be very little difference in tone between Canadian and American literature; but what there is now in Canada is a literature of extraordinary vigor and historical significance.

"National Consciousness in Canadian Culture." First published in *Transactions of the Royal Society of Canada*, 4th series, 14, 1976.

Across the River and Out of the Trees

The first issue of the *University of Toronto Quarterly* appeared in 1931. Its appearance was not exactly a breathtaking novelty: *Queen's Quarterly* and the *Dalhousie Review* were already in existence, and there had even been an earlier version of the *Quarterly* itself. But it was an important historical event none the less. The opening editorial statement attached the journal's traditions firmly to those of the "gentleman's magazine" of the eighteenth and nineteenth centuries. It was not to be a specialized learned journal: there were already enough of those, the editor implied, perhaps meaning that there were too many. Nor was it to be an outlet for creative talent in poetry or fiction: it published a poem or two at the beginning, but apologized editorially for the digression. It tried to cover a broad spectrum of academic interest for a while, but soon restricted itself in effect to the humanities, though it did not acknowledge this by calling itself a "Journal of the Humanities" until some years later. Within a very short time it had inaugurated "Letters in Canada" as an encyclopaedic critique of everything published in Canada, so for all its exclusion of poetry and fiction it clearly had no intention of slighting the Canadian cultural scene, much less ignoring it.

There were some remarkable people first associated with the journal. There was G. S. Brett, the first editor, a philosopher of vast erudition whose *History of Psychology* is still a standard work on the subject. There was E. K. Broadus, one of an extraordinary group of scholars in Alberta, and an early Canadian anthologist. There was Pelham Edgar, interested mainly in what was then contemporary fiction, author of a pioneering work on Henry James, and deeply concerned with Canadian writing as well. There was E. K. Brown, whose book on Canadian poetry was crucial in consolidating the sense of the context and tone of Canadian poetry up to that time. There was Watson Kirkconnell, whose prolific output and fantastic linguistic abilities enabled "Letters in Canada" to include a survey of Canadian writing in languages other than English and French, all of which he could read. A malicious but admiring legend said that when he became President of Acadia he took to shaking hands with his left hand so as not to interrupt his writing. An early issue contained an article by Kirkconnell on "Canada's Leading Poet," who according to Kirkconnell was Stephan Stephansson, a poet living in Manitoba and writing in Icelandic up to his death in 1927.

I was preoccupied with getting through my sophomore year when the *Quarterly* first appeared, and I should perhaps not have been aware of its existence for some time if Brett and Edgar had not been teachers of mine. If I adopt a personal, even to some extent an autobiographical, tone in what follows, the reason is not simple egotism or garrulity: one needs a point of view for a survey, and a personal point of view is the obvious one for a surveyor who has lived entirely within the territory he surveys. In retrospect, *Quarterly*'s early editorial policy decision seem to me to have been prophetic of my own interests in criticism, and objectified much of what I have tried to do since. They also seem to me to mark a most significant cultural change, which was among other things a change in the university's relation to society, and which was already taking place, in Canada as elsewhere.

The learned journals the *UTQ* was separating itself from belonged mainly to the philological tradition, with its headquarters in nineteenth-century Germany, that had dominated American scholarship for half a century. The scholars who wrote in them generally knew the standard classical and modern languages, and for the most part did not include contemporary literature in their purview — at least not as scholars, whatever their general level of cultivation. Their scholarship thus gave the impression of being an activity independent of the creative life of their time. This was particularly true of Canadian scholars in 1930, many of whom had not only moved to Canada from elsewhere but have done much of their seminal work before they arrived. But the number of university people who gathered around *The Canadian Forum,* established in 1920, indicated that other things were happening.

My own college of Victoria had produced a monument of philological scholarship, Andrew Bell's *The Latin Dual and Poetic Diction* (1923), a work so obsessively specialized that the Classicists themselves hardly knew what to do with it. Yet the genial and urbane scholarship of Douglas Bush, another graduate of Victoria, who in his early years was a lively contributor to *The Canadian Forum,* grew directly out of this environment. Edgar's contemporary interests I have noted: he also influenced Brown's interest in twentieth-century American and Canadian writing, besides getting E. J. Pratt into his own English department at Victoria. Pratt was not a "writer in residence," but a full-time teacher until his retirement, and all the more influential as a link between creative and scholarly interests for both students and colleagues. He was portent of the modern university's acceptance of some responsibility for encouraging writers and fostering a discriminating public for them.

In 1930 Canadian literature was still in a provincial state. Pratt and Morley Callaghan had established themselves as twentieth-century writers, and in 1936 a little anthology of six poets, including Pratt, called *New Provinces*, indicated that newer and more contemporary poetic idioms were taking shape. Morley Callaghan's books, I think I am right in saying, were sometimes banned by the public library in Toronto — I forget what the rationalization was, but the real reason could only have been that if a Canadian were to do anything so ethically dubious as write, he should at least write like a proper colonial and not like someone who had lived in the Paris of Joyce and Gertrude Stein. More recent scholarship has revealed that there was a good deal of remarkable, even astonishing, writing produced in Canada before 1930, but a mass of writing with good flashes in it is still not a literature. Articles proclaiming the imminent advent of literary greatness had been appearing for a long time, giving to Canadian literature, or its history, the quality that Milton Wilson[1] has described, in a practically definitive phrase, as "one half-baked phoenix after another."

The excuse normally given for this state of affairs was that Canada was a "young" country, that its priorities had to be material ones, and that literature and the other arts would come along when economic conditions were more advanced. First the primary forms of communication, railways, bridges, canals, then the secondary ones. This argument makes very little sense: seventeenth-century Puritans in Massachusetts wrote poetry and carried on with their pamphlet war against the Anglican establishment. And in a genuinely primitive community, like those of the indigenous peoples, poetry leaps into the foreground as one of the really essential elements of life, along with food and shelter. It was no more "natural," and no more in accord with the historical process, for Canada to build the Victoria bridge or the Welland Canal than to have produced major poets and novelists. But the argument was accepted because it was a mercantilist argument, and was part of Canada's acceptance of its role as a provider of raw materials for manufacture in large centres. The reverse movement of imported goods brought the standard of culture set up in London and Paris back to the boondocks, and efforts were made to imitate them.

In 1930, again, the depression settled into Canadian life, and the depression was also a hampering and delaying influence on culture.

---

[1]Milton Wilson (1923-), a prominent Canadian literary critic and anthologist. He is best known for his essay, "Other Canadians and After," 1958 and for the anthologies *Recent Canadian Verse*, 1959, and *Poets between the Wars*, 1967.

There was not only the difficulty of getting books and pictures marketed (A.Y. Jackson remarked to me some time before his death that he still had guilt feelings when a picture of his sold for more than thirty-five dollars), but a theory of culture developed which was a modified form of mercantilism. According to it the creative person was to produce the raw material of his experience as part of an attempt to affect the ownership of production. There has always been a strong realistic and documentary slant to Canadian writing and painting, for obvious reasons, and this stereotype, after confusing a number of writers and spoiling one or two quite decent painters, hung around for several decades, though it shifted to a more psychological basis in the fifties. Clearly this was still another way of reducing literature to rhetoric, and focusing attention on content, or what a writer thinks he is saying, rather than on what he constructs, or says in spite of himself.

When I was reviewing Canadian poetry in the fifties, I noted the emergence of a curiously interconsistent language of symbolism and imagery among the poets who most obviously knew what they were doing. The language had close affiliations with that of contemporary British and American poets, but was a quite distinctive language, a direct response, as I felt, to an environment that was taking on a new significance for them. I have spoken of what I call a garrison mentality and of the alternating moods of pastoral populism and imaginative terror (which has nothing to do with a poet's feeling terrified) in earlier Canadian writing. These were set up mainly as historical markers, like roadside plaques telling a motorist that something happened here two centuries ago, but they also attempted to define elements in a cultural tradition that was taking clearer shape as the contemporary writing matured. For those who felt that a poet ought primarily to express either sexual passion or social indignation, and was doing so if he said he was loudly enough, my comments on the emergence of a a new variety of symbolic language sounded like a preference for poetry that was academic and inhibited. I myself felt that a quality was forming in Canadian poetry that I could only call professional. I finished my survey in 1960 convinced that Canadian literature was about to become a phoenix again, and a properly cooked one this time.

Well, I think I was right: Canadian literature since 1960 has become a real literature, and is recognized as one all over the world. We are told that there are Canadian authors who sell better in Holland or Germany than they do in their own country — and it has never been fair to say that the Canadian public has ignored its own literature, as far as buying and reading books goes. I doubt if there are any real causes for such a development, but there are some obvious conditioning factors. The Massey Report, published in 1951, was a landmark in the history of Canadian culture, not merely because it recommended a Canada Council, but because it signified the end of cultural *laissez faire* and assumed that the country itself had a responsibility for fostering its own culture. Back in 1930, Pelham Edgar was trying to organize voluntary societies for the relief of indigent authors, and there was an all too frequent assumption that society should concern itself with literature only when it felt like denouncing or censoring it. But the principle of social responsibility was established with the Massey Report, and without that principle Canadian literature would perhaps still be in its nonage. Federal support has been supplemented in the wealthier provinces, to the advantage of all concerned.

In his book *Odysseus Ever Returning* George Woodcock quotes a review by Oscar Wilde in which Wilde praises an American writer for being concerned with the literature he loves rather than the country in which he lives, adding "the Muses care so little for geography." As usual, Wilde's critical instinct is sound: a writer cannot try to be anything except a writer, and a poet must adhere to literature, which is where his technical equipment comes from, not to the false rhetoric of the factitious and the *voulu*. But the last comment seems to me dead wrong. No Muse can function outside human space and time, that is, outside geography and history. Wilde himself owed his whole being as a writer to the tiny area of Anglo-Irish ascendancy which provided his own space and time. So while a Canadian writer may go anywhere and make any sort of statement about the place of Canada in his life, positive or negative, his formative environment and his ability as a writer will be interdependent, however different. Our knowledge of "Canada" is inferred from what for example, Jack Hodgins tells about Vancouver Island or Robertson Davies about southwestern Ontario or Roger Lamelin about the *pente douce* in Quebec City. A writer working outside Canada, like Mavis Gallant, is evidence that Canadian literature is diversified enough to have its expatriates as well, as American literature had its T. S. Eliot and Gertrude Stein.

In an "instant world" of communication, there is no reason for cultural lag or for a difference between sophisticated writers in large centres and naive writers in smaller ones. A world like ours produces a single international style of which all existing literatures are regional developments. This international style is not a bag of rhetorical tricks but a way of seeing and thinking in a world controlled by uniform patterns of technology, and the regional development is a way of escaping from that uniformity. If we read, say, Wilson Harris's *Palace of the Peacock* and then Robert Kroetsch's *Badlands* one after the other, we find that there is no similarity between them, and that one story is steeped in Guyana and the other in Alberta. But certain structural affinities, such as the fold over in time, indicate that they are both products of much the same phase of cultural development.

II

In 1930 native Canadian scholarship in the humanities was spotty, and in a state of uneasy transition from nineteenth- to twentieth-century conceptions of humanism. Within the next twenty years a remarkable change had taken place. In 1950 I had a year off on a Guggenheim Fellowship and went to Harvard, and on my first visit to the bookstores I was startled at the prominence in them of books by my colleagues at home. I knew about the books, naturally, but seeing them in that context was a different experience. There were Cochrane's[2] great book on Christianity and Classical culture, Barker Fairley's[3] second book on Goethe, Kathleen Coburn's[4] edition of Coleridge's *Philosophical Lectures,* F. E. L. Priestley's[5] edition of Godwin's *Political Justice,* my own book on Blake, Woodhouse's[6] edition of the Clark Papers with its epoch-making introduction, Arthur Barker's[7] book on Milton and Puritanism, still standard after nearly forty years — there were several others, but I remember seeing those. Not a bad showing, I thought, for Canadian scholarship with its very inadequate libraries and travel grants (I am speaking of 1950). There were other signs too, like the establishment of the Pontifical Institute of Medieval Studies under

---

[2]Charles N. Cochrane (1889-1945). Author of the influential *Christianity and Classical Culture,* 1940.

[3]Barker Fairley (1887-1986) was one of the foremost German scholars, author of two epoch-making books: *Goethe as Revealed in His Poetry,* 1932, and *A Study of Goethe,* 1947.

[4]Kathleen Coburn (1905-91) is best known for her outstanding work on Coleridge. The first two volumes of *Coleridge's Notebooks* appeared in 1959, the second in 1961, and the third in 1973. She is also general editor of *Coleridge's Collected Works.*

[5]F. E. L. Priestley (1905-88), Professor Emeritus, University of Toronto, author of *Language and Structure in Tennyson's Poetry,* 1973, and editor of *John Stuart Mill 1806-1873,* 1963.

[6]A. S. P. Woodhouse (1895-1965) was one of Canada's leading literary critics, an influential teacher and a passionate humanist. His best-known works are *Puritanism and Liberty,* 1938, and "The Argument of Milton's Comus," 1941.

[7]Arthur E. Barker (1911-90). Author of *Milton and the Puritan Dilemma,* 1942.

Gilson,[8] which indicated that Canadian scholarship in the humanities had become a genuine presence in the world. The scholarship had come to maturity rather earlier than the literature, and the fact nagged my subconscious for the next decade.

The expansion of scholarly activity represented by the setting up of the "Letters in Canada" column of *University of Toronto Quarterly* meant that some scholarship, at least, was becoming assimilated to reviewing, even to journalism. And this kind of criticism has been traditionally regarded as a subordinate, even a parasitic activity. It was recognized that writers needed honest and informed criticism, but such criticism was the blest office of the epicene, of the bee who carries the pollen for the flower but does not fertilize it himself. I felt when criticism and scholarship were the same activity (and an academic critic surely ought to apply the same principles to whatever he writes about) this parasitic relation to the writer disappeared. The academic critic is primarily concerned with the expansion of knowledge and sensitivity rather than with evaluation and "maintaining standards," which the writer must meet or else. He and the writer represent rather, I thought, the theory and practice respectively of the same activity. That did not mean, and could never possibly mean, that the critic's function was to influence the poet or tell him how he should write or what he should write about. But I felt that poetry and criticism, *Dichtung* and *Wahrheit,* imaginative expression and conceptual expression, were linked on equal terms in a dialectical relationship none the less, whenever they appeared in the same culture.

It was clear that to follow up this conviction one would need to expand and redefine the conception of criticism. If I was right, what I said would be confirmed by the cultural developments taking place around me. Matthew Arnold, in his essay on "The Function of Criticism at the Present Time" and elsewhere, had spoken of the essential role of criticism in the maturing of a culture, from which the poet would directly benefit. But he also assumed that the critical faculty was "lower" than the creative one, and I felt that this Romantic baggage of high and low metaphors was getting to be a nuisance. Some of my colleagues, notably A. S. P. Woodhouse, were absorbed by a scholarly interest to which they gave the name "history of ideas." It seemed to me

---

[8]Étienne Gilson (1884-1978) helped found the Institute of Medieval Studies at St. Michael's College, University of Toronto, and was appointed its first director in 1928. In 1939 the Institute was given a charter from the Vatican and became the separate Pontifical Institute of Medieval Studies. His influential books in the field of Medieval philosophy include *The Spirit of Medieval Philosophy,* 1936, and *History of Medieval Philosophy in the Middle Ages,* 1955.

that these "ideas" were really elements or units in what Tillyard[9] calls a world picture, the conceptual aspect of a kind of cosmology of imagery and metaphor that every poet who works on a large scale seems to work with, and that seems to preserve its main outlines for centuries, however much it may alter in detail from one age to another. Earlier poets could take such a world picture for granted, as something already formed by religious and political thought. In such passages as Ulysses' speech on degree in *Troilus and Cressida* we glimpse something of a framework of theoretical assumptions that Shakespeare depended on his audience's possessing. But these traditional frameworks had largely collapsed by the end of the eighteenth century, and new poetic structures would need new conceptual ones. Hence when Arnold spoke of "criticism," he meant partly what was traditionally meant by that word, but he was also speaking of something new, something just coming into being that had barely taken form in his day.

Reviewing, of which I did a good deal in the fifties, is a hermeneutic activity, which means that it is a form of writing in which understanding and the articulating of that understanding become the same thing. It is also a species of translation: the poet writes in a specific language of symbolism, myth, imagery and metaphor, and the reviewer renders that language in a different conceptual framework. Literature is one of the practical imaginative arts: criticism is one of the scholarly areas loosely called the humanities. It was clear that a great deal of shifting and regrouping of forces in the humanities was taking place. Toronto has always emphasized the importance of undergraduate teaching, and the undergraduate teaching of English literature is a very large activity, as it will be for the foreseeable future. But literary scholarship was beginning to resemble the well-known caterpillar, staring at a butterfly and saying "you'll never catch me going up in one of those things." As a student in the early thirties I had had to answer vague examination questions about a writer's "style;" as a teacher in the early forties I had to learn something quite specific about stylistic and rhetorical devices. No colleague or student of Woodhouse could avoid the challenge of the fact that history and philosophy were not just "background" for literature but were an essential part of literary criticism itself. Writers beyond the Toronto horizon at that time told me that anthropology and psychology were no less relevant.

---

[9]E. M. W. Tillyard (1889-1962), British literary critic and editor, best known for his study of English Renaissance sensibility. His books include *Elizabethan World Picture*, 1943, *The English Renaissance*, 1952 and *The Metaphysicals and Milton*, 1956.

The question then arose, what was this larger body of criticism of which literary criticism, as traditionally practiced, seemed to be forming a smaller and smaller part? It was evidently something like "human science" of the kind adumbrated by Dilthey[10] and others, but its total shape was still vague. The social scientists would have nothing to do with the suggestion that they were the applied humanities, nor did psychologists and anthropologists take much interest in the kind of use literary critics made of their material. I was aware of the rapid rise and influence of linguistics, especially synchronic linguistics, but, in striking contrast to the humane flexibility of nineteenth-century philology, linguistics was still a somewhat sectarian activity, not greatly interested even in literature, which it sometimes seemed almost to regard as a disease of language. But other movements were overriding this attitude, if I am right in thinking it existed. Gadamer,[11] who is naturally thinking in a German context, says that the modern hermeneutic attitude, based on identifying *intelligere* and *explicare,* was established by the Romantic philosophers following Kant, and he adds that the effect of this was to move language from the periphery into the centre of the human science. It was not until mid-sixties, with the rise of European structuralism and the conception of the "linguistic model," that I began to see something of the shape of what was emerging, and to see also where such figures as Wittgenstein and Heidegger belonged in the pattern. I am not sure how deeply Canadian criticism even yet has been affected by these developments: Dennis Lee's *Savage Fields* is an example of a critical approach that one hopes will soon be less exceptional. But I did learn three things of relevance to this question while writing about Canadian culture. One came from the editorial committee that had gathered under Carl Klinck to plan the *Literary History of Canada.* It was obvious to all of us from the start that a history of what would conventionally be called Canadian literature would be an utterly pointless cream-skimming operation. The book had to be an exhaustive survey of writing in Canada, whatever the subject written about, if the real "literary" element in Canadian culture was to be captured. The second came from the fact that I was drawing support and suggestions and in-

[10]Wilhelm Dilthey (1833-1911), German philosopher whose numerous contributions to the history of Western civilization belong among the classics of historical analysis and literary criticism.

[11]Hans-Georg Gadamer, German philosopher and author of numerous books and essays, is best known for his contribution to the study of hermeneutics in philosophy. His *Hegel's Dialectics: Five Hermeneutical Studies,* 1976, is available in English translation.

sights from such writers as George Grant, Abraham Rotstein, Carl Berger, Frank Underhill, who represented a great variety of academic "disciplines," but whose writing I could not think of as anything but Canadian "criticism." The third came from my personal knowledge of Canadian scholars, such as the authors of the books I saw at Harvard. I could not feel that their scholarship would have been exactly the same wherever they lived. I knew that my own interest in Blake had been sparked by the way he made imaginative sense out of the Nonconformist attitude that I had been brought up in myself. And whenever a Canadian scholar makes a personal statement, as, say, Kathleen Coburn does in her autobiography, *In Pursuit of Coleridge,* it becomes clear that scholarship, no less than poetry, grows out of a specific environment and is in part a response to it.

It is no great credit to me that I entirely missed the significance, at the time, of the later work of Harold Innis, which appeared around 1950-52. I found the prose style impenetrable and the subject matter uncongenial. But, of course, as is widely recognized now, Innis was defining a central issue in the Canadian imagination which ultimately affected the interest of practically everyone concerned with words. Innis had first, as an economist, studied the fur trade and the fishing industry, and had gained from that study a vision of the "Laurentian" centrifugal economic development of the country, with the traders and trappers fanning out from the Great Lakes into the far north. This in turn provided him with the underlying pattern of the primary modes of communication in Canada, the network of railways and canals mentioned above. After that, he asked himself the fateful question: "O. K., what happens next?" This took him into a panoramic vision of secondary communication through words, as conveyed by papyrus, paper, parchment, clay bricks, manuscripts, books and newspapers. He saw that verbal communication was an essential instrument of power, and that an ascendant class will naturally try to control and monopolize it. In *Empire and Communication,* and in the more accessible essays in *The Bias of Communication,* he sketched the outlines of a philosophy of history, based on the theme of the production and the control of the means of communication, on a scale as comprehensive, at least potentially, as anything since Marx. Like Marx, too, he left a large mass of *Grundrisse* to be published after his death.

Innis's influence, in Canada as elsewhere, will grow steadily, because with practice in reading him he becomes constantly more suggestive and rewarding. He was a curiously tentative writer, which may account for something of his rather spastic prose rhythms. He saw that every new form or technique generates both a positive impulse to exploit it and a negative impulse, especially strong in universities, to resist it, and that the former of course always outmanoeuvres the latter. But he had something of what I call the garrison mentality in him, the university being still his garrison for all the obscurantism in it that he comments on so dryly. Perhaps it is not possible to hold a vision of that scope and range steadily in one's mind without a more passionate commitment to society as well as to scholarship.

Marshall McLuhan, a literary critic interested originally in Elizabethan rhetoric and its expression in both oral and written forms, followed up other issues connected with the technology of communication, some of them leads from Innis. His relation to the public was the opposite of Innis's: he was caught up in the manic-depressive roller coaster of the news media, so that he was hysterically celebrated in the sixties and unreasonably neglected thereafter. It is likely that the theory of communications will be the aspect of the great critical *pot-pourri* of our time which will particularly interest Canadians, and to which they will make their most distinctive contribution. So it is perhaps time for a sympathetic rereading of *The Gutenberg Galaxy* and *Understanding Media* and a reabsorption of McLuhan's influence, though no adequate treatment of this topic can be attempted here.

I have often noted that many nineteenth-century writers in Canada, especially poets, spoke in what could be called, paraphrasing the title of Francis Sparshott's remarkable poem, the rhetoric of a divided voice. Up above was vigor and optimism and buoyancy and all the other qualities of life in a new land with lots of natural resources to exploit; underneath were lonely, bitter, brooding visions of cruelty without and despair within. This division in tone is still in Pratt, in a different way, and can even be traced in later writers, such as Layton, though the context naturally changes. It is by no means confined to Canada, as a reading of Whitman would soon show, but it is traditional here. McLuhan put a similar split rhetoric into an international context. On top was a breezy and self-assured butterslide theory of Western history, derived probably from a Chestertonian religious orientation, according to which medieval culture has preserved a balanced way of life that employed all the senses, depended on personal contact, and lived within "tribal," or small community units. Since then we have skittered down a slope into increasing specialization (McLuhan defines the specialist as the man who never makes a minor mistake on his way to a major fallacy), a self-hypnotism from concentrating on the visual stimuli of print and mathematics, a dividing and subdividing of life into separated "problems," and an obsession with linear advance also fostered by print and numbers. The electronic media, properly understood and manipulated, could reverse the direction of all this. Below was a horrifying vision of a global village, at once completely centralized and completely decentralized, with all its senses assailed at once, in a state of terror and anxiety at once stagnant and chaotic, equally a tyranny and an anarchy. His phrase "defense against media fallout" indicated this direction in his thought.

In the sixties both the anti-intellectuals, who wanted to hear that they had only to disregard books and watch television to get with it, and the "activists" pursuing terror for its own sake, found much to misunderstand in McLuhan. Many of his theses involved research in linguistics, anthropology, sensory psychology and economics which has still to be done or established even in those fields, and his recurring tendency to determinism involved him in prophecies not borne out by events. Media may be hot or cool, but societies do not turn hot or cool in consequence of adopting them. Canada is a cool country with cool people in it, hence all its media are cool. But McLuhan raised questions that are deeply involved in any survey of contemporary culture, and in any attempt to define the boundaries of the emerging theory of society that I call "criticism" in its larger context.

Meanwhile Canada's own involvement with new media, more particularly film and radio, had been a decisive influence in maturing the culture of the country and giving it a place in the international scene. I have no space or expertise to tell the story of the golden age of the NFB and CBC radio in the forties and early fifties. That has been done before, and it is generally recognized that film and radio are the media of much of the best work produced in Canadian culture. The benefits extended into literature, through radio plays and such programmes as *Anthology,* and Andrew Allan and Robert Weaver[12] are names of the same kind of significance in Canadian writing that publishers like William Briggs[13] had in the nineteenth century. Radio also influenced, I think, the development of a more orally based poetry, more closely related to recitation and a listening audience, and popular in a way that poetry had not been for many centuries. As I write this, an anthology of "sound texts" comes in, poems based on sound and removed from ordinary

---

[12]Robert Weaver (1921-) is identified with a popular radio program, "Anthology," begun in 1953, which introduced Canadians to their current literary production. In addition, he has been a prominent anthologist of Canadian short fiction. He has published, for Oxford, three volumes: *Canadian Short Stories: First Series,* 1960, *Second Series,* 1968 and *Third Series,* 1978.

[13]William Briggs (1836-1922), prominent Toronto publisher and promoter of Canadian writing in the closing decades of the nineteenth century. Literary works — especially poetry — by such writers as William Kirby, Charles Mair, Charles G. D. Roberts and others appeared under his imprint.

syntax, and I notice that Canadian poets are deeply involved in this movement.

But there were difficulties that the coming of television made painfully obvious. These three new media, film, radio and television, are mass media, and consequently follow the centrifugal and imperial rhythms of politics and economics more readily than the regionalizing rhythms of culture. This was not too crucial a problem for CBC radio, though it was certainly there, but the NFB had to struggle with problems of distribution created by the fact that movie houses had been monopolized by American syndicates. I remember a *Spring Thaw* skit which was a takeoff of on an NFB film, ending with the line "on view in your local Sunday-School basement." So when television came the government passed a Broadcasting Act and set up the CRTC as a regulating agency for both radio and television, and both private and subsidized networks. I became an advisory member of the CRTC in 1968, when the Broadcasting Act still made a good deal of sense. The feeling was that the distribution of books, newspapers, movies and magazines had been very largely sold out to American interests, and that if television were the same way there would be no Canadian identity left.

For the next decade what seemed like a completely autonomous technological development started to explode: microwave, cable, satellite, and now a metamorphosis of pay-TV. It was not autonomous, of course, but Canadian identity, in that area, began to look as desperate as a Spartan at Thermopylae. Nor could a regulating agency even count on the support of public opinion: Canada was, in the stock phrase, "flooded with American programmes," it was clear that the majority of Canadians preferred the flood to any Canadian ark that would float above it. Further, television is expensive to produce, and there have been many complaints that not only the CBC but the educational stations set up by the wealthier provinces have become mired in real estate, bureaucracy, and vested interests. Many viewers living in or near Toronto say that they cling to the PBS station in Buffalo, looking for a standard of programming from it that they no longer expect from Canadian sources, and some of them, noting the frequent PBS appeals for money, draw the inference that limited funds may be a stimulus of livelier thinking. The provinces are demanding a larger share of control of communications, but their motives for doing so are not cultural ones.

So a "mass culture" which follows expanding economic rather than regionalizing rhythms complicates the situation I have been outlining very considerably. Certainly there is much in it at present which is not Canadian in any sense and expresses very little creative energy. On the other hand all the mass media seem to have an entire cultural history to recapitulate, from the most archaic crudity to the greatest technical, and eventually creative, sophistication. There are still bad movies and dull radio programs, just as there are still bad books, but a listener to FM radio today or a moviegoer is a long way from the world of Amos and Andy or the Keystone Cops. Television is more frustrating and is still largely formulaic, but it too seems to be maturing in obedience to an inner process of development. I think the inherent tendency of television, as of film and radio, is to decrease the distinction between highbrow and lowbrow listeners, and within its widening central area of appeal to find more room for a greater variety of tastes.

In the sixties a resistance movement against the mass culture of (mainly) television grew up in the United States, and the magic word that explained everything that was then going on in this area was the word "sub-culture." But a sub-culture, whether its interest was in rock or drugs or meditation, showed a strong tendency to become mass news, featured on television networks or being reflected in fashion advertising. In other words these sub-cultures seemed to be really specialized forms of mass culture. Perhaps genuine culture is also the genuine form of subculture. No matter how complex the technical means of communication, the elements communicated are still words, tones, and images, the same elements that have been around since the earliest stone age. And I feel there is hope that the genuine article will continue, quietly but persistently and increasingly, to filter through the new technology.

"Across the River and Out of the Trees" in: *University of Toronto Quarterly*, Vol. 50, No. 2, fall, 1980.

Culture and Society in Ontario, 1784-1984

Most of the cultural factors that exist in Canada as a whole also exist in Ontario in a reduced but identical form. Geographical displacement is the most obvious. The entire province is half as large again as Texas, but most of its people are huddled near the American border, in a territory no larger than Michigan. The hinterland in the north has been explored by painters, but in this paper I have time and space only for the literary aspect of Ontario culture, and northern Ontario does not seem as yet to have found a Rudy Wiebe[1] to interpret it. The chief exception, so far as I know, is Wayland Drew's[2] remarkable but rather neglected story *The Wabeno Feast*, and Drew has also written essays on what this vast territory ought to be contributing to our imaginations. It is a type of irony familiar in the modern world that in most respects it is easier to get from Toronto to Moscow or Tokyo than to get to Moosonee, at the other end of the province. It may be an irony more typical of Ontario that it seems to be easier to get into a genuine social contact with Asians or Africans than with the indigenous peoples. The impact of native Indian consciousness on white settlers has been remarkably narcissistic: Pauline Johnson was very much a whitecomer's Indian, and when Grey Owl turned out to be an Englishman obsessed with noble-savage ideology he repeated a pattern set up in Ontario's earliest historical novel *Wacousta*, where the allegedly Indian hero is actually a rejected suitor of the heroine's mother, back in Great Britain.

In the nineteenth century the central activity was the clearing of the land for farming. "Clearing" meant for the most part cutting down

---

[1]Rudy Wiebe (1934-), Professor Emeritus of English and Creative Writing, University of Alberta, and author of numerous works of fiction, including such well-known novels as *Peace Shall Destroy Many*, 1962, and *The Temptations of Big Bear*, 1973.

[2]Wayland Drew (1932-), author of a single novel, *The Wabeno Feast*, 1973, in which the relation between contemporary life and Algonquin native customs is explored.

trees, the trees being regarded not as a potential resource but simply as obstacles. Catharine Parr Traill remarks in her *Backwoods of Canada*:

> Man appears to contend with the trees of the forest as though they were his most obnoxious enemies; for he spares neither the young sapling in its greenness nor the ancient trunk in its lofty pride; he wages war against the forest with fire and steel.

Anna Jameson[3] makes the same observation, but carries it a step further:

> A Canadian settler hates a tree, regards it as his natural enemy, as something to be destroyed, eradicated, annihilated, by all and any means... [She goes on to say that there are two ways of killing a tree, by burning it and by draining the sap out of it.] Is not this like the two ways in which a woman's heart may be killed in this world of ours — by passion and by sorrow?

Leaving this terrifying remark to speak for itself for the moment, we note that clearing the forest means, among other things, a slaughter of the animals who are thereby made homeless. Here is Samuel Strickland, the male literary representative of that celebrated family:

> The deer are not now (1853) nearly so numerous as they formerly were... To give my readers some idea how plentiful these wild denizens of the forest were some years since, I need only mention that a trapper with whom I was acquainted, and four of his companions, passed my house on a small raft on which lay the carcasses of thirty-two deer — the trophies of a fortnight's chase near Stoney Lake. The greater number of these were fine bucks. I once had seventeen deer hanging up in my barn at one time — the produce of three days' sport, out of which I had the good fortune to kill seven... I do not know anything more pleasant than these excursions... This is one of the great charms of Canadian life, particularly to young sportsmen from the Mother Country, who require here neither licence nor qualifications to enable them to follow their game; but may rove in chase of deer or other game at will.

There are any number of ways in which such activities can be defended or rationalized; but to begin one's culture by severing so many

---

[3]Anna Brownell Jameson (1794-1860), wife of a colonial official stationed in Toronto, was a distinguished writer and art critic whose *Winter Studies and Summer Rambles*, 1838, provides an early, sharply observed account of Toronto's colonial life.

links with nature and the earlier inhabitants poses the most formidable problems for its development. As Anna Jameson suggests, can one really destroy so many trees without stunting and truncating human lives as well? I have often had occasion to notice the curiously powerful resonance that the killing of animals has for Canadian writers: Irving Layton invests the death even of a mosquito with dignity. Among Ontario writers, we notice how the action in Margaret Atwood's *Surfacing* is directed toward reversing the current of the destroying and polluting of nature: the heroine, searching for what is both her father and the as yet unspoiled source of Canadian life, wants "the borders abolished... the forest to flow back into the place his mind cleared." Al Purdy's "The Death of Animals," a very intricate and subtle poem among many of his that deal with similar themes, shows us how the real horror in man's attitude to nature is not so much deliberate cruelty as total indifference, a feeling that man and nature have no life in common whatever:

> When mouse died, a man coughed, stirred,
> Went to the bathroom. No connection, of course.
> When the lady slit her lover's throat with a nail file,
> The owl was already dead. Again, no connection.
> Fox screamed, but the lady with lacquered nails
> Already owned a fur coat. No real connection.
> Deer died later of a bullet wound, having trailed
> A broken leg through miles of red snow...
> What's the point of all this? None at all, really.

It is also Purdy who, in "Watching Trains," depicting some Indian boys staring at a railway train, shows us, without wasting a syllable on moralizing, an abyss between two ways of life too wide even for conflict: the boys might as well be on a different planet, as in some respects they are. And I doubt if any other book on the First World War calls our attention more distinctly to the suffering of animals than Timothy Findley's *The Wars,* when describing a situation in which men have started to treat each other the way they have always treated wild animals. The slaughter of animals, so often ignored as a feature of war, is one of the major element in the demoralizing of the hero, and toward the end of the book we have a description of a mare and a dog, mute and helpless victims in a nightmare, and remember that this episode is repeated verbatim from the opening page, as a central emblem of the story.

It is often said that if it hadn't been for Niagara Falls, Ontario would have been a most idyllic and pastoral community. Of course the sense of something idyllic and peaceful represents only a pause, a sort of plateau, in the "clearing" of nature. Technology, however, is a second twist in the destruction of so many of its features, and the cultural opposition to it is vocal and versatile. Lampman's poem "The City of the End of Things" is a familiar example, as is Grove's late Ontario novel *The Master of the Mill*, where the theme is mechanophobia hitched to a sorcerer's apprentice myth, the mill compulsively continuing to grind flour after the world has been smothered with it. George Grant's *Technology and Empire* approaches a similar theme philosophically. Canada, as I have often had occasion to remark, missed out on eighteenth-century enlightenment, and has no counterparts to such cultural heroes as Jefferson and Franklin. But, as Grant insists, it did participate, very fully, in the Hegelian antithesis that the enlightenment turned into, the oligarchic exploiting of the country. It is probably Grant's influence that lies behind the sombre brooding opening poem of Dennis Lee's *Civil Elegies:*

> Buildings oppress me, and the sky-concealing wires
> bunch zigzag through the air. I know
> the dead persist in
> buildings, by-laws, porticos — the city I live in
> is clogged with their presence, they
> dawdle about in our lives and form a destiny, still
> incomplete, still dead weight, still
> demanding whether Canada will be.

Marshall McLuhan is often regarded as a prophet on the opposite side, but actually he thought of the coming of electronic media as bringing about a political reversal of development from technological imperialism back to a new form of tribalism, and was sustained by that belief as long as it was possible for him to hold it. No one has spoken more strongly of the dehumanizing effects of technology than he has:

> When the perverse ingenuity of man has outered some part of his being in material technology, his entire sense ratio is altered. He is then compelled to behold this fragment from himself "closing itself as in steel" [the quotation is from Blake]. In beholding this new thing, man is compelled to become it.

The question that this paper faces me with is one that I have never dealt with in depth, and trying to cut through the jungle of jargon in contemporary critical theory will give one no help whatever. The question is this: when a new society begins to develop some cultural interest, that culture is bound to be, for some time, a provincial culture — I am not using this as a putdown term but as a characterizing one. After a culture has matured, it begins to show a decentralizing movement, as more and more commitments become articulate through the writers that grow up in them. For about 150 of the 200 years I am considering, Ontario had mainly a provincial culture, and a rather sparse one at that. For the last 25 years, at least, with the writers I have mentioned and others I have still to mention, it has had a regional culture, and a remarkably rich and varied one. Obviously there are affinities as well as contrasts between the provincial and the regional: what are they, and how does one get from one to the other? The central social process at work is the shift from a rural-based to an urban-based lifestyle, but the cultural changes accompanying this must involve more complex factors than that. I should say at once that I am not going to solve this question, merely to raise it, along with a few suggestions that I hope will be useful.

I arrived in Toronto to take up what turned out to be permanent residence there, in September of 1929. Toronto was then mainly a quiet Scotch-Irish town, its Yonge Street a curious mixture of an English midland and a middle-west American appearance, both of them deceptive. It was English midland in its array of second-hand bookshops and small grocery or butcher shops, with what appeared to be practically live rabbits hanging from the ceiling. The mean architecture, the grid plan, and the uniformity of the drug stores and branch movie houses were middle-western American features. It was a homogeneous city, with very little of the ethnical mix that Montreal and Winnipeg had: perhaps this is connected with the fact that the Jewish community in Toronto did not make the impressive contribution to Canadian literature that its counterparts in the other two cities did.

Toronto's spiritual life began on Saturday evening, where many downtown corners had a preaching evangelist, and continued through Sunday, a day of rest of a type I have never seen paralleled except in Israeli Sabbaths. One could then learn from a celebrated preacher that God was in his heaven and that the only events that bothered him were produced by the machinations of the Roman Catholic hierarchy. The Orange Order kept a firm grip on municipal government, demonstrating Communists, who began to appear in the depression, went to jail with broken heads, and, in imitation of the United States, the word ethic had expanded to the point of making any form of alcoholic drink illegal, drinking being bad for working-class morale. Outside Toronto there was a good deal of ridicule of "Hogtown's" somnolence and sexual prudery. It is still true that Ontario gives too much authority to censors, originally out of panic, though the real reason now is probably that censoring is a genuinely popular sport, with many votes to be got out of it. Even so, prudery in Ontario at its worst is mild enough compared to what one would find in Islamic or most Communist countries today.

What one noticed at once was the curious double-think about the loyalty to the British connection. There had been a good deal of resentment in the nineteenth century about some of the more spectacular ineptnesses of British colonial rule, and its obviously greater respect for American than for Canadian interests. One might have expected the aftermath of the First World War to have weaned Canada from much of its colonial fixation, the casualties being so hideously large in proportion to the population of the country. A holocaust is not less a holocaust for being a voluntary one. George Grant, speaking of Canada after 1918, says: "Those who returned did not have the vitality for public care, but retreated into the private world of money-making." Yet this was mainly imitative of American life in the twenties, where the Republicans, who thought of a president as an idol carried in the processions of big business, had a permanent majority. The imperialism which thought of Canada as one more exit from the globe-girdling highway of the British Empire was already in decline: its epitaph had been written, though few realized it at the time, in Sara Jeanette Duncan's *The Imperialist* (1904), where one of the main characters, an earnest but fairly articulate bore, keeps flogging what is clearly the very dead horse of "imperial federation."

So by 1929 the loyalty to the British connection in Ontario began to have a suspiciously vociferous quality to it: obviously it masked the fact that Canada was rapidly ceasing to be a British colony and was becoming an American one. A few years later, Frank Underhill said this openly, and the furor that resulted showed, first, that he had hit a social neurosis squarely in the bullseye, and, second, that is a genuine necessity for academic freedom, even though he left the university early to disappear into the civil-service vortex in Ottawa. I remember that the fiercest condemnation of Underhill I heard came from Charles G. D. Roberts, who had spent much of his productive career in the United States, but had received a new lease of imperial loyalty along with his knighthood.

And yet the ignoring of Canada by Americans effectively prevented much loyalty from going in that direction. American arrogance was all the more galling in that it was so largely unconscious. Apart from a few Fenians,[4] who, like the murderers of the Donnellys,[5] had brought their

---

[4]Fenians were members of a movement initiated in 1857 by Irish-Americans to secure Irish independence from Britain. It was a powerful organization, with

feuds from Ireland with them, there was little awareness in the United States that a different country bounded them on the north. In the year 1826 the citizens of Ancaster were insulted by a travelling American exhibition showing a diorama of the glorious American victory over the British at New Orleans ten years earlier. Doubtless, like their descendants today, the showmen had forgotten or never realized that the war that ended at New Orleans had begun with an invasion of Upper Canada.

It was much more important, of course, that in proportion as the United States began to exert its strength as a world power, the continentalism of the Liberals, as expressed in the later Underhill and elsewhere, began to look increasingly reactionary. Nineteenth-century Canadian critics of the American way of life had tended to attack from both the right and left, criticizing the absence of social standards in American democracy but also reflecting on the gross inequalities, including the retention of slavery in the South, in American oligarchy. In the depression the new CCF party, which hoped to become the Labour Party of Canada and force the Conservatives and the Liberals to unite against them, represented a new kind of British-centered ideology. The British model faded along with the party, but an uneasy kind of Tory and radical mixture, expressed in very different ways by Donald Creighton, George Grant and Dave Godfrey,[6] continues the fight to try to define just what kind of social contract Canada in general, and Ontario in particular, does have to hold it together. The fight has not been made any easier by the more childish aspects of French separatism, which tend to divide the continent into Quebec and the United States.

With so much agreement that Ontario probably does not exist, it is hardly surprising that earlier studies of its culture, such as E. K. Brown's *On Canadian Poetry* (1943), should have expressed some wonder, not that it had a provincial culture, but that it had any at all. Tracing the criticism of Canadian literature back into the nineteenth

---

10,000 American Civil War veterans organized in military clubs. One section of the movement, led by John O'Mahony, favoured attacking Canada. The first attack, against the New Brunswick frontier in 1866, was unsuccessful, as were subsequent incursions across the border into Ontario and Manitoba.

[5]The Donnellys, of the village of Lucan, Ontario, were brutally murdered in 1880 by a group of men later brought to trial and acquitted. The killings were the result of a feud that had begun in Ireland three decades earlier.

[6]Dave Godfrey (1938-), co-founder of one of Canada's most important literary presses, House of Anansi, 1966, and author of a collection of short stories, *Death Goes Better with Coca-Cola*, 1967, and a novel, *The New Ancestors*, 1970.

century, it is extraordinary to find so unflaggingly persistent a desire to produce a literature, so constant a hope that a few contemporary seeds will burgeon into a bumper crop. The desire and the hope were genuinely heroic, and right in that our provincial heritage has become an essential cultural asset, not something to repudiate or get away from. The continuity between provincial and regional literature is primary: if we understand something of that, most of the differences will fall into line. An English friend once remarked to me that a Canadian's conversational opening gambit seemed to be invariably "Where you from?" Two of our most memorable novels, Margaret Atwood's *Surfacing* and Margaret Laurence's *The Diviners*, trace the development of their heroines backward to its source, in an effort to answer the same question to the satisfaction of the heroine herself. But novels are Ontario-based, even though one heads east to Quebec and the other west to Manitoba. Often such a journey to the source includes the cultural sources. Margaret Atwood's *Journals of Susanna Moodie* indicate how creative an act it can be to absorb and exploit one's own cultural tradition, and Susanna's sister Catharine Parr Traill plays a significant role at the end of *The Diviners*.

These two novels employ, in reverse, the commonest formula of Canadian fiction, the *Bildungsroman*. The theme of "How I Grew Up in Zilch Corners" is inevitable for the young writer who as yet knows nothing except his own impressions, and of course the great bulk of all writing, in every age, consists of filling up prescribed and fashionable conventions. You will note that I fell into the idiom myself a moment ago. Even so, the theme seems to have an unusual intensity for Ontario writers: the best and most skilful of them, including Robertson Davies and Alice Munro, continue to employ a great deal of what is essentially the Stephen Leacock *Mariposa* theme, however different in tone. Most such books take us from the first to the second birth of the central character. Childhood and adolescence are passed in a small town or village, then a final initiation, often a sexual one, marks the entry into a more complex social contract.

In Ontario literature the large proportion of women writers comes out of a tradition established at the very beginning of settlement. It was not that nineteenth-century women had any more leisure than their husbands, or that the physical effort involved in the work they did was less intense. But they did have a more creative notion of what to do with the leisure they had: we may compare Samuel Strickland's three-day-orgy of deer-killing with his sister Catherine's delighted discoveries of new plants and birds in her environment. The Strickland sisters worked mainly in a genre which had an actual market, of sorts: diaries, journals, reminiscences aimed, not at readers in Ontario, but at prospective immigrants "back home." We owe many of our clearest insights into the social and cultural development of the country to such work. Very occasionally we see some awareness of its function: thus Anne Langton,[7] writing in 1840:

> ... The bride looked much better than on ... her first appearance. Her dress was of another shade, richer than the former. I think it would have stood erect by itself ... If the follies and extravagances of the world are to be introduced upon Sturgeon Lake, we might as well, I think, move on to Galt Lake. I am afraid women deteriorate in this country more than the other sex. As long as the lady is necessarily the most active member of her household she keeps her ground from her utility; but when the state of semi-civilization arrives, and the delicacies of her table, and the elegancies of her person become her chief concern and pride, then she must fall, and must be contended to be looked upon as belonging merely to the decorative department of the establishment and valued accordingly.

The woman who loses her commanding position in a household to become part of the furniture is familiar enough today: in the literature we are considering, the dead end of the process is reached by the heroine of Margaret Atwood's *The Edible Woman,* the victim of a cellophane-wrapped consumerism. It is more common, however, for Canadian fiction writers to feature the woman who is determined to hold on to that commanding position even after her real function is past. Male-dominated societies are constantly turning into matriarchies and vice versa, and some reflection of this is perhaps what has produced the literary convention described, again, by Margaret Atwood in *Survival*:

> If you trusted Canadian fiction you would have to believe that most of the women in the country with any real presence at all are over fifty, and a tough, sterile, suppressed and granite-jawed lot they are. They live their lives with intensity, but through gritted teeth.

One of the earliest of such women, though not one she mentions, is the mother of the heroine of Raymond Knister's novel, *White Narcissus* (1929), a book I shall come to again in a moment. This is a story of how a young man's love for a young woman is frustrated by the latter's parents, who are emotional vampires sucking all the life out of her. They are feuding with each other for some reason, communicate only

---

[7]Anne Langton, aunt of Hugh Hornby Langton (1862-1953), was a prominent historian and librarian. Her letters and journals were published under the title *A Gentlewoman in Upper Canada,* 1950.

through her, and the mother retreats into an epic sulk and raises white narcissi. The funeral colour, the sickly-sweet smell, and the mythical overtones of "narcissus" provide the central image of the novel. A rather forced ending breaks up this pattern of frustration, but the type itself marches across Canada from sea to sea. I have occasionally wondered if some psychological transfer from a political dependence on a "mother country" has affected Canadian feeling about female establishment. Scott Symon's[8] *Place d'Armes,* for example, has castrating mother symbols all over it, and ends in an apocalyptic prophecy of the fall of the "mommy bank," the Bank of Montreal. The setting is Montreal, but the psychological focus is clearly Ontario.

In writing a *Bildungsroman* about one's early surroundings, especially if one is not thinking of the people one writes about as forming any large part of one's readership, it is often difficult to avoid a patronizing tone that isolates the characters from the rest of the world. That is, the author knows that his milieu is provincial, and his knowledge is apt to work against him into identifying with it. Hence a certain self-conscious archness in earlier Canadian fiction, in Ralph Connor, or even in Leacock's *Sunshine Sketches.* Leacock, however, is aware of this tone and feels defensive about it, and so adds a sentimental epilogue to the book, describing a returning railway journey to Mariposa after a life misspent in the big city:

> Don't bother to look at the reflection of your face in the window-pane shadowed by the night outside. Nobody could tell you now after all these years. Your face has changed in these long years of money-getting in the city. Perhaps if you had come back now and again, just at odd times, it wouldn't have been so.

It is easy to locate, and still easier to caricature, the limitations of a provincial culture. There is, for example, its resentment of realism, its feeling that it should not be studied before it has had time to put on its best clothes. There are the querulous complaints against academic critics, who know how it should be done but can't do it, through which one can always hear the voice of the provincial appeal "Please go away until we get better." And there are all the fallacies engendered by the wrong kind of literary study, such as the notion that poetry is an ele-

---

[8]Scott Symons (1930-), a controversial journalist and author of such experimental works of fiction as *Place D'Armes: A Personal Narrative,* 1967, and *Civic Square,* 1969. Symons' unconventional life is the subject of Charles Taylor's fascinating book, *Six Journeys: A Canadian Pattern,* 1977.

gant varying of meaning instead of a higher concentration of it. Thus Wilson MacDonald in *The Song of the Ski:*

> I land erect and the tired winds drawl
> A lazy rune on a broken harp

where the skier may have landed erect but his metaphors are a basket case. I am more interested, however, in the genuine difficulties encountered by dedicated and isolated writers. May I turn again to White Narcissus:

> He smiled bitterly. "It is always of her you speak," he added, with a surprising acrimony, for this thwarted feeling was being transferred to annoyance in behalf of the representative of his own sex in this generation-long quarrel. "Doesn't your father feel? Do you think he doesn't know the bitter of loneliness and misprision as well as your mother?"
>
> "Father, of course. I know that, and it is why things are as they are. Possibly if I could take sides, there could be some outcome, even to strife. But I see, I understand too well, so that there is no hope. I see the sadness of both, and how oblivion awaits it all... across a mist of pathos like dreaming."

This is provincial style: the heightening of tone, so that the conversational idiom is smothered in rhetorical rhythms, and the conscientious tracing of motive, indicate a writer who thinks of the highest standards of his craft as being already established outside his community (Henry James is the chief ghost haunting this passage, I should think), and as having to be met by very deliberate efforts.

It was a similar concern about meeting external standards that produced the dream of "The Great Canadian Novel," by which was apparently meant a Victorian type of character-crowded panorama, on the model of *Bleak House* or *Middlemarch*, or, if one ventured to hope so high, *War and Peace.* But such forms now exist, so far as they do, chiefly in historical romance, which is an international commercial product for the most part, though Antonine Maillet's[9] *Pélagie-la-Charrette* indicates that something much more could be made of it. In any case, as we saw, prose in Ontario began with the documentary realism of journals and memoirs, and when fiction developed, that was the tradition it recaptured. Documents, when not government reports, tend

---

[9]Antonine Maillet (1929-) is the creator of a large fictional world centered on her native region of Canada, `L'Acadie.' In English Canada she is best known for her novel *Pélagie,* 1982.

to have short units, and the fact may account for the curious ascendancy in Canadian fiction of the novel which consists of a sequence of inter-related short stories. This form is the favourite of Alice Munro, and reaches a dazzling technical virtuosity in *Lives of Girls and Women.*

As a way of approaching cultural through social phenomena, let me give one example of how a provincial situation is affected, first, by the rural-urban population shift, and then expands into a more complex social issue. I remarked earlier that it was impossible to get legally any kind of alcoholic drink in Toronto in 1929. I forget whether the first tentative post-prohibition beers were available then or not, but I should not consider them an exception if they were. Many Protestant churches, at least, seemed to attach more importance to abstaining from liquor than they did to all the clauses in the Apostles' Creed together. Whenever we have a token anxiety symbol of this kind, we should look for unacknowledged change in the social process. The process here, as mentioned, was the rapid shift to an urban-based ethos. The churches adhered almost obsessively to the rural one, and in rural communities there was some justification for assuming that one either did not drink or took to drink. Where the industry was strongly seasonal, as with Newfoundland fishing, this was proportionately more true. However, according to Catharine Parr Traill:

> Intemperance is too prevailing a vice among all ranks of people in this country; but I blush to say it belongs most decidedly to those that consider themselves among the better class of emigrants.

The word "emigrants" goes a long way to annotate the remark: the "better class" in Ontario at that time had not come to Canada so much as left Britain or the United States, and like other refugees they felt a lack of social context, especially in moments of leisure. Ontario is a place to stand, we are told: the cultural complications begin with sitting down.

So "temperance," meaning total abstinence, may have been so vigorously supported by the more evangelical churches partly as a native protest against manners imported by the self-styled gentry. If so, this would explain why the political affinities of temperance movements were liberal to the verge of radical. A very easy generalization from denouncing "the liquor interests" and their control of politicians and the press would soon bring one to radicalism, or at any rate a kind of radical populism. The alliance between the evangelical and the populist was noted as early as Tiger Dunlop[10]:

> It is long since the French reproached the English with having twenty religions, and only one sauce. In Canada, we have two hundred religions, and no sauce at all... The mode by which religion and politics are joined is, I believe, peculiar to the American continent, viz., by newspapers inculcating the tenets of a sect, and at the same time the politics of the leaders of it; and this unholy alliance have the Methodists set up to blend treason with the Gospel.

I became aware of the blending of "treason" and the gospel from some of my contemporaries who came from missionary families, and had spent much of their childhood in China or Japan. The Student Christian Movement, a very influential organization among students at the time, drifted rapidly leftward, partly under their influence. The tragic career of my classmate Herbert Norman[11] is perhaps too well known to need more than a reference. So it should not be surprising that if, on a Sunday afternoon in 1931, there were 18,000 people at Denton Massey's York Bible Class in Maple Leaf Gardens, the children or grandchildren of those people should be listening to left-wing speakers imported from third-world countries in the same place in the late sixties.

If we add to this issue a dozen others, we can begin to understand how it was that Toronto was able, in half-a-dozen years after 1945, to transform itself from the "Hogtown" of the thirties into a cosmopolitan city with a minimum of ethnical tension. The immigration of those years was not of course confined to Toronto, though it was most dramatic there, and it was not the cause of the contemporary transformation of Ontario literature from the provincial to the regional, though it accompanied it and had many connections with it. The process itself by which a provincial writer isolated in a part of the world becomes a regional writer who from a sense of being in the world strikes his roots in his social environment remains a mysterious one. James Reaney has a poignant poem called "The Upper Canadian":

---

[10] William 'Tiger' Dunlop (1792-1848) developed Canada's brand of travel literature — an autobiographical sketch in which the narrator dramatizes himself in the process of discovering a new place. His *Statistical Sketches of Upper Canada*, 1832, made him one of the most celebrated literary men of his time.

[11] Herbert Norman (1909-1957), Canadian diplomat and scholar who committed suicide in Cairo when the U.S. Senate accused him of being a security risk. The accusation stemmed from the fact that Norman was a Communist.

I shall always sit here in this hovel
Weeping perhaps over an old
Victorian novel
And hear the dingy interwinding tunes

Of country rain and wind
And lame fires of damp wood.
Especially shall I hear that starved cricket
My mind, that thinks a railway ticket
Could save it from its enclosed, cramped quality.
That mind where thoughts float round
As geese do round a pond
And never get out.

Alvin Lee,[12] in his book on Reaney, identifying the narrator of this poem with Reaney himself, remarks that his way of handling the problem "was not to export himself elsewhere but rather to learn an order of words or literary language comprehensive enough to swallow up the place and society which had brought him into being."

Lee is certainly right in pointing to language as the key to the process: it is a new sense of language that makes a writer realize that he must establish his own standards and not try to meet those of someone or somewhere else. There are many other factors: sometimes a railway ticket does help, as a ticket to Toronto helped E. J. Pratt to become a Newfoundland poet. Sometimes one can see a definite influence. One of the first Ontario writers to whom this metamorphosis occurred was Morley Callaghan, and the impact of Maritain[13] on Ontario Catholic culture was operative there. But critics, when they identify such an influence, are apt to exaggerate it, because the actual process eludes them as much as it does the writer himself.

The point is that the transformation did occur, however it occurred. If the Nobel Prize Committee were to ask for Canadian nominees, anyone reasonably conversant with the field could name eight or ten people in English Canada alone, without feeling in the least apologetic about

---

[12]Alvin A. Lee (1930-), Professor of English, McMaster University, Hamilton, Ontario. Author of *James Reaney*, 1968, and *The Guest-Hall of Eden*, 1972. He co-edited *The Legacy of Northrop Frye*, 1984.

[13]Jacques Maritain (1882-1973), French Catholic philosopher and one of the leading exponents of the thought of St. Thomas Aquinas and of its relevance for the modern world. His numerous books include *The Angelic Doctor*, 1930, *The Degree of Knowledge*, 1937 and *Art and Poetry*, 1953.

any of them, and a good proportion of them would be Ontario writers. At the beginning Ontario struggled along in what Douglas LePan calls "A Country Without a Mythology," having both obliterated the Indian mythology and discarded its own. A mythology is a framework of thematic imagery within which a literature operates, hence a country without one is a country with a provincial literature and a largely undeveloped imaginative potential. A mythology emerges when the mental landscape of a group of writers begin to fuse with their physical environment. In another article I have tried to show this process at work among some contemporary Canadian poets. If I had another hour of my own (which I do not), I might attempt a similar study of Ontario fiction, showing how the *Bildungsroman* form, and others closely related to it, so often works through to some intuition or private epiphany that is an aspect of an emerging coherent mythology. LePan's own novel *The Deserter* affords an impressive example, as does each of the three Deptford novels of Robertson Davies, especially *Fifth Business.* Fable and fantasy forms, such as Marian Engel's *Bear,* Timothy Findley's new novel *Not Wanted on the Voyage,* or still in a different way Graeme Gibson's *Perpetual Motion,* have an important role to play here. Predictably, perhaps, the unifying theme of the fantasies is nearly always a renewed relation between humanity and nature. And there is also, of course, the ironic version of the *Bildungsroman.* To win through to a genuine mythical vision means casting off any number of false ones, and the failure of some characters to do this is quite as significant as the success of others. An example would be the heroine of Margaret Atwood's *Lady Oracle,* who exchanges a physical obesity for equally overstuffed myths, because, as she says, "the truth was not convincing."

When an imaginative coherence of this kind emerges within a literature, it becomes genuinely communicable, and provokes an immediate response in other parts of the world. It is not geographical curiosity about Canada, and certainly not its political importance, that has caused universities in Germany and Italy, in China and Japan, in Holland and Scandinavia, to set up centres of Canadian studies. Perhaps, as has been suggested, Canada has passed up or abandoned a genuinely political identity. But as long as it retains its imaginative one, it will do infinitely more for the benefit of the world.

"Culture and Society in Ontario, 1786-1984." Address at McMaster University (Ontario Historical Series, 7 September 1984). First published in *On Education.* Markham: Fitzhemry & Whiteside, 1988.

Levels of Cultural Identity

I suppose that nowhere in the world is there a relationship between two countries even remotely like that of Canada and the United States. The full awareness of this relationship is largely confined to Canada, where it has churned up a good deal of speculation about "the Canadian identity," the extent to which Canadians may be said to be different from non-Canadians, meaning, ninety per cent of the time, Americans. I am not concerned with this approach to the question, which seems to me futile and unreal. A nation's identity is (not "is in") its culture, and culture is a structure with several distinct levels. On an elementary level there is culture in the sense of custom or life-style: the distinctive way that people eat, dress, talk, marry, play games, produce goods, and the like. On this level culture in Canada, including both English and French Canada has been practically identical with the northern part of American culture for a long time. This fact is not, in my view, one of any great significance. The time is past when we could speak of the "Americanizing" of this aspect of Canadian life: what faces us now is the homogenizing of the entire world, including the United States, through twentieth-century technology. Today Canadians, like other people, are hardly more Americanized in their lifestyle than they are Japanned or common-marketed.

Then there is a middle level of cultural identity, which is the product of tradition and history, and consists of the distinctive political, economic, religious, and other institutions that shape a nation's life and give direction to the main currents of its ideology. This is an area where Canadians have always felt beleaguered and threatened by American influences, and where, by an inevitable irony, that influence keeps increasing through divisions among Canadians themselves. In every part of Canada there are strong separatist feelings, and separatism can lead only to increased American penetration, especially economic and ideological. This is not to say that such penetration must be sinister, merely that it is the opposite of what separatism aims at.

Finally, there is an upper level of culture as the product of a nation's specialized creative powers. In Canada it seems to be particularly literature, painting, film, and radio drama that have attracted most attention, both within the country and outside it, and we should now add architecture, as this building [the new Canadian Embassy[1]] is one of three at least to achieve such recognition in the present year. In theory, culture in this more specific sense is the product of the people as a whole and the shared heritage of all the people. In practice, it is the product of an often neglected minority, and in its appreciation there is a strongly elitist element. To bridge this gap between theory and practice is largely what the process known as education is all about.

The middle level, the specific nation formed by an historical process, is the place where the conception "Canada" is to be found, but it is not the place to look for cultural symbols. Those come from either the life-style level or the creative level. On the life-style level, Canada has shown an extraordinary ability to absorb ethnical groups without essentially violating their folkways. The treatment of the indigenous peoples is an exception to this that I shall return to later. But the Icelandic and Ukrainian immigrants of the nineteenth century, the Italians and Portuguese and Jamaicans of the twentieth, have been able to preserve much of their life-style cultures: the extent to which they have been eroded, as just said, is due to world-wide rather than national pressures. The same thing was true of the original British and French groups: in fact John Kenneth Galbraith, with no sense of incongruity, wrote a book called *The Scotch*, which was concerned entirely with a community of Scottish origin in Southern Ontario.

In life-style culture there is little that is typical of Canada as a whole: a satiric revue of forty years back called *Spring Thaw* pretended to make a search for authentic Canadian symbols, and emerged with a mounted policeman and a bottle of rye. Canada is the Switzerland of the twentieth century surrounded by the great powers of the world and preserving its identity by having many identities. Its distinctive identity is represented by its creative culture, in its literature and painting and the other arts just mentioned.

As for the American awareness of Canada, one may say that Americans are conscious of Canada first of all as insulation. And perhaps one should not ignore the importance of Canada as a geographical object, apart from its inhabitants, in sealing in the United States on one point of the compass much as the oceans seal it on two others. The physical existence of Canada helped to confirm the American sense of separateness from the world up to the earlier decades of this century, and perhaps later had something to do with the fact that the Cold War re-

[1]The Canadian Embassy in Washington was designed by one of Canada's leading architects, Arthur Erickson (1924-). His other commissions include Simon Fraser University, Vancouver, Museum of Anthropology, Vancouver, and Roy Thomson Hall, Toronto.

mained relatively cold. But of course there are people in Canada, and it has been of immense benefit to the United States, whether it knows it or not, to have across its northern border not merely a friendly ally but another nation with a different history and traditions, closely related to and yet contrasting with its own.

The contrasts relate to what I have called the middle level of culture, the distinctive paths formed by history. The American revolution was a Whig revolution, and one of the things it revolted against was the mercantilist theory that the function of colonies was merely to produce raw materials. English Canada was settled, in upper Canada and much of the Maritimes, largely by disaffected Tories. This made common cause to some degree, with the former enemies in French Canada, who felt doubly betrayed, first by the lack of interest in Canada shown by the government of pre-revolutionary France, and secondly by an atheistic French Revolution. It is perhaps fair to say that France has never shown any real concern for Canada since, except when promoting its own interests. And English-speaking Canadians, even those who remained uncritically loyal to Britain, had to put up with massive ineptitude, indifference, and an attitude that showed much more respect for the independent United States than the dependent colonies. The feeling of not being wanted except as a place of exploitation, forms a ground bass under Canadian themes, and among other things has forced Canada to retain the dependence on commodity exports which makes its economy so different from the American one.

One always has to oversimplify situations like this, unless one is writing scholarly history but in the forming of Canada there was something like this Tory-Whig division of ideology and one that went much deeper than the Republican-Democrat or Conservative-Liberal divisions arising later in the separate countries. The revolution produced a written constitution and a deductive attitude to social problems, whereas the Canadians, in rejecting the revolution, adopted something more like an Edmund Burke theory of a continuous contract including the dead, the living and the unborn, an unwritten constitution based on precedent, and a tendency to look for solutions to crisis by safeguarding the rights of both sides. Canadian history is a series of *ad hoc* compromises, in contrast to the American practice of re-interpreting and amending an eighteenth-century document. Each crisis brings with it a settled belief in the minds of many Canadians, that this is really the end, that the country is at last irremediably torn apart by its own inner contradictions. So far such feelings have proved to be mistaken, but if a sculptor were making a statue symbolizing Canadian loyalty to Canada he might well portray someone holding his breath and crossing his fingers.

The entrenched Tory oligarchy in nineteenth-century Ontario, known as the Family Compact, provoked a rebellion of sorts in 1837, though the history of that rebellion, at least in Ontario makes very curious reading. Canadians have always refused to believe in any kind of political logic, whether the logic of revolution or the logic of repression. The liberal opposition that began to take shape was continentalist in tendency and some of the more myopic liberals, such as the English Goldwin Smith,[2] who resided for some time in Toronto before going to Cornell, assumed that the union of the British colonies was a chimerical fantasy, and that annexation to the United States was only a matter of time. But even Toryism in Canada has always had a radical element in it that opposed American tendencies from the left as well as the right. This element emphasized the gross inequalities of wealth and privilege building up in the United States, and it was more aware than the liberals of the aggressive and imperialistic side of American development. The Monroe doctrine,[3] through much of the nineteenth century, seemed to imply that the Americans were claiming the right to exploit the New World for themselves. The effects in Canada included the War of 1812, the Fenian raids, the "Fifty-four forty or fight" crisis, and various other incidents. But as regards Canada the United States seems to have realized very early that, to paraphrase Clausewitz, economic penetration is the continuing of war by other means, and with a far greater chance of success.

There was also the Canadian opposition to slavery. During the Civil War, the liberal John Stuart Mill in England attacked the Tories of his time for supporting the South and rejoicing over the apparent disintegrating of the great republican experiment. One might have expected Canadians to take a similar view, and some did, but Canadian volunteers produced a sizable contingent for the Union army. Much earlier, the Nova Scotian writer Haliburton, who was about as Tory as one

---

[2]Goldwin Smith (1823-1910), distinguished professor of history at Oxford, moved to the newly founded Cornell University in 1868, and settled in Toronto in 1871. While in Toronto he established a number of journals and periodicals, including *The Week* (1883-96), which became an important forum for debate on domestic and international issues. He generated a great deal of public hostility over his political views, according to which the destiny of Canada was to form a commercial and political union with the United States. Smith's anti-imperialist arguments are most cogently presented in *Canada and the Canadian Question*, 1891.

[3]The Monroe Doctrine, named after James Monroe (1758-1831), the fifth president of the United States, regarded any interference in the internal affairs of the American states as an unfriendly act.

could get, made his stage American Sam Slick[4] refer to the Fourth of July as "fifteen millions of free men and five millions of slaves a-celebratin' the birthday of liberty."

The point all this is leading up to is that the continuity of certain British elements in Canadian life are not simply vestigial relics of Canada's colonial past or reactionary nostalgia. One very obvious example is the retaining of the monarchy, along with a Governor-General as, so to speak, the resident Canadian crown. When there is no question of British rule any more, keeping this memento of the fact that we were once a British colony is one way of qualifying the extent to which we are now an American colony. In any case the monarchy in both Britain and Canada seems to be genuinely popular, its connection with an aristocratic class having largely disappeared.

The monarchy is a symbol of a national unity transcending the conflicts of all political and religious pressure groups. The corresponding symbol of such a unity in the United States is the flag, something Canada did not even have until it acquired one along with the new Third World nations a quarter-century ago. The real point about a monarchy is that it puts the cult of personality where it belongs, in the area of ceremonial symbolism. A flag, however useful for covering the mental nakedness of political speeches, lacks the accessibility of a personal symbol like a royal family: it is pointless to complain about it, and impossible to gossip about it. A parliamentary system, where a leader stands or falls with his party, reduces the personality cult in other ways, although there is a growing emphasis on leadership conventions and the like in Canada which reflects American influence.

Then again, Canada has had, for the last fifty years, a Socialist (or more accurately Social Democrat) party, which is normally supported by twenty-five to thirty per cent of the electorate, and has been widely respected, through most of its history, for its devotion to principle. Nothing of proportional size or influence has emerged among socialists in the United States. When the CCF, the first form of this party, was founded in the nineteen-thirties, its most obvious feature went largely unnoticed. That feature was that it was following a British rather than an American tendency, trying to assimilate the Canadian political structure to the British Conservative-Labour pat-

---

[4]Sam Slick is the main character in T.C. Haliburton's *The Clockmaker; or, the Sayings and Doings of Samuel Slick, of Slickville.* Composed of a series of satirical sketches, *The Clockmaker* is a sharply observed commentary on the political and economical state of Nova Scotia. As an energetic and aggressive Yankee peddler, Sam Slick is the embodiment of American entrepreneurship. His principal function was to satirize Nova Scotia's colonial apathy.

tern. The present New Democratic Party, however, never seems to get beyond a certain percentage of support, not enough to come to federal power. Principles make voters nervous, and yet any departure from them towards expedience makes them suspicious.

The American ideology of assimilation, expressed in such phrases as "hundred percent American," "un-American activities," and the like, can hardly operate in Canada, with its roots in a coalition of two founding groups. Recently Canadians have become aware that a large proportion of the population, including of course the indigenous peoples, comes from an ethnical and linguistic background which is neither English nor French. Hence the policy of bilingualism, so sharply intensified in the Trudeau era, has been qualified by the newer buzzword of "multiculturalism." In Toronto, for example, where the teaching of French in elementary schools is heavily stressed, the Italian-speaking population is much greater than the French-speaking one. The result, or so an irritated educator once remarked to me, is to send an Italian child to schools to destroy his native language and make him illiterate in two others. Not that it is all that easy to destroy a native language.

I am entering an area here which is thickly sown with emotional minefields, and any advance into it has to be cautious. I have first to return to my three levels of culture, a level of lifestyle, a level of ideology and historical process, and a level of creativity and of education in the arts and sciences. On the level of lifestyle there are immense pressures towards uniformity, including uniformity of language. Economic forces in particular make for increasing centralization. One frequently sees the statement that such trends are changing and becoming more decentralized, but applied to Canada the statement is nonsense.

The creative arts, on the other hand, have to be planted in a very limited environment. Literature, in particular, is intensely regional in Canada, as it is in the United States, and even in the much smaller Great Britain. Canadian critics have realized for a century that the more Canadian a writer tries to be, the less chance he has of becoming a really distinguished writer. The reason is that the conception "Canadian" belongs to a different aspect of culture, and can have little direct or positive influence on the creative one. At the same time, the aggregate of writers in Canada will produce a Canadian body of literature, which is felt by both Canadian and non-Canadian readers to be distinctive of the country.

Regional literature grows out of provincial literature. The provincial writer assumes that literary standards have been established for him outside his environment. English and French writers in nineteenth-century Canada both tended to follow models in their ancestral countries. But the notion of meeting established external standards is a fallacy: literature changes too rapidly, and standards are no longer mainstream influences by the time the provinces get around to imitating them.

As a provincial culture matures, it becomes more aware of the variety of new ideas and ideologies, new techniques of narrative, new forms of imagery, that are sweeping across the world, and it begins to respond to them and becomes part of an international idiom. Such an idiom does not, like lifestyle fashions in food or clothing, makes for uniformity or mass production: it works in quite the opposite direction, though in ways too complex to go into here. What it does not do either, or does very seldom is uproot the writer from his localized place in his own community. There is a curious law in culture, at least literary culture, which says that the most specific settings have the best chance of becoming universal in their appeal. It is clear that a multiplicity of ethnical backgrounds is highly favourable to a culture, and any writer or artist will exploit everything he has that is distinctive in his regional, ethnical, or religious background. But as he matures as a writer and his horizon expands, he wants to be read on his own merits and not as an ethnic specimen, however unusual. Similarly with the consumer. A reader interested in Canadian literature may feel in the position of one who has bought a box of candy and discovered from the fine print on the box that he has acquired a melange of twenty-three food, chemical, and additive substances. But he still expects some unity of taste in the final product, not a mere recognition of the subtle contributions made by invertase or lecithin. As for minority languages, they seem to be one area where privatisation actually does seem to work. I think that among the Celtic languages in the British Isles, Welsh has fared better than Irish, because Welsh has been spoken and studied by the people who wanted to speak and study it, whereas Irish was made compulsory in schools and given the rank of an official language, to the great detriment of its popularity.

There remains, however, the unique historical development which has made Canada a bilingual country with two recognized Canadian languages. I suppose no reasonable Canadian denies the extraordinary advantages of a bilingual culture, despite all the complaints one may hear in English Canada about "shoving all that French down our throats," though those who use such phrases are unlikely to have much French in their throats. Corresponding complaints can be heard in French Canada. But one should keep in mind the different aspects of cultural life already referred to, and the fact that a creative benefit may be a political burden. The conception "Quebecois," for example, belongs culturally to the area of political leverage, not to anything genuinely creative.

Many languages, including earlier English, have no word for space but only for place, or space-there. For the imagination of, say, Shakespeare's original audience, the entire cosmos was filled up by objects or beings with assigned places. Nature abhors a vacuum, the philosophers said, at a time when vacuum and empty space meant much the same thing. But as the influence of Copernicus and Galileo began to make itself felt, the imaginative responses changed. The French who settled Quebec and Acadia belonged to the seventeenth-century world of Descartes and Pascal. Descartes was, I think, the first to make the conception of space as pure extension, apart from whatever it contained, functional in philosophy. Pascal, certainly no Cartesian, expressed his terror of "these empty spaces and their silence," in one of the most famous epigrams ever uttered. By "these empty spaces" he meant much more than what is now called "outer spaces" beyond the sky, but the phrase reflects a time when, to adapt a remark of Blake, the human imagination was beginning to be more impressed by the amount of space between the stars than by the stars themselves.

It was the sense of space without place, descended to earth to become the natural environment, that confronted the Canadian imagination in its formative years. A universe of places means a hierarchical universe: earlier human imagination was dominated by the sense of a natural hierarchy, with everything occupying the place that God had assigned it. As the sense of natural hierarchy waned, distinction of ranks in human life seemed increasingly to be imposed simply by human will expressed in violence. Some time ago I used the phrase "garrison mentality" to describe the psychological effects in Canada of the Anglo-French wars, fear of Indian attacks, and protection against an implacably indifferent nature, with its cycle of intense heat, intense cold, and the coming of spring along with the black flies. I grew up in a town in the Maritimes about thirty miles from where, in the eighteenth century, a French and a British fort scowled at each other across the isthmus that separates New Brunswick from Nova Scotia. It was an eloquent if primitive symbol of the "two solitudes" that Hugh Mac Lennan later described in his novel of that name about Anglo-French relations in Montreal. Similar survivals of this "two solitudes" construct were still all around me in my early years. My phrase, however, has been rather over-exposed since, and like other over-exposed images has got blurred and fuzzy, its specific historical context being usually ignored.

As I understood it, a garrison brings social activity into an intense if constricted focus, but its military and other priorities tend to obliterate the creative impulse. In one brief interval of relaxation, after the peace of 1763, a novel called *Emily Montague* was written by a woman named Frances Brooke in the garrison town of Quebec. It is not only the first novel written in Canada; it is one of the earliest novels to be written anywhere. But a more typical garrison attitude survived psychologically in the rural and small-town phase of Canadian life, with its heavy pressures of moral and conventional anxieties. Canadians are now, however, one of the most highly urbanized people in the world and the garrison mentality, which was social but not creative, has been replaced by the condominium mentality, which is neither social nor creative and which forces the cultural energies of the country into forming a kind of counter-environment.

The same paradox of space without place confronted American life too, but the Americans lived in a two-dimensional country, and were able to fill up their empty space more systematically, with the aid of a frontier. Canadians were compelled by geography to live in much more scattered communities, the main divisions of the country being widely separated from one another. The writers or speakers who eventually emerged from this environment were confronted first of all by the physical problems of being able to communicate at all. De Tocqueville, in his magisterial survey of democracy in America, says only one thing about Canada, but what he says bears on our present point. "In Canada," he says, "the most enlightened, patriotic and humane inhabitants make extraordinary efforts to render the people dissatisfied... more exertions are made to excite the passions of the citizens there than to calm them elsewhere." He is speaking mainly of French Canada, but the remark applies to the whole country. One reads between the lines the desperate frustrations of the earlier communicators, and the massive indifference of those they attempted to address. The silence of the eternal spaces remained at the bottom of the Canadian psyche for a long time, and in many respects is still there. Communication is of course a major preoccupation, almost an obsession, with Canadians, but in the nineteenth century the impressive part of it was a matter of building railways and bridges and canals. Articulate communication has now taken its normal place in Canadian life, but with rare exceptions Canada has avoided the movements of mass hysteria that have swept over the United States so frequently during the last century.

Some time ago, in looking through an anthology of American poetry, I came across Theodore Roethke's poem "Journey to the Interior." The "interior" in this poem is both a landscape and a psyche, but the journey is out of the self and not into it. We begin with the image of driving a car or jeep over rough and dangerous roads. Then the car goes faster and soon we are travelling at a breakneck speed past a place where "some idiot plunger" had previously met his death. The car disappears and the poet's spirit expands to become merged with the nature around him, as all the dormant powers within him break into renewed life. I had read the poem before, but had not realized how superbly it caught a dominant mood in American imaginative experience: the conquering of nature through the sheer force of technology, the exhilaration of danger and high speed that comes as technology develops, and the arrival through the speed at an ecstasy of an expanding consciousness.

I remembered too that there was a Canadian poem also called "Journey to the Interior," in Margaret Atwood's first volume, *The Circle Game*, so I turned to it. Here the "interior" is again both psychic and physical, but the journeying narrator is apparently walking through woods, moving very cautiously as much aware of the rough going and the tangles of branches as her counterpart, but with a total uncertainty about her direction. The Atwood narrator wonders if she is going in circles; Roethke speaks only of "detours" in a straightforward quest. But if the Atwood traveller has no trust in direction she is intensely aware of presences, which may be menacing presences. It is important, she says, to keep one's head but useless, perhaps dangerous, to call out or utter words in such a wilderness. Roethke in contrast, is aware of no presence except his expanding self. I am not of course comparing the poems in merit, merely looking at them as documents illustrating two kinds of sensibility. Both poems come from the sixties, Roethke's being a late poem, composed near his death, and Atwood's being early and experimental. I know how easy it is to deceive oneself in such matters, but I feel sure that one sensibility represents something centrally American as it was twenty years ago, and the other something centrally Canadian. One is preoccupied with speed, machinery, progress, and intensity of consciousness, the other with loneliness, diffidence, uncertainty of direction and a divided consciousness. In the twenty years since then great changes have come over the imagination of both countries, to the point almost of a merging of attitudes.

According to the Canadian economist Harold Innis, the development of techniques of communication tends to create a "bias" in culture. There are two main biases according to Innis, a bias toward time and a bias toward space. Innis felt that the Canadian sensibility has a time bias and the American a spatial one. This is not as a rule the type of observation that I find very cogent, but let us follow it up for a moment. It may seem to contradict what I said earlier about the impact of space on the Canadian imagination, but the contexts are very different.

Countries that have a long record of oppressive foreign rule are intensely aware of their history: Ireland and Poland are obvious examples. Nations expanding into empires think in terms of acquiring space, and English Canada felt something of this by proxy when it was part of a British empire on which the sun was alleged never to set. French

Canada, on the other hand, has been very conscious of its history and traditions: Quebec automobile license plates still bear the motto *je me souviens,* I remember. But in fact all Canada, with its sense of precedent and continuous contract, seems oriented to history in a way that the United States until quite recently, never has been. The sense of irreversible progress that has been so central in American imagination seems to carry with it the sense of an escape from history itself.

The bias toward time may become neurotic, preoccupied with Don Quixote's vision of some imaginary historical idea that ought to exist now. Ideological terrorism in particular is usually inspired by an obsession with reshaping the past. But the same bias may go in a genuinely creative direction, recognizing that it is tradition more than anything else that creates identity. From about 1960 on English Canada began to achieve something of the sense of self-definition that French Canada had had for much longer, and a renewed historical sense began to realize how much Canadian cultural traditions had been mutilated by the coming of two European peoples who refused to continue, in fact did their best to extinguish, the culture of the Indian and Inuit peoples already there.

Of course appreciation for the arts and culture of native peoples has not been lacking. The Haida mask from the early documentary *The Moon's Necklace* has been practically a Canadian logo for some time, and the outpouring of Inuit (Eskimo) sculpture and painting has been one of the most remarkable cultural developments in modern history. A great deal of scholarship has been devoted to collecting the oral literary culture of the indigenous peoples, who of course still produce it. What is more recent is the sense of the absurdity of regarding native peoples as foreigners, and their culture as an exotic curiosity. Clearly it forms a tradition which should be at the head-waters of our own and should be absorbed into our traditions in the same way that English and French traditions are. In Canadian literature, one could point to many examples of such absorption in the works of Susan Musgrave, John Newlove, Robert Kroetsch, M. T. Kelly, Yves Thériault, and others. Even careless popularizers are more hesitant about writing such sentences as "Jacques Cartier was the first man to set foot on Canadian soil," which were fairly frequent usage not so long ago. Even when the word "white" was inserted the implication "first genuine human being" was often there.

But the new sense of cultural kinship with the indigenous people was not really an expanded historical or temporal awareness: it was part of a new attitude to space, specifically the space within Canada. The closer relationship of the indigenous peoples to their natural environment was what gave them a new significance in Canadian imagination. The nineteenth-century sense of a hostile and amoral nature, the early twentieth-century sense of a land of mystery with its huge and so seldom visited lakes, rivers, and islands, has been almost reversed in a world where anything that is natural may be precious. Rupert Brooke spoke seventy years ago of the "unseizable virginity" of the Canadian landscape, but this will hardly apply to a situation in which even uninhabited land may still be polluted.

Of course a concern for the environment is a worldwide movement, politically as well as culturally, but the Canadian economy has been marked by a peculiarly reckless exploiting of natural resources, in which trees, fish, and furbearing animals were sacrificed on a scale that has left a cultural residue of intense guilt feelings in the Canadian consciousness. There has hardly ever been a time when Canadian writing has not expressed some resentment or apprehension at the treatment of the environment. But it is fairly recently that large numbers of people have come to feel that the exploiting of nature is just as wrong and immoral as the exploiting of other human beings. There is an essay by Heidegger, "The Origin of a Work of Art," which has been a strong influence on two very distinguished works of Canadian criticism, Dennis Lee's[5] *Savage Fields* and Bruce Elder's[6] *Image and Identity,* the latter concerned mainly with film. Heidegger's argument turns largely on a distinction between "World" and "Earth." "World" means the universe of human consciousness, "Earth" the universe of animals, plants, and inanimate nature. "World" tries to dominate and enslave "Earth," but "Earth" has its own modes of survival, and it is dangerous to violate it beyond a certain point. In a poet of an older generation, E. J. Pratt, the main themes are still "World" themes. He wrote narrative poems about whaling expeditions, shipwrecks, the building of the Canadian Pacific railway, the martyrdoms of Jesuit missionaries in which the Iroquois are assimilated to a mindless and ferocious nature. But even he has a late poem called "The Good Earth" in which he warns:

---

[5]Dennis Lee (1939-), author, song lyricist, editor and literary critic. He co-founded the House of Anansi Press and was poetry consultant for MaClelland & Stewart 1981-84. His best-known publications are a book of poems, *Civil Elegies,* 1968, a critical study of Canadian writing, *Savage Fields,* 1977, and a popular book for children, *Alligator Pie,* 1974.

[6]Bruce Elder (1947-), artist, writer and film-maker, best known for his epic film cycle *The Book of All the Dead,* of which thirty-five hours have been created. He is author of *The Body of Film,* 1989, and *Image and Identity: Reflections on Canadian Film and Identity,* 1989.

Hold that synthetic seed, for underneath
Deep down she'll answer to our horticulture:
She has a way of germinating teeth
And yielding crops of carrion for the vulture.

In the last two or three decades there has been a remarkable growth of the feeling that "nobody owns the earth," as bill bisset says (a poet who chooses lower cases and unconventional spellings). There have been startling works of fiction, such as Marian Engel's *Bear*, where an erotic relation between a woman and a pet bear has clearly an allegorical implication that Canadians have to learn to love their environment instead of exploiting or ignoring it. Some poets, again, have internalized the nineteenth-century landscape, with all its fears and loneliness, realizing that the real fears are there and not outdoors. The developments in painting has run closely parallel. When I spoke in Washington some years ago, there were two exhibitions of Canadian painting on view, representing two phases of "World" culture in Canada. One was concerned with the early twentieth-century painters, the "Group of Seven" and their contemporaries, who were the pictorial successors of the explorers and missionaries of earlier centuries. The other and more highly publicized exhibit gave us the Clement Greenberg[7] version of painting in Canada, the trend to abstraction which was at once the climax of the "World" view and the beginning of something else, although the something else was even then much more present in Canada than the exhibit suggested. Techniques in painting and film of directly confronting natural imagery, such as the one often called "magical realism," are part of the evidence that a new kind of spatial consciousness has come into Canadian imagination, in all its arts, and has given it a new confidence and stability.

I spoke earlier of the Tory ideology in early English Canada: it was never associated with an aristocracy, though some of the family compact may have regarded themselves in that light. But of course their Tory counterparts in England did include a good many of the aristocracy, who devoted a large part of their energy to preserving their game, working up anxieties about poachers and the like. Consciously, there was nothing to this but the selfishness and arrogance of privilege, a subculture of what Matthew Arnold accurately called "Barbarians." But in unconscious symbolism there was some preservation of "Earth" from the encroachments of "World." Canadian consciousness may be

[7]Clement Greenberg (1909-94), was a well-known American art critic who launched the career of Jackson Pollock and helped to established Abstract Expressionism as a major artistic movement.

slowly moving toward a conception of Canada as something like a gigantic national park, with a string of cities along or near its southern border. Some years ago Buckminster Fuller[8] used the metaphor of "spaceship earth," but this suggested an overcrowded ship with all its space outside. The writers, painters, and film-makers whose function it ought to be, in part, to tell us what the rest of the public will be thinking fifty years later, are providing us with a different metaphor, an internal reservoir of space, an "Earth" that can live with "World."

Great changes have come over the American consciousness too in the last few decades, and I suspect that the more strident and readily politicized issues, such as feminism or racial prejudice, are not the really underlying ones. I spoke earlier of a certain sense, in American imagination up to about 1950, of outrunning history, of a linear progress that would still move in a straight line even if it were headed for disaster. It seems to me that the Vietnam war has brought about the beginning of a profound shift of perspective. In the days when I taught for brief periods in American universities, my students would ask me if I noticed any difference between American and Canadian students. I said that students conditioned from infancy to be part of a world empire must necessarily be very different from students conditioned to be part of a secondary power, observing history from the sidelines rather than playing a major role in it. But I think American consciousness since then has acquired a new sensitivity to history, including its own history, and seeing its recent ascendancy as part of a parabola that goes up and comes down. History has no record of any empire that did not, qua empire, decline and fall, and the process is still inevitable, even though the decline and fall of the Russian and Chinese empires has still to come. There is nothing to regret in this, because the phrase decline and fall, in this context, means only the straightening out priorities, throwing away phony ones and, with luck, acquiring more genuine ones.

Of course it takes some effort to become more self-observant, to acquire historical sense and perspective, to understand the limitations that have been placed on human power by god, nature, fate, or whatever. It was part of President Reagan's appeal that he was entirely unaware of any change in consciousness, and talked in the old reassuring terms of unlimited progress. But the new response to the patterns of history seems to have made itself felt, along with a growing sense that we

---

[8]Buckminster Fuller (1885-1983), American engineer, inventor, designer, mathematician and philosopher, best known for his development of the geodesic dome. His numerous publications include *No More Secondhand God,* 1962, and *Critical Path,* 1973.

can no longer afford leaders who think that acid rain is something one gets by eating grapefruit. I wish I could document this change from recent developments in American culture, but I am running out of both time and knowledge. It seems clear to me, however, that American and Canadian imaginations are much closer together than they have been in the past.

I make no apology for having talked mainly in terms of the creative aspect of culture. In the first place, you can get better informed political commentary by turning on a television set. In the second place, imaginative developments give one the real clues to political and economic ones. Third, and most important to me, fifty years of teaching have only confirmed my conviction that only the arts and sciences are stable social realities: everything else simply dissolves and re-forms. The world of 1989 is no more like the world I was born into in 1912 than it is like the Stone Age, but nothing has improved since then except scientific and scholarly knowledge, and nothing has remained steady except human creative power.

The students crushed under tanks in Tienanmin Square may have been in a way, as much in the grip of illusion as the thugs who crushed them. But they showed very clearly that all human beings want the same things, freedom and dignity and decent living conditions, that those are very simple and reasonable things to want, and that nothing but the release of the power to apply our knowledge and creative energies can get them. If the process I have tried to trace in the cultural history of Canada and the United States has any validity, that is what it has for its moral.

"Levels of Cultural Identity." Address at Canadian Embassy 1989. First published in *Northrop Frye Newsletter*, Vol. 2, No. 1 (Winter 1989-90).